# THE INTEGRITY OF THE JUDGE

*To Elia, Vera and Christiaan*

# The Integrity of the Judge
## A Philosophical Inquiry

JONATHAN SOEHARNO
*Utrecht University, The Netherlands*

ASHGATE

Published by
Ashgate Publishing Limited
Wey Court East
Union Road
Farnham
Surrey, GU9 7PT
England

Ashgate Publishing Company
Suite 420
101 Cherry Street
Burlington
VT 05401-4405
USA

www.ashgate.com

**British Library Cataloguing in Publication Data**
Soeharno, Jonathan
The integrity of the judge : a philosophical inquiry. -
(Law, justice and power series)
1. Judicial ethics 2. Judicial independence 3. Judicial power
I. Title
347'.014

**Library of Congress Cataloging-in-Publication Data**
Soeharno, Jonathan, 1977-
The integrity of the judge : a philosophical inquiry / by Jonathan Soeharno.
p. cm.
Includes bibliographical references and index.
ISBN 978-0-7546-7409-2
1. Judicial ethics. 2. Judicial independence. 3. Judicial power. I. Title.

K3367.S64 2008
347'.014--dc22

2008040221

ISBN 978 0 7546 7409 2 (hardback)
ISBN 978 0 7546 9124 2 (e-book)

Mixed Sources
Product group from well-managed forests and other controlled sources
www.fsc.org Cert no. SA-COC-1565
© 1996 Forest Stewardship Council
FSC

Printed and bound in Great Britain by
MPG Books Ltd, Bodmin, Cornwall.

# Contents

# Preface

The importance of judicial integrity is undisputed. It is seen as a constituent for the legitimacy of judicial authority, as a condition for sound judicial decision-making and as a prerequisite for public trust. Across the world, many initiatives are taken to safeguard judicial integrity. The concept of integrity and its normative implications are, however, clouded by obscurities. Does integrity concern merely the absence of misconduct or does it also refer positively to specific norms or values? If so, is it a norm in its own right or is it merely a 'buzz word' for everything good in the judiciary?

In light of the need to safeguard the integrity of the judge,[1] the normative questions concerning what the integrity of the judge is and along which lines it should be safeguarded are the central questions of this book. These questions are complicated by the fact that little has been written about the subject in philosophical literature. It would seem that the vast amount of attention that integrity receives in practice is at odds with the understanding of the subject in theory. Therefore, in order to say anything meaningful about the nature of judicial integrity, this book also sets itself the task of developing a theory about professional integrity of public officials. In doing so, this book aims not only to contribute to our understanding of judicial integrity, but also to a philosophical understanding of integrity in general.

There are good reasons to explore the concept of the integrity of the judge via a philosophical inquiry. Research on the legal realization of a system of control or research into the effectiveness of integrity management within the judiciary is only useful after one has established a normative concept of integrity that is applicable to judges. The present lack of clarity about the meaning of judicial integrity is also an obstacle to undertaking sociological or legal research. For what would one research? Or which statutes or practices fall within its scope? It is a task of philosophy to provide such a normative analysis. Moreover, notions by which integrity is often described – amongst others conscience, conviction, good conduct, moral steadfastness and prudence – are philosophical terms or at least philosophically laden. It requires a philosophical investigation to re-articulate these notions in relation to the concept of integrity.

The method of this philosophical inquiry is hermeneutical. I come to an understanding of the phenomenon of judicial integrity by carefully exploring the circle between fact and norm, discourse and theory, opinion and argument,

1 Although the focus of this book is on professional judges, the treatment may apply to any person exercising judicial power, however designated.

thus spiraling down to an apparent understanding of judicial integrity. This understanding is thus not the result of analytical deduction – to which the literature does not yet lend itself – but of a careful phenomenology. Specific philosophical discussions, which fall outside of the scope of this phenomenology, will be treated in the footnotes.

This philosophical inquiry is to be applied to the practice of judges. The applicability to judges is an important feature, as practices in the judicial world, which are concerned with integrity management, are nowadays often inferred from corporate ethics. These default methods do not do justice to the specific problems that surround judicial integrity, especially the problem of judicial independence.

This book is organized around five questions, to which the chapters correlate: (1) Is judicial integrity a norm? (2) Can a theory of professional integrity of public officials be developed? How can this theory be applied to judges with respect to (3) decision-making and (4) conduct? (5) Finally, by which parameters must judicial integrity be safeguarded?

In Chapter 1, an inventory is made of the discourses about judicial integrity. I will first look at the discourse about violations of integrity in both established and developing democracies. I will then look at practices of safeguarding judicial integrity and at deeper undercurrents that have led to an awareness of judicial integrity. I conclude this chapter with an analysis of the role of judicial integrity against the broader framework of democracy and rule of law: is judicial integrity a norm in its own right?

In Chapter 2, I will develop a theory of professional integrity of public officials. In order not to be blinded by the practices connected with one profession, I will also take into account discussions about professions that have had to deal with integrity problems prior to the judiciary having had to do so. These discussions show some important features that must be accounted for in a theory of integrity. With these features in mind, a theory of professional integrity of public officials will be developed through the consideration of philosophical literature.

In the next chapters this theory is applied to the judge. Chapter 3 is concerned with the core activity of the judge, namely judicial decision-making. What does it mean to be a person of integrity in decision-making? What is the relation between the character of the judge and the process of adjudication? How is a judge to render external accountability for his decisions so that they enhance public trust? These questions will be treated in light of the theory of integrity as developed in Chapter 2.

Chapter 4 is concerned with judicial conduct other than decision-making. As Lord Devlin once put it, 'the judge who gives the right judgment while appearing not to do so may be thrice blessed in heaven, but on earth he is of no use at all'.[2] How is the conduct of the judge to be perceived as an exemplification of the judicial institution? How ought judges to behave outside court? These questions will be treated in light of the theory of integrity.

2 Devlin (1981:3).

In Chapter 5 I will examine safeguarding professional integrity. This chapter sets the parameters for safeguarding integrity and considers their applicability to the process of selection and appointment, to judicial decision-making and to the conduct of judges. As this book is a philosophical inquiry, it will not cover the empirical question concerning the effectiveness of specific safeguarding measures. The emphasis lies on setting the parameters for safeguarding and showing their interconnectedness and their relation to institutional values. The exact implementation of these parameters in a concrete legal culture, however, takes shape in a discourse that lies beyond the scope of this book.

Three final remarks need to be made. First, this book is not about the integrity of law,[3] nor does it postulate a theory of judicial integrity from a theory about the integrity of law. Equally, the matter of competence in respect to the separation or balance of powers is not a central focus of this book.[4] The subjects of judicial integrity and the integrity of law cannot, however, be entirely separated. Since the discussion about the integrity of law falls outside of the scope of this thesis, suffice it to say that judicial integrity presupposes societies, which are a democracy under the rule of law. I understand the rule of law to encompass general principles, such as classic and social human rights.[5]

Second, as the discussion about integrity is still in its infancy, I am venturing into uncharted territory. As a result, some parts of this book are more technical than others as they go into primary philosophical texts – especially in Chapters 3 and 4. Such a treatment raises specific hermeneutical questions about the use of these texts. Every time that I discuss a philosopher, whether Aristotle or Hegel, I take the following approach. I do not treat these philosophers within the broader framework of their own metaphysics and ontology. Rather than taking a 'top-down' approach I look at their philosophy from a 'bottom-up' angle. This 'bottom-up' approach finds its justification in the fact that the viability of their thoughts can be demonstrated by showing how they work in dealing with specific philosophical problems.[6] Thus,

3 See Dworkin (1986). Dworkin's notion of the integrity of law has been criticized widely, especially with respect to its clarity, cf. Gaffney (1996), Honeyball & Walter (1998) and Raz (2004). In so far as the integrity of law is understood as coherence, I concur with Raz when he argues that this principle may be inferior to some other alternatives in justice and in fairness (2004.289). I am therefore hesitant to connect the theory of integrity, which I will develop in this book, with a notion of the integrity of law as there is much obscurity about the latter.

4 This problem area is referred to as judicial activism (Thomas 2005:88–107), judicial policy-making (see the classic work of Bell 1983) or in a more pejorative sense, as judicial politics (cf. Stone Sweet 2000; Sunstein, Schkade, Ellman & Sawicki 2006).

5 As I will argue, I adopt a broad approach to the rule of law that nears the idea of the *Rechtsstaat* (see Section 3.1 of Chapter 1; see Soeharno 2006 for a comparison of the notions of rule of law and *Rechtsstaat*).

6 In taking this approach, I follow Peperzak (2001:80), Quante (1997:46) and Siep (1997:14). They have developed this approach to deal with Hegel's philosophy, which – as is well known – has some preponderant claims. Their stance can be summarized as follows:

I will not adopt the metaphysical underpinnings of Aristotle or the holistic claims of Hegel – but merely look at their analysis of specific problems.

Third, I refer to the judge in male terms. This is done for mere practical purposes.

---

overarching claims need only to be considered *after* the relevance of their plausibility in dealing with a specific problem has been shown.

# Acknowledgements

At the outset of this book I wondered whether this topic was suitable for a solitary research project. Yet I was glad to find academia to be a forum for a meeting of minds. In that respect many have contributed to the thoughts articulated in this book.

This book is the result of a four-year research programme at Utrecht University and I express deep gratitude to my supervisor, Professor Anthony Hol (Utrecht University), who continually stated his confidence in both this project and my abilities. I owe much gratitude to my co-supervisor, professor Peter Rijpkema (University of Amsterdam), for our valuable discussions. I also thank my colleagues in the Legal Theory section at Utrecht, especially my (former) roommates Theo Rosier, Tina van der Linden and Suzanne Heeger-Hertter, and my colleagues at the Wiarda Institute, especially Professor John Vervaele, Corrie van Rooijen and Mila Putters. I thank Philip Langbroek (Utrecht University) for his invitation to participate in a wide-ranging research project into the Dutch judiciary (within the framework of the Deetman Commission), which allowed me to speak to many judges about current developments.

I thank the Netherlands Organization for Scientific Research (NWO) for a grant to spend research leave as a visiting scholar at Pembroke College Cambridge in 2006. I thank Professor John Bell (Pembroke College), Professor Trevor Allan (Pembroke College), Professor J.A. Jolowicz QC (Trinity College) and Professor Matthew Kramer (Churchill College) for the discussions. I thank the staff at Pembroke College for their kind reception.

Many others have read and commented on parts of this book. I would like to thank especially Professor Antoine Garapon (Institut sur la Justice, Paris), Professor Leo Huberts (Free University of Amsterdam), Marcel Becker (Radboud University of Nijmegen), Professor Edith Brugmans (Radboud University of Nijmegen), Professor Erik Claes (Catholic University of Leuven), Liesbeth Huppes-Cluysenaer (University of Amsterdam), Professor Anne Ruth Mackor (University of Groningen) and Professor Mark Bovens (Utrecht University). I thank the PhD students at the Netherlands School for Research in Practical Philosophy (NSRPP) for valuable comments. I thank Alison Morley and Emily Gibson for editing the English in this book.

I would like to thank warmly those with whom the line between academic sparring partner and friend is or has become vague: Johan Roeland, Kees Quist, Iris van Domselaar, Judith Leest, Anna Gerbrandy, Jill Coster van Voorhout, Irena Rosenthal, Hendrie van Maanen, Teunis van Kooten, Jaron van Bekkum and Giovanni Zampetti. I thank Steve Rutt and Marijke Breeuwsma for their encouragement to pursue the path of academia.

Finally, I would like to express my gratefulness to my parents, Elia and Vera Soeharno, and my brother, Christiaan Soeharno; it is not a cliché to say that I learnt much about personal and moral integrity from your examples.

# Abbreviations

| | |
|---|---|
| *Cat.* | *Aristotelis Categoriae et De Interpretatione*. Edited by I. Bywater. Oxford: Oxford University Press (1949). |
| *EN* | *Aristotelis Ethica Nicomachea*. Edited by I. Bywater. Oxford: Oxford University Press (1954). |
| *EN* (*Irwin*) | *Aristotle, Nicomachean Ethics*. Translated with introduction, notes and glossary by T. Irwin (2nd ed.). Indianapolis: Hackett (1999). |
| *EN* (*Ross*) | *Aristotle, Nicomachean Ethics*. Translated by W.D. Ross. Oxford, Clarendon Press (1908). |
| *EN* (*Rowe*) | *Aristotle*, *Nicomachean Ethics*. Translated (with historical introduction) by C. Rowe. Philosophical introduction and commentary by S. Broadie. Oxford: Oxford University Press (2002). |
| *Grl* | *G.W.F. Hegel, Grundlinien der Philosophie des Rechts (Naturrecht und Staatswissenschaft im Grundrissen*) [1820]. Edited by J. Hoffmeister. Hamburg: Meiner (1995). |
| *GrlE* | *G.W.F. Hegel, Elements of the Philosophy of Right*. Edited by A.W. Wood and translated by H.B. Nisbet. Cambridge: Cambridge University Press (1991). |
| *Pol.* | *Aristotelis Politica*. Edited by W.D. Ross. Oxford: Oxford University Press (1957). |
| *Ret.* | *Aristotelis Ars Rhetorica*. Edited by R. Kassel. Berlin: De Gruyter (1976). |

# Chapter 1
# Is Judicial Integrity a Norm?

## 1. Introduction

This chapter aims at providing an inventory of the discourse on the integrity of judges[1] and at providing an analysis of the role of integrity as norm in the context of a democratic rule of law.

In section 2 I explore the scope of judicial integrity: its violations, its safeguarding and the developments which explain its upsurge. First, the debates about violations of judicial integrity are outlined. I will look at both established democracies, where 'traditional' integrity violations such as fraud or corruption are practically absent, and developing democracies, where several forms of judicial corruption infringe the rule of law. I will then look at safeguarding activity with respect to judicial integrity on both international and national levels. Lastly, I will look at factors that contribute to the upsurge of the concept of integrity. Why is it a buzz word now, but was hardly mentioned a few decades ago?

In section 3 the concept of integrity is placed in a broader normative framework of rule of law and democracy. The question is asked if integrity can be reduced to this normative framework or if it is a norm in its own right. I will defend the latter position. Integrity is a norm that serves the legitimacy of public functions. I conclude that there is a need for a philosophical theory of what integrity as norm entails.

## 2. The Rise of the Concept of the Integrity of the Judge

### *2.1 Judges on Trial: Debates on Judicial Integrity*

Although there is hardly a consensus about the nature of the concept of integrity or about its practice, this does not seem to hinder people from complaining about violations of judicial integrity. Let us therefore look at some discussions in which explicit reference to judicial integrity is made. The selection below is by no means exhaustive and the question whether these discussions have actually to do with judicial integrity will not be asked at this point. The purpose is to give the reader an impression of some of the issues that are often referred to as a violation of judicial integrity.

1 I do not follow the method of discourse analysis (cf. Coulthard 1977), for it would require a well-defined discourse. It is rather an inventory of the relevant discourses.

I distinguish between established democracies and developing democracies. In established democracies there are debates about miscarriages of justice, the ancillary functions of judges, corporate bias, misbehaviour of judges, the independence of judges and neo-managerialism within the judicial organization. In developing democracies there is also the difficult issue of corruption: bribery, political interference and organizational corruption within judicial organizations have a grave impact on the rule of law.

*2.1.1 Integrity issues in established democracies*

'Established democracies' and 'developing democracies' are types,[2] whereby 'established' and 'developing' refer to the quality of public institutions. In established democracies, traditional integrity problems such as fraud and corruption are practically absent and trust in the judiciary is relatively high. Developing democracies are democracies with developing institutions. Here traditional integrity problems take centre stage in the discourse on integrity. Of course, as these are mere types, exceptions confirm the rule.

*Miscarriages of justice* Due to higher media scrutiny, investigative journalism and new evidence science such as DNA analysis, judicial miscarriages are more likely to be detected. These miscarriages have a severe impact on the trust in the judiciary.

For example, in two high profile cases in the Netherlands, a case concerning the murder of a 23-year-old stewardess in Putten in 1994[3] and a case concerning the murder and rape of a 10-year-old girl and the sexual abuse of an 11-year-old boy in a public park in Schiedam in 2000,[4] the suspects were convicted of murder in all instances up to the highest appeal court, the *Hoge Raad*.[5] During both cases it was journalists who questioned the judgments and in particular the evidence on which the judgments were based. Their doubts were dismissed at the time but in the end the journalists proved to be right and the cases still make headlines today. The problem of miscarriages of justice is not confined to the Netherlands. For instance, in England a number of miscarriages, the *Birmingham Six*, *Guildford Four* and the *Maguire Seven*, caused a great stir.[6] It is fair but unfortunate to say that every country has its own landmark miscarriages.

---

2 The distinction is common in the literature. For examples of the usage of the terms, see Malleson & Russell (2006) and Gloppen, Gargarella & Skaar (2004).

3 Rb Zutphen 06-01-1995 LJN AE1685; Gh Arnhem 03-10-1995 LJN AE1892; HR 16-09-1996; HR 26-06-2001 LJN AA9800.

4 Rb Rotterdam 29-05-2001 LJN AB1823; Gh 's-Gravenhage 08-03-2002 LJN AE0013; HR 15-04-2003 LJN AF5257; HR 07-09-2004 LJN AQ9834; HR 25-01-2005 LJN AS1872.

5 For an older but very elaborate discussion on miscarriages of justice in the Netherlands see Crombag, Van Koppen & Wagenaar (1992).

6 For an extensive treatment see Griffith (1997:204–213).

*Increasing interest in the personalities of judges and their ancillary functions* In common law countries, interest in the personality of judges is traditionally high, which gives rise to intimate curiosities. These curiosities are nurtured by the notably personalized completion of the judicial role. Not only does the style of judgments bear the touch of the judge's individuality,[7] but also the performance at trial is unique to every single judge. It must be observed that these are not *eo ipso* benign to the trust that the parties or the public have in the judiciary.[8] Although in the civil law tradition the personality of judges is traditionally seen as subsidiary to their office,[9] there is an increasing interest in their personal profile that is concerned with their ancillary functions.[10] Sometimes it is initiated by a group of perturbed citizens who publish a 'revealing' account.[11] Some judiciaries publish their own list.[12]

Extra-judicial activities are often seen as a societal responsibility. For example, in common law countries judges are frequently called upon to chair Royal Commissions, Committees or 'independent' inquiries.[13] This is interesting in respect of the separation of powers, for in this capacity they cannot always avoid giving overt opinions on the investigated, who are sometimes politicians.[14] These opinions may arouse suspicions of bias when they return to act as judges.[15] Interesting in respect of natural justice are cases in which personal impartiality is challenged on an objective level, such as in the Pinochet case, where Lord Hoffmann failed to declare his links with Amnesty International. This led to the unprecedented setting aside of a judgment of the House of Lords.[16]

7 An outstanding example being a code put into a judgment by Peter Smith J in the case concerning Dan Brown's *Da Vinci Code* (*Baigent v. Random House Group Ltd* [2006] EWHC 719).

8 See the instance where the judge allowed a 33-year-old sex attacker to avoid jail on the condition that he write a letter of apology to his victim. Cause for his mild punishment was the fact that he, as a millionaire's son, had led a 'sheltered life' in India and was led into temptation. 'Apologise and you won't go to jail, judge tells "sheltered" sex attacker', *The Times*, 11 August 2006.

9 In line with Montesquian tradition that the judge should be a '*bouche de la loi*', Montesquieu (1868:XI.6).

10 According to Di Federico (1997:193:196) in Italy the number of ancillary functions runs into 'tens of thousands'.

11 For the Netherlands see Van der Voort, *Rechtspraak in opspraak. Over schurken in jurken* (2006) and Stichting WORM, *Rapport Integriteit Rechterlijke Macht* (1996). They also have a website where the ancillary functions and education of lawyers and judges are – not very accurately – listed (www.pj-design.nl/burhoven/antecedenten-2005.htm).

12 For instance in the United Kingdom (www.publications.parliament.uk/pa/ld/ldreg/reg01.htm) and in the Netherlands (namenlijst.rechtspraak.nl).

13 For a critical discussion of the arguments against and in defence of this practice in England and Israel, see Beatson (2005).

14 Cf. Stevens (2005:186–189) and Griffith (1997:25–57).

15 One has only to remember the impact of the UK Report of Lord Hutton, which was to clarify the circumstances surrounding the death of Dr Kelly.

16 *Bow Street Metropolitan Stipendiary Magistrate ex p. Pinochet Ugarte [1999] 1*

Another issue concerning extra-judicial activities is membership of the Freemasonry or like organizations. The secrecy of these organizations has been viewed in many countries as incompatible with the trust that one needs to have in the judges. For example, after the 'clean hands' operation in Italy, all memberships of secretive organizations were forbidden for judges.[17]

*Corporate bias* Corporate bias concerns worries about the over- or under-representation on the basis of gender, minority, social class, region, political preference or religious background.

In some countries, there is a serious lack of women in the judiciary. In many countries, this has led to active policy. For example, vacancies in Germany state that with equal qualifications women are privileged.[18] Sometimes there is no under-representation in the judiciary as a whole, but merely at the higher court levels, such as in the Netherlands.[19]

Another corporate bias issue concerns minority groups. For example, in France there are questions about the under-representation of Muslims. Even though they comprise about 8 per cent of the population, they have been for a long time 'practically invisible' in the judiciary.[20] In Canada under-representation has led to affirmative action whereby a policy of active encouragement rather than quotas was used.[21]

Sometimes political bias can be experienced as a problem. In France there are debates about the role of judges in political scandals[22] and in the United States political preference of judges form a constant point of discussion.[23]

*Misbehaviour of judges* Every now and then there are incidents involving the misbehaviour of judges in private or in court. A rather horrific example is that of a district court judge for the Oklahoma 10th circuit (USA). In July 2006 he was accused of using a penis pump, while hearing a murder trial, after a 'wooshing' sound was heard by members of the jury. Police found semen on the chair and floor behind the bench and on his robe. The jury found him guilty and recommended a one-year imprisonment, which was raised to four years by the presiding judge.[24]

---

*All ER 577.*

17 On corruption within the Italian judiciary and ties with the *Cosa Nostra* see Della Porta (2001).

18 See Böcker & de Groot-van Leeuwen (2006:20).

19 Cf. de Groot-van Leeuwen (1997:103–116). For the latest numbers see www.rechtspraak.nl.

20 See Provine & Garapon (2006:190).

21 See Böcker & de Groot-van Leeuwen (2006:97).

22 See Roussel (2002).

23 For an older but well-documented overview on the development of judicial politics in the United States see Wolfe (1986).

24 It came to light that he had exposed himself more than 15 times. 'Penis Pump Judge Gets 4-Year Jail Term', *USA Today*, 18 August 2006.

Debates may also concern the behaviour of the judge in private. A Belgian judge, KA, who frequented sadomasochistic (SM) clubs and participated in SM practices with his wife and others, was found guilty in 1997 of assault which led to bodily harm and of incitement to immorality and prostitution, as he suggested to the management of an SM club that his wife be employed there as a 'slave' to indulge in extremely violent practices.[25] His defence, that it was a private matter and consensual, was rejected up to the European Court of Human Rights due to the severe gravity of the acts. The Court remarked for example that KA, as a judge, must have been aware of the principle that the victim's consent had no bearing on the unlawfulness of the acts committed or on the perpetrator's guilt.[26]

Such misbehaviour raises questions as to a disciplinary system for judges. Due to judicial independence, supervision and discipline are – to a large extent – internal matters. The public simply has to trust that judges behave well. This situation is justified by strict selection procedures or by a tradition where one has to have a well-established reputation prior to becoming a judge.[27] A growing question is, however, whether this situation is fitting in an open democracy. Can suspicions be dealt with adequately when things go wrong?

*Neo-managerialism* Recent reforms in the judiciary have put more emphasis on the issue of efficiency. This is seen as part of rendering external accountability: to heighten accountability with respect to spending taxpayers' money, but also with respect to the requirement that judgments will be delivered in due course.

This may raise some integrity problems, especially with integrity on a case level. For example in the Netherlands,[28] the fact that funding is related to output[29] gives

25 The *Cour de Cassation* eventually dismissed him (25 June 1998) and thereby stripped him of his pension.

26 An important factor was the fact that the men rented private venues rather than visit SM clubs because the clubs would not allow the acts perpetrated upon the woman. Cf. ECHR, 17 February 2005, *KA and AD – Belgium* (appl. no. 42758/98 & 45558/99), §§ 46–61.

27 Guarnieri & Pederzoli (2002:66–68).

28 In the Netherlands, the judiciary is very much an organization (the name of the main statute wherewith the judiciary is regulated, '*Wet op de rechterlijke organisatie*' says as much). In the jargon of the Council for the Judiciary, the judiciary is an organization with a production, personnel, work processes, performance norms and the like. Among the objectives in its 2002–2005 agenda were: improving the efficiency of the organization and gaining more insight into the costs of adjudication (*Agenda voor de rechtspraak* 2002–2005, *Continuïteit en vernieuwing* at www.rechtspraak.nl). This was to aid the financing structure of the courts. Since the funding of the courts was linked to output productivity, it comes as no surprise that the output productivity of the courts has grown significantly; see Sociaal Cultureel Planbureau & Raad voor de Rechtspraak, *Rechtspraak: produktiviteit in perspectief*, 2007. For a defense of the necessity of efficiency see Rottier (2003:36).

29 See 'Besluit financiering rechtspraak 2002', in *Staatsblad* 2002, nr. 390 and 'Besluit financiering rechtspraak', in *Staatsblad* 2005, nr. 55. For an English translation (Decree of 28 January 2005 containing new rules on the funding of the court sector in

managerial judges a dual focus: good adjudication and speed in order to save funds. These aims may collide. At a case level, a judge may feel burdened when calling upon an extra witness or when rethinking a verdict. Similar problems, but related to under-funding, occur in England. The listing procedures have become so strict that judges fear that it might harm their integrity or autonomy.[30]

This discourse, which is at times labelled 'new public management' or 'neo-managerialism'[31] has proved itself in tackling bureaucracy in various public services – such as healthcare or the schooling system – by ensuring that the organizations work more efficiently. With regard to such public services, however, efficiency accounts for only a part of the satisfaction of the 'customer'. With respect to these examples, health, education or justice seem to be preferable. In the Dutch situation, where judges are to cope with a high and increasing workload, the interlocking between performance norms and financing structure has led to a discussion on the neglect of the primary process of judging.[32]

*Judicial independence* There are continual debates about whether judges are sufficiently independent. For instance, in the United States there is an ongoing controversy about the political nature of the appointments in the US Supreme Court.[33] The matter of raising campaign funds for judicial elections in the United States is also fiercely debated as is voting on the retention of judges.[34] In other countries there are debates about whether judges are too independent, for instance in Italy where judicial independence seems to stand in the way of an effective system of evaluation of professional qualifications.[35]

In Europe, the case law of the European Court of Human Rights on Art. 6 of the European Convention on Human Rights has expanded the scope of judicial

---

connection with the introduction of an accrual budgeting and accounting system and the netting of output differences (Court Sector (Funding) Decree 2005), see www.recht.nl/doc/BesluitFinancieringRechtspraak_Engels.pdf.

30 Cf. Flood, Whyte, Banakar & Webb (2007:158, 183).

31 See Osborne & Gaebler (1992) and Terry (1998).

32 See Boone & Langbroek (2007) and Ng (2007). The relationship between a high workload and mistakes in judging has been suggested in various discussions. See for instance the conclusion of N. Jörg, the then Attorney General of the *Hoge Raad* (HR 25-01-2005 LJN AR6190 conclusion 16-44) and the discussion that followed (cf. 'Rechters maken teveel fouten', *NRC Handelsblad* 29 January 2005; Tonkens-Gerkema & Van Kesteren (2005)).

33 Cf. Tolley (2006). See Sunstein, Schkade, Ellman & Sawicki (2006) for empirical research on the voting behaviour of Democratic and Republican judges.

34 Cf. Transparency International (2007:26–31); on 'retention elections' see Friedman (2004: 121–122).

35 See Di Federico (1997:201), who states that 'The guarantees of professional qualifications should not be sacrificed in the name of judicial independence (as in Italy), nor should the value of independence be sacrificed by too strict a control on the content of judicial decisions'.

independence – thus sparking debates about the nature of judicial independence. The Court looks *in concreto* whether the requirements concerning judicial independence are met. Its case law is casuistic and does not provide a dogmatic standpoint. It adopts a broad approach: judicial independence may comprise aspects of personal, functional, constitutional, factual and internal independence. The requirement of not being subject to any authority in the exercise of the judicial function seems to be the most important.[36]

### *2.1.2 Integrity issues in developing democracies*

In developing democracies similar problems occur as in established democracies. For example, corporate bias is equally an important issue, but here it may concern racial divides such as in post-apartheid South Africa[37] and some other African countries,[38] or religious divides, such as in Israel.[39] The main difference is that – typically – in developing democracies, corruption is the first thing to battle when it comes to judicial integrity. This corruption is systemic and has affected the whole public sector, thus weakening public institutions.

Transparency International defines corruption as 'the abuse of entrusted power for private gain'. It understands gain to mean 'both financial or material gain and non-material gain, such as the furtherance of political or professional ambitions'. Judicial corruption then 'includes any inappropriate influence on the impartiality of the judicial process by any actor within the court system'.[40] I

36 It has for instance ruled the following. Judicial *appointments* by the executive are not *eo ipso* in breach of the Convention but additional safeguards may be demanded (ECHR, 28 June 1984, *Campbell and Fell – United Kingdom* (Series A-80), § 79). For instance, the involvement of an independent third party is desirable (ECHR, 8 July 1986, *Lithgow a.o. – United Kingdom* (Series A-102), § 202). With regard to *duration* of term, the Court has ruled that short terms, such as three years, may be permissible – it would not necessarily affect the independence of the judge (ECHR, 28 June 1984, *Campbell and Fell – United Kingdom* (Series A-80), § 80). In respect of *irremovability*, the Commission considered the situation a breach of the Convention where civil servants act as judges while being employed under the same conditions as other civil servants, and can thus be dismissed by the Crown without any formal guarantees (ECHR, 20 November 1995, *British-American Tobacco Company Ltd – Netherlands* (Series A-331), §§ 68–77). The power to dismiss does not have to be exercised in practice – the existence of such power to remove a judge is sufficient to breach the Convention (ECHR, 22 November 1995, *Bryan – United Kingdom* (Series A-335-A), § 38). With respect to the *separation of powers*, the Court held that even the existence of a legal provision allowing the executive to invalidate a judicial decision retroactively leads to a breach of the Convention – irrespective of the fact that it has never been used in practice (ECHR, 19 April 1994, *Van de Hurk – Netherlands* (Series A-288), §§ 44–55).

37 See Du Bois (2006:287–299).

38 For example in Namibia (Bukurura 2006:316–325) and Zimbabwe (Matyszak 2006:331–347).

39 See Salzberger (2006:150).

40 Transparency International (2007:xxi).

distinguish between three forms of corruption: bribery, political interference and organizational corruption.

*Bribery* Bribery may include accepting gifts[41] and monetary incentives in exchange for favourable rulings,[42] to accelerate resolutions, to avoid due process or to 'lose' files or case materials.[43] For example, in 2005 a Russian think tank calculated the cost of obtaining a decision in Russia at 9,570 roubles (then $358).[44] Bribery may extend to all levels. In 2002 the Chief Justice of Zambia, who was until that point considered to be a man of great integrity, resigned after an independent newspaper revealed that he had illegally accepted a large sum of money from the government.[45] Bribery is likely to occur when judges are severely underpaid, for example in Vietnam and Laos.[46]

Bribery may also extend to the police department or the prosecution, so as to cause the disappearance of evidence or confiscated possessions, or to fail to bring cases before a judge. It may also be used to influence experts.[47]

*Political interference* Another form of corruption is political interference.[48] Transparency International names Russia and Argentina as examples of countries with vast political influence within the judiciary.[49] In Russia, the trial against oil tycoon Khodorkovsky was perceived by many to be highly politicized,[50] whereas in Argentina an impeachment tribunal consists of a majority of politicians.[51]

Political interference comes about by – among other means – threat, intimidation or bribery of judges. For example, in Guatemala, no trials followed

41 This may also include sexual extortion, Transparency International (2007:122).

42 For example, in Estonia before the Riga Regional Court in Riga, prosecutors demanded an 8-year sentence of imprisonment for two judges who were found guilty of taking bribes in exchange for favourable rulings. 'Corrupt judges face lengthy jail time', *Baltic Times*, 30 January 2008 (www.baltictimes.com/news/articles/19734/).

43 The 370 complaints filed against 30 judges in Guatemala cover pretty much the whole spectrum (www.prensalibre.com/pl/2006/diciembre/16/index.html).

44 Transparency International (2007:33); based on the survey of a Russian think tank (www.indem.ru).

45 See Gloppen (2004:119).

46 See O'Brien (2006:369).

47 Cf. Transparency International (2007:281).

48 Again, I assume that the countries I speak of are democracies under the rule of law. In other contexts, some of these forms may not even have to be labelled as corruption – as for instance cultural specifics may demand that the public/private distinction is not a shared value (see Velasquez 2004).

49 Transparency International (2007:xxiii, 31–34).

50 The website www.khodorkovskytrial.com has been taken off the Internet, but see the website by his lawyers: www.khodorkovsky.info. On political interference in Russia see also Solomon (2004).

51 Transparency International (2007:46). On political dependence see also Gargarella

from the Truth Commission, which had confirmed thousands of human rights violations, out of fear of reprisals.[52] And in Peru, Venezuela, Argentina, Ecuador, Paraguay and Bolivia, national presidents forced out justices or entire Supreme Courts, or provoked massive dismissals.[53] Sometimes political interference is latent, for instance in Tanzania where judges are reluctant to put their foot down when government officials do not comply with their mandate.[54] Sometimes it is constitutionally sanctified. In China, the provision that judges have the right to adjudicate without interference from 'administrative organs, social groups and individuals' does *not* include interference by the 'Party' itself or interference by court presidents, adjudication committees and higher level courts.[55]

It may also come about by manipulation of appointments, for instance when judges are not selected on merit but on partisan connections or 'flexibility'.[56] In Russia, politicians interfere with judicial selection rules[57] and in Vietnam and Laos, the ruling party closely scrutinizes appointment and promotion.[58]

Political interference is not limited to the judiciary but is also aimed at other independent institutions, such as the media or academia. In turn, this paralyzes checks and balances for a viable judiciary, as the media loses its scrutinizing power and academia is unable to criticize bad judicial decisions openly.

*Organizational corruption* Another form of corruption is organizational corruption. This may concern the misuse of private funds for corporate or personal enrichment, when hiring friends or family members, or refurbishing court buildings for excessive amounts of money. For example, in Brazil, one judge was discovered to have placed 63 relatives on his court payroll.[59]

As well as such instances of nepotism or cronyism, corruption may also involve the creation of 'internal mafias' within the judicial organization. Transparency International mentions Venezuela as the prime example, where courts were divided among the judges so that they could appoint their own protégés to lower positions, and noticed these practices in Mexico, Paraguay, Nicaragua and Bolivia as well.[60] These 'internal mafias' make the judicial organization susceptible to infiltration by organized crime. Organized crime may also use threats to weaken

(2004).

52 Cf. Sieder (2004:150) and Transparency International (2007:211–214).

53 Although this happens in most cases on the pretext of corruption, personal or political interests appeared to be at stake, Transparency International (2007:139).

54 See Gloppen (2004:118).

55 See Hawes (2006:409–410).

56 Transparency International (2007:138).

57 See Trochev (2006:390).

58 See O'Brien (2006:372).

59 See Transparency International (2007:45). In Brazil, there are also complaints about unaccounted overspending by the judiciary, see Santiso (2004:172).

60 Transparency International (2007:139).

judicial impartiality.[61] For instance, the systematic threat of *plomo o plata* ('lead or silver') by drug cartels in Mexico and Venezuela severely weakens the judicial organization.

Organizational corruption may, when understood in a wider sense, also concern downright mismanagement. For example, in India delays and disposals of cases, shortage of judges, complex procedures and new laws caused a congestion of the judicial apparatus.[62] This is also the case in Brazil, where measures aimed at enhancing efficiency caused exactly the opposite: a vast bureaucracy.[63]

### *2.2 Developments with Regard to Safeguarding*

In the last two decades[64] there have been remarkable developments on both international and national levels, which are associated with the topic of judicial integrity. Some of the most notable are the following.

#### *2.2.1 International and European Developments*

*International developments* At the sixth United Nations Congress on the prevention of crime and the treatment of offenders, the Committee on Crime Prevention and Control was instructed to elaborate guidelines relating to the independence of judges and the selection, professional training and status of judges and prosecutors. As a result the United Nations drafted the Basic Principles on the Independence of the Judiciary in 1985.[65] As a 'human rights instrument' it is to ensure the realization of intentions, such as are expressed within the Charter of the United Nations, 'to establish conditions under which justice can be maintained to achieve international co-operation in promoting and encouraging respect for human rights and fundamental freedoms without any discrimination' and principles, such as are found in the Universal Declaration of Human Rights, of equality before the law, of the presumption of innocence and of the right to a fair and public hearing by a competent, independent and impartial tribunal established by law. The Basic Principles are primarily concerned with the criminal administration of justice and contain mainly instruction norms to the member states.

The Bangalore Principles of Judicial Conduct cover a wider scope. On the invitation of the United Nations Centre for International Crime Prevention and Transparency International, the Judicial Group on Strengthening Judicial Integrity put forward the first draft in 2000 in Vienna, which was based on a large number of

61 For examples see Transparency International (2007:77, 139, 225).

62 See Transparency International (2007:215).

63 See Santiso (2004:171).

64 In the next paragraph I will turn to the question concerning why the attention on safeguarding integrity has grown especially in the past decades.

65 This document can be found on the website of the Office of the High Commissioner for Human Rights (www.ohchr.org, under 'International Law').

ethical codes for judiciaries. This group consisted of a Special Reporter of the UN-Commission, who was entrusted with the subject of the independence of judges and lawyers, and seven chief justices from African and Asiatic countries. It was presided over by Judge Weeramantry, vice-president of the International Court of Justice in The Hague. The first draft was revised a number of times in order to become an adequate reflection of principles of both common law and civil law traditions. In its final form, as adopted in 2002, it is set up around six fundamental values: independence, impartiality, integrity, propriety, equality, and competence and diligence.[66]

Safeguarding judicial integrity is also conducted by non-governmental organizations. For example, the Geneva based International Commission of Jurists, founded in Berlin in 1952, is 'dedicated to the primacy, coherence and implementation of international law and principles that advance human rights'.[67] To that end it provides legal expertise to judicial organizations. Another example is the work of the already mentioned Transparency International, a global civil society organization founded in 1993, with a mission to 'create change towards a world free of corruption'.[68] In 2007, it published a report about corruption in judicial organizations.[69] The World Bank and the International Monetary Fund also help in efforts to fight corruption in judiciaries.

*European developments* In the aftermath of the Second World War, vast reforms have taken place in Europe in order to strengthen the rule of law. These reforms have obviously included the judiciary.

The Council of Europe boasts a tradition of supporting the role of the judicial office. In Recommendation R(94)12 'The independence, efficiency and role of judges', the Committee of Ministers urges governments of the member states to take all necessary measures to promote the role of judicial power and the individual judge. In 1998 the European Charter on the Statute for Judges was put forward, 'conscious of the necessity that provisions calculated to ensure the best guarantees of the competence, independence and impartiality of judges should be specified in a formal document intended for all European States'. The Council of Europe also set up the Consultative Council of European Judges (*Le Conseil Consultative des Juges de l'Europe*) in 2000.[70] This is an advisory body of the Council of Europe on issues related to the independence, impartiality and competence of judges. It was, for example, among the bodies advising on the above mentioned Bangalore Principles.[71]

66 The Bangalore Principles can be found on the website of the United Nations Office on Drugs and Crime (www.unodc.org).

67 See www.icj.org.

68 See www.transparency.org.

69 Transparency International (2007).

70 It has a website on the site of the Council of Europe (www.coe.int).

71 As the Bangalore Draft was initially conceived by – for the main part – common

Perhaps the strongest incentive for discussions on the integrity of the judge is the case law of the European Court of Human Rights on Art. 6 of the European Convention on Human Rights. In a legal respect, the notion of judicial integrity is usually treated in the context of the right to a fair trial. The importance of the notion of fair trial for the rule of law is undisputed. It is seen by the European Court of Human Rights as a cornerstone of the rule of law, securing impartiality and equality.[72] The case law which has developed on the notion of fair trial has had a major impact on European traditions.[73] For example, the demand to ensure 'objective impartiality' has sparked discussions on disqualification and recusal.[74]

### *2.2.2 National developments*

*Examples from established democracies* In response to violations, a wide array of safeguarding mechanisms has emerged on national levels, a number of which are highlighted here.

In the Netherlands, miscarriages of justice were regarded as such a danger to trust in the rule of law[75] that a permanent Committee was set up under the name *Posthumus* II, later renamed CEAS (*Commissie Evaluatie Afgeloten Strafzaken*

---

law judges, the CCJE was very keen to point out civil law tradition sensitivities. It recommended, for example, abandoning the title 'code' and replacing it by 'principles', especially in view of the prescriptive and exhaustive connotations of codes in civil law countries (cf. Comment no 1 of the Working Party of the Consultative Council of European Judges on Code of Judicial Conduct Bangalore Draft (2002)).

72 ECHR, 26 April 1979, *Sunday Times – United Kingdom* (Series A–30), § 55: '... Article 6 (art. 6), which reflects the fundamental principle of the rule of law' with reference to ECHR, 21 February 1975, *Golder – United Kingdom* (Series A – 18), § 34: 'It may ... be accepted ... that the Preamble does not include the rule of law in the object and purpose of the Convention, but points to it as being one of the features of the common spiritual heritage of the member States of the Council of Europe. The Court ... considers ... that it would be a mistake to see in this reference a merely "more or less rhetorical reference", devoid of relevance for those interpreting the Convention'. See also ECHR, 17 January 1970, *Delcourt – Belgium* (Series A – 11) § 25: 'In a democratic society within the meaning of the Convention, the right to a fair administration of justice holds such a prominent place that a restrictive interpretation of Article 6 para. 1 (art. 6-1) would not correspond to the aim and the purpose of that provision'. With regard to 'fair trial' Article 6 aims to ensure in the first place both the absence of bias and also a fair hearing (Cf. ECHR, 24 May 1989, *Hauschildt – Denmark* (Series A – 154); ECHR, 1 October 1982, *Piersack – Belgium* (Series A – 53)).

73 For example, on the impact of the ECHR on the English 'rule of law' see Tamanaha (2004:56–58).

74 In *Piersack – Belgium* and *Hauschildt – Denmark* the Court has, however, given no concrete ruling as to the scope of objective impartiality, see Kuijer (2004:343–346).

75 Illustrative is the newspaper commentary by Professor H.F.M. Crombag, who argued that miscarriages of justice were the symptom rather than the disease, '*Strafrechtpraktijk heeft therapie nodig. Fouten in zaak Schiedamse parkmoord zijn symptoom van ernstige ziekte*', *NRC Handelsblad* 25 January 2005.

– 'Committee for the Evaluation of Closed Criminal Cases).[76] Its mandate is not to scrutinize *ex post* the integrity of judges but of the prosecution, to see whether serious shortcomings have occurred in tracing criminal facts and/or in the treatment of the subsequent criminal cases, which have obstructed a balanced assessment of the case. In spite of these nuances, popular opinion has it that this committee provides an extra possibility to seek acquittal,[77] which sits uncomfortably with the judges.[78] Similar developments have occurred in other countries.[79]

With respect to judicial ethics, a shift can be observed from relying on informal checks to a more active approach towards judicial ethics. For example, in England the topic of judicial integrity has long been left to informal peer leadership, relying on the hierarchical structure of the English judiciary.[80] In an attempt to meet the broader concern over departures from standards of public conduct[81] the Standards Committee was set up in 1994. In its first report it defined Seven Principles of Public Life, also called the Nolan Principles after the first chairman, Lord Nolan

76 The Committee was named after F. Posthumus, who wrote the official evaluation report on the '*Schiedammer Parkmoord*' case on the orders of the Public Prosecution Office.

77 Recently, some scholars have sought publicity to plead for a commission with a wider remit in line with the English Criminal Cases Review Commission (see footnote 79 below), cf. '*Strafkamer van Hoge Raad voldoet niet*', *NRC Handelsblad* 13 March 2007.

78 See '*Rechterlijk tekort*', in *NRC Handelsblad*. 11 April 2006 and '*Het ongemak van rechters over Buruma*', in *NRC Handelsblad* 18 April 2006. For this reason its president, Professor Y. Buruma, does not cease to emphasize that the Committee does not sit on the judge's chair. It investigates on the initiative of third parties – not the parties involved – whether the process of gathering and presentation of evidence has been a fair one. If this is not the case, the Committee will advise the Public Prosecution Office to review the case.

79 In England, on the recommendations of the Royal Commission on Criminal Justice, the Criminal Appeal Act 1995 established the Criminal Cases Review Commission. Its primary task is to review suspected miscarriages of justice and refer convictions to an appropriate court of appeal where it is felt that there is a 'real possibility' that they would not be upheld. It is also 'to investigate and report to the Court of Appeal on any matter referred to the Commission'. Lastly it is 'to consider and report to the Secretary of State on any conviction referred to the Commission for consideration of the exercise of Her Majesty's prerogative of mercy' (see for an overview of its role www.ccrc.gov.uk). Because of its successes, its objectives have been widened to general standards such as 'enhancing public confidence in the criminal justice system'. Due to this wide mandate and the media attention which its successes have received, the caseload of the Commission has grown causing an immense backlog, cf. Brants (2006:51).

80 See Paterson (1982:chs 2, 5 & 6).

81 This concern was brought about by a series of scandals involving, among others, Members of Parliament, cf. Griffith (1997:36).

of Brasted.[82] These are understood to apply to the whole of the public sector,[83] including the judiciary, and have become the common ground for an extensive ramification of codes, principles and regulations in regard to public standards. The Judicial Studies Board, established in 1979, has also been active on the subject of judicial ethics, providing ethics courses and producing, for example, an Equal Treatment Bench Book.[84]

A relatively new development are independent 'councils for the judiciary' such as the *Domstolverket* in Sweden, the *Domstolsstyrelsen* in Denmark, the Department for Constitutional Affairs in the UK, the *Conseil Supérieur de la Magistrature* in France, the *Consiglio Superiore della Magistratura* in Italy and the *Raad voor de Rechtspraak* in the Netherlands. A council for the judiciary is typically 'a self-governing judicial organization, which functions independently from the government and parliament but acts as an intermediate institution between the legislative-executive branch of government and the judiciary. It does not administer justice as such, but performs "meta-judicial" tasks such as disciplinary action, career decisions by judges, the recruitment and professional training of judges, coordination between courts, general policies and service related activities such as IT'.[85] As it is independent on the one hand but may facilitate peer accountability and the transfer of peer knowledge on the other, it is well able to safeguard and further judicial ethics.[86] It is therefore not surprising that a number of these councils have a mandate with respect to discipline, correction, education, training and promotion.[87]

*Examples from developing democracies* In some countries there are major judicial reforms. These reforms commonly have two dimensions. The first dimension concerns the internal structure, administrative efficiency and quality of judging, the second dimension concerns the role of the judiciary vis-à-vis

---

82 These are: selflessness, integrity, objectivity, accountability, openness, honesty and leadership. Cf. the *First Report of the Committee on Standards in Public Life*, Cm. 2850-I (1995). It can be found on the Committee's website (www.public-standards.gov.uk).

83 Cf. the wide objective of the Committee, announced by Prime Minster John Major: '… to ensure the highest standards of propriety *in public life*' and '… to examine concerns about standards of conduct of *all holders of public office*', in *Parliamentary Debates, House of Commons*, Sixth Series, vol. 248 (1993/94), col. 758.

84 See its website (www.jsboard.co.uk).

85 Voermans (2007:149).

86 For example, the first objective of the Dutch *Raad voor de Rechtspraak* in its agenda for 2005–2008 (www.rechtspraak.nl) was to implement best practices of integrity. This has resulted in the possibility for every judge to do a course in moral dilemmas, to help in developing integrity codes and in projects on integrity risk management within the court organizations.

87 For an earlier comparison of the mandates in this respect, see Voermans & Albers (2003).

other state powers.[88] It involves the introduction or reconfiguration of a range of measures: new selection systems, higher salaries, guaranteed tenure, ethical training, courtroom automation, improved monitoring and discipline et cetera.[89] Reforms that aim at the first dimension rarely succeed. In Guatemala, corruption is still high after expensive and vast reforms.[90] In Brazil, it led to a congestion of the judicial system.[91] An important difficulty is an educational lag, for instance in Cambodia and Vietnam, where there are simply too few qualified judges and where legal university training is in its infancy.[92] Reforms which aim at securing the independence of the judiciary from political interference – and which may to that end promote for instance tenure or the abolition of impeachment by the executive – at times lead to excessive independence. For example, in Brazil, few incentives exist within the judicial system to discipline itself and fight corruption.[93] In fact, when judicial independence is too high, accountability with respect to the first dimension seems to be low.

An instrument that is frequently used to safeguard judicial integrity is the implementation of codes of conduct. For example, in India the higher judiciary adopted a code of conduct for judges, the Restatement of Values of Judicial Life,[94] at the Chief Justices Conference of India in 1999. As the name suggests it is not an enforceable code but provides mere guidelines as to cases involving family members and the acceptance of gifts.[95] In Israel a code of ethics was introduced in 2006 comprising guidelines for professional and daily life, as well as guidelines for disqualification.[96] South Africa equally adopted an 'informal' code of conduct which merely laid out guidelines. Yet in order to strengthen judicial accountability, a 'formal' code of conduct has been proposed in combination with procedures for complaints and discipline.[97]

Lastly, actors within civil society – especially NGOs – play an important role in safeguarding judicial integrity.[98] For example, in Guatemala an NGO (MINUGUA) documented the threats, intimidations and attacks against judges

88 See Santiso (2004:174).

89 Cf. Transparency International (2007:138).

90 See Sieder (2004:145–147).

91 See Santiso (2004:171).

92 Cf. O'Brian (2006:369–371).

93 See Santiso (2004:170).

94 See the website (nja.nic.in).

95 See Transparency International (2007:217).

96 See Transparency International (2007:220).

97 Transparency International (2007:273). The status of this new code – laid out in the Judicial Conduct Tribunal Bill – is still unclear. Cf. the address by Brigitte Mabandla, MP, Minister for Justice and Constitutional Development, on the second reading before parliament in Cape Town (www.info.gov.za/speeches/2007/07112016451003.htm).

98 NGOs also play an important role in combating corruption in non-judicial justice systems, Transparency International (2007:129–137).

from 1996-1999[99] and another NGO (CALDH) threatened to go to the Inter-American Court to find compensation for those involved in genocide.[100] NGOs often join hands, for instance in the Philippines where 30 NGOs are involved in combating corruption.[101] Sometimes they cooperate with other local actors within civil society. For instance, the World Bank and the International Monetary Fund operate in many countries, often joined by local banks and companies as they see a strong judiciary as a backbone for economic reform.[102] Actors within civil society are also concerned with the first dimension of judicial reform: modernizing the judicial organization to standards of transparency and efficiency. NGOs may perform the evaluation of institutional control mechanisms, for example in-depth review of controversial cases or systematic review of guidelines for judicial performance. They sometimes establish 'judicial observatories' designed to monitor the implementation of reforms and the administration of justice.[103]

### *2.3 Understanding the Growing Attention on Integrity*

How can this growing attention on the integrity of the judge be explained? After all, the discourse on integrity is only a few decades old, both within the judiciary and within other sectors. Here, I will look into three factors that are acknowledged in the literature to contribute to the upsurge of the concept of judicial integrity: the growth of judicial power, the growth of public scrutiny and the resulting call for professionalism. These are usually not the *trigger* for the attention to judicial integrity. The trigger can be found in for instance debates about violations, which were discussed previously, or in wide-ranging reforms such as in Latin America or in Eastern Europe after the fall of the Berlin wall.[104] The factors that are discussed here form rather the undercurrent of the growing attention on judicial integrity.

#### *2.3.1 The growth of judicial power*

One reason for the specific attention to judicial integrity lies in the growing power of the judiciary.[105] Although the political and constitutional contexts may vary

99 Private insurance companies considered judges to be such a high risk that they refused to grant them life insurances, Sieder (2004:147).

100 See Sieder (2004:147).

101 Transparency International (2007:262).

102 For example in Brazil, cf. Santiso (2004:161–162).

103 See for a more elaborate treatment Transparency International (2007:115–121).

104 On the latter reforms see Bárd (2004).

105 For general accounts on the growing role of the judiciary in established democracies, common law democracies such as the United States, the United Kingdom, Australia and Canada; and civil law democracies such as Italy, France, Germany, Sweden, the Netherlands (for a detailed account of the growing role of the Dutch judiciary see Soeharno 2006) and Malta; and in developing democracies such as Israel, Russia, the Philippines and Namibia, see the contributions in Tate & Vallinder (1995) and the works of Stone Sweet (2000) and Guarnieri & Pederzoli (2002).

considerably, the following trends are common to many civil law and common law countries: the role of the judge in court has grown, with respect to a more complex society and with respect to international (and European) law.

First, the power of judges has grown *in court*. Typical in this respect is the reform of civil procedure in England. New Civil Procedure Rules were implemented in 1998 as a result of reforms suggested by Lord Woolf and his committee.[106] In this reform, the judge was to abandon its traditionally passive role in civil procedure. Instead, he must seek to give effect to the overriding objectives, which include: ensuring that the parties are on an equal footing, saving expense, dealing with the case in ways which are proportionate, ensuring that it is dealt with expeditiously and fairly and allotting to it an appropriate share of the court's resources.[107] Other countries have implemented similar reforms that give the judge more power in court.

The power of the judge has also grown with respect to a *more complex society*. In a complex society, citizens fulfil multiple roles. This creates more occasions for conflict and it is therefore likely that people will increasingly seek recourse to a judge. In order to meet the complexities of society, the legislator may be more inclined to the use of open norms and flexible law, which does not always have a positive effect on the quality of law. The judge is then looked to, to correct law or to render laws inoperative when necessary. This gives rise to the more fundamental question concerning the grounds on which the judge can do so. Also, the legislator and executive might be inclined to work together to meet the complex needs of society adequately. This changes the critical relationship between both powers and heightens the need for a stronger controlling function for the judiciary, with more powers to review.[108] The vast number of public authorities and their permeation of society has contributed significantly to this development.[109]

With respect to *international and European law*, the judiciary has been given a central place in maintaining the rule of law.[110] It is in many cases the judge who may test national law against international – or European – law, and may as a consequence render national law inoperative. Since the national legislator and

106 For the new Civil Procedure Rules see the website of the Ministry of Justice (www.justice.gov.uk/civil/procrules_fin/index.htm), for the committee's report see Lord Woolf, *Access to Justice: Final Report*. Stationery Office, July 1996 (www.dca.gov.uk/civil/final/index.htm). Cf. Andrews (2003) for a comprehensive treatment.

107 Civil Procedure Rules 1998 rule 1.1(1) and (2).

108 For a compelling overview of the rise of judicial review in the United States see Wolfe (1986).

109 This process is also called 'horizontalization' (Ommeren & Zijlstra 2003:1). It works from two angles. On the one hand, the expansion of government machinery has caused it to permeate society thoroughly. On the other hand, the contours of civil society seem to be wavering more than ever. For example, on the principle of 'exit the nation state, enter the tribes', the philosopher Bauman has observed that today's society consists of groups which change according to preferences of individuals (Bauman 1993:141).

110 Scheltema (1995 & 2005).

executive cannot always keep up with the speed and volume of international and European regulations, and since it is the judiciary that decides on the interpretation and method of interpretation of international and EU law, we may at times certainly speak of a considerable shift in the balance of power from the legislative bodies to the judiciary.

That the role of the judiciary has grown is not to say that judges *misuse* their accumulated power.[111] In light of the growing role of the judiciary it is, however, understandable that in response to incidents involving the judiciary – few as they may be – there is an increasing awareness of the issue of judicial integrity.

*2.3.2 The growth of public scrutiny*

The rise of the attention to judicial integrity is not merely a result of the growing power of judges, but also of the growth of public scrutiny. I will discuss three aspects of this growth: media attention, the upsurge of individualism and the lack of moral homogeneity.

Independent media are a powerful check in a democratic society and their influence on public scrutiny from open internet sources, televised broadcasts of trials[112] or investigative journalism is indisputable. The media promote the awareness of adjudication: they may force judges to formulate clearly and to treat litigants respectfully. In developing democracies it is often the media that expose corrupt judges.[113] For example, in 2004 a prize for investigative journalism was awarded to Arturo Torres, who revealed the illicit enrichment of a Supreme Court judge and in turn unmasked other corrupt judges.[114] On the other hand, trust seems easily undermined in societies where the media do not shy from using their occasional shattering power. High profile cases involving serious crimes often receive sensational coverage, especially miscarriages of justice exposed by journalists. Such coverage seriously affects consideration for the judiciary. Although the image that judges are untrustworthy is, in established democracies, fortunately in many cases wrong, it requires but a few incidents that find their

111 Judges are very keen to show restraint. In England, this sometimes leads to remarkable judgments, cf. the cases *Bentley* [1993] 4 All ER 442 and *Reckley* [1996] 1 All ER 562 (see in this respect *Lewis* [2000] 3 WLR 1785). Similarly, in the Netherlands judges have shown restraint in devising their own regulations to ensure equality of decision, cf. Teuben (2004).

112 On the effect of televised broadcasts of trials see Cohn and Dow (2002), who have critically analysed the effect of landmark media trials, such as those of OJ Simpson, the Menendez brothers and Kennedy Smith.

113 Transparency International (2007:108).

114 The 'Prize for Best Investigative Journalism Report on a Corruption in Latin America and the Caribbean' was launched by Transparency International and the Press and Society Institute and is funded by the Open Society Institute (www.opensocietyinstitute.org). For more information on this price see the website of the Press and Society Institute (www.ipys.org/premio2.shtml).

way through the media into public consciousness to undermine public trust. Its aftershocks can be felt for a long time.

Other factors leading to public scrutiny are the *upsurge of individualism* and the *lack of moral homogeneity*. Since 1960, economic and normative dependencies on the direct social environment – as partners, parents, neighbours, etc. – have shifted to more anonymous collective contexts – as employer, insurer, government, etc. This has caused more balanced relations to emerge between individuals and their direct social environment. The individual, who is now better informed and educated, familiarizes himself according to preference with norms and values, by means of cross-border information technology, consuming the products of multinationals and donating to NGOs. Consequently, the individual has become more critical of the authority of institutions.[115]

Lastly, in a situation of moral homogeneity, a number of elements that have to do with the subjectivity of judges are tacitly shared. For instance, an infilling of open norms such as 'good faith' and 'equity' at times requires moral evaluation which in turn requires moral views. Also intuitions and conscience may be regarded to be of influence in this regard. Due to the rise of moral heterogeneity, as a result of secularization and multiculturalism,[116] distrust may arise about these tacit elements. For example, if a judge takes an oath, we do not know to which God he swears or as to what he fears when violating his conscience. This may lead to a call for a professionalism of these former tacit elements: of judicial intuitions, judicial moral evaluations or a judicial conscience.

### *2.3.3 The call for professionalism*

These developments call for more professionalism on the part of the judges: as judicial power grows, so should their competence and as scrutiny increases, so should judicial accountability.[117] The process of the professionalism of judges 'must find a means of enhancing competence while balancing the competing precepts of independence and accountability'.[118] These problems will be discussed in Chapter 5.

The call for professionalism is wider than just the judge. Professionalism has in many countries taken place on the side of the prosecution, the bar, forensic institutes, public servants and the police forces. This creates higher demands for judges. For example, increased professionalism on the part of the prosecution, with more focus on numbers and statistics, a more professional approach towards

115 Dumont (1986).

116 On the relation between multiculturalism and moral pluralism see Joppke & Lukes (1999) and Kymlicka (1995).

117 On the rise of judicial professionalism in Europe see Baas (2000) and Bell (2006).

118 Armytage (1996:7).

evidence and access to more materials puts pressure on the judiciary to raise its performance.[119]

## 3. The Normative Framework: Democracy, Rule of Law and Integrity

Before exploring the philosophical merits of integrity in the next chapter, the question must be addressed as to whether integrity is a norm at all.[120] Here, I look at the place that integrity occupies in the normative landscape of democracies under the rule of law.

For what does the foregoing inventory say about the concept of integrity? We see that in respect to violations or suspicions the term integrity is freely used. We also see that, in respect to safeguarding, integrity seems almost to be a 'buzz word' for everything good in the judiciary. And in explaining the growing attention on integrity, it could only be explained *why* it has become important – but not yet what integrity entails. If a term has so many connotations and can be used so vaguely, is it then useful to speak of integrity? Is judicial integrity not merely a portmanteau term for all good practices? Or may we be able to understand it as a *norm*?

### *3.1 Integrity in the Context of Rule of Law and Democracy*

In both established democracies and developing democracies, the normative framework in which the judge operates is a democracy under the rule of law. I understand the rule of law[121] to be the *legal* framework in which he operates.[122] Its normativity is derived from law: the judiciary is a legal institution and should act as such. I understand democracy to be the *factual*[123] framework in which he

119 See Freidson (2001) on the necessity of professionalism as other areas have evolved.

120 Here, I use the term 'norm' in the widest sense possible. In the next chapters, the normative constellation of integrity – which is highly complex – will be elaborated upon.

121 The legal legitimacy that the rule of law provides, rests in a broader debate about the legitimacy of the rule of law per se (for an inventory of these debates see Tamanaha 2004). Since Lon Fuller (1969) it has become commonplace for rule-of-law theorists to formulate 'basic' rule-of-law principles, such as the principles of promulgation and of generality (see Marmor 2004 for a refurbishment). General principles of the rule of law are indispensable ingredients for any discussion of the legitimacy of the judiciary. In this book I adopt a broad approach to the concept of the rule of law, whereby I take general principles to also include classic and social human rights (see preface). Evidently, not all of the countries I discussed previously meet these standards. Unfortunately, a further discussion on the matter falls outside of the scope of this book.

122 By characterizing the rule of law as a legal framework, I adopt a notion of the rule of law that comes close to the idea of the *Rechtsstaat* (on the differences and similarities between the two concepts see Soeharno 2006).

123 The factuality here denoted is not at odds with being a *normative* framework. It is

operates. Its normativity is derived from the idea of de facto acceptance:[124] in order to be legitimate, its existence and its actions should be acceptable.[125]

In this manner the ideas of rule of law and democracy secure the normative legitimacy of public functions such as the judiciary. Classically, it is by these principles that the mores of such functions are understood. Professional ethics come with the legal and democratic understanding of the function. For instance, the ethic that the judge should not be too actively engaged in political discussions must be seen in connection with his position under the rule of law. And the ethic that a judge should show exemplary behaviour in and out of court has meaning in respect of a democratic society. This brings us to the question whether integrity is a 'separate norm' or whether it simply denotes this spectrum of professional ethics.

### *3.2 Integrity as a Condition for Legitimacy*

Thus, according to the rule of law, the legitimacy of public functions rests in law, while according to democracy, the legitimacy of public functions rests in the de facto acceptance thereof. These two forms of legitimacy I consider to be the two pillars of the legitimacy of public offices. Let us look closer at these notions.

From a rule of law perspective, institutions are erected and endowed with rights and duties. Without the professional character of persons, however, these institutions remain an empty shell. For these institutions factually to act in the public interest, persons who are of integrity are needed, whose intentions are aimed at the public interest and whose deliberations adequately reflect the purposes of the institution.[126] Thus, from a rule of law perspective, the integrity of the persons

---

rather a factuality to which specific norms correlate. See section 3.2 below and also section 3.3 of Chapter 2.

124 The manner in which acceptance is institutionalised may differ according to the institution: for instance, for the legislator it is in many countries provided by general elections.

125 The relationship between authority and acceptance is illustrated by the European Court for Human Rights in the *Sunday Times* case: 'The phrase "authority of the judiciary" includes, in particular, the notion that the courts are, and are accepted by the public at large as being, the proper forum for the ascertainment of legal rights and obligations and the settlement of disputes relative thereto; further, that the public at large have respect for and confidence in the courts' capacity to fulfil that function', ECHR, 26 April 1979, *Sunday Times – United Kingdom* (Series A-30), § 55.

126 Some would object that institutions can be fashioned in such a way that they are indifferent to the integrity or non-integrity of office-holders. What is then demanded from office holders is only technical competence but not moral competence. Although the effort to guard institutions from the non-integrity of its holders is laudable (see Chapter 5 at section 2.3), this position is untenable. It overlooks both the axiological structure of public institutions and the prudence required to aptly enact institutional values against the demands of concrete situations. For more on my stance on the issue see Chapter 2 at section

acting on behalf of public institutions seems to be presupposed as a distinct norm: integrity seems to be the norm that officials are to be of the right professional character.

From a democratic perspective, according to which the legitimacy of public functions rests in the de facto acceptance thereof, we are faced with the question *why* one would accept the power of the judges.

At the basis of the idea of acceptance lies the idea of trust.[127] For in a free society acceptance is ideally a choice from a consciousness that institutions can be trusted with powers that profoundly impact the lives of individuals.[128] An important observation in this respect is that trust in judges is characterized by an *asymmetrical relationship*. This can be illustrated by two epistemic problems.

The first problem is that the citizen can never know the true motives behind a decision. A litigant cannot 'check' the 'real' reasoning of the judge. He has to trust the judge in his deliberations, that these are upright and that his final motivation is not a matter of legal window dressing. The discretion of the judge is in its essence something not fully controllable. The same is true for dependence on government officials for a building licence or accepting a government's decision to raise a new kind of tax – to a certain extent one has to trust that the decision is taken in the public interest.

The second problem is that many citizens lack the legal knowledge to check the rightness of the decision. In this respect, the judge has a qualitative advantage: just as we trust a doctor because he knows about medicine, we trust the judge because he knows about law and the application of rules.The notion of trust correlates to the norm of trustworthiness of institutions. Nowadays trust is not understood anymore solely as the citizen's fate but also as the norm for the institution. Why would a citizen accept the authority of an institution merely for the sake of it, now that his money, freedom or properties might be at stake? As the nature of institutional decision-making is obscure, the institution has to render external accountability.

In this respect it is important to note that the trustworthiness that is demanded concerns first of all the institution and, only secondarily, the office holder. To a citizen, it may be a matter of indifference which official deals with his case – as long as it is done in a manner that is fitting with the integrity of the institution.

Thus, against the normative framework of the rule of law and democracy, integrity seems to be a vital condition for the legitimacy of public offices. As the rule of law presumes the professional character of the judge and democracy

---

3.2, Chapter 3 at section 2.3.3 and Chapter 4 at section 2.

127 On the notion of trust as the final end of democracy see Adams (2004).

128 O'Neill (2002:18–19) comments sharply on an often mentioned '*crisis* of trust'. She calls it exaggerated to speak of a crisis, for evidently people still trust enough in public institutions to vote for them or turn to them. Instead, she speaks of a culture of suspicion: 'perhaps claims about a crisis of trust are mainly evidence of an unrealistic hankering for a world in which safety and compliance are total, and breaches of trust are totally eliminated'.

demands that the institution renders external accountability, integrity seems to be the right candidate for the term to cover these problem areas, as it has bearing on both professional character and the 'purity' or 'inviolability' of a public institution within the public domain. In other words, it is concerned with both an aspect *internal* to the institution, namely the character of the person holding the function, as well as an *external* aspect, namely the need for external accountability of the institution in relation to a democratic society.

### *3.3 Judicial Integrity as Norm*

From this analysis I conclude that, from a rule of law perspective, integrity is presupposed as a norm. This norm holds that officials are to have the right professional character. From the perspective of democracy, integrity also appears as a norm, namely to be accountable in respect to public trust. Here, the emphasis lies on the external accountability of the institution.

This dynamic between the professional character of the individual official and external accountability of the institution I regard as the specific domain of integrity. It is in this sense that integrity has a role of its own to play in the normative discourse on professional ethics. Here it does not merely concern the relationship between the professional and his organization, between professionals or between the professional and a third party, but the relationship between the ethics of the professional and the external accountability of the institution.[129]

Hereby a norm appears to have been laid bare that deals with a key domain of the question of legitimacy of public functions, which cannot be reduced to democratic or rule of law legitimacy.

## 4. Conclusion

Judicial integrity is widely debated in both established and developing democracies. In established democracies there are debates about miscarriages of justice, the ancillary functions of judges, corporate bias, misbehaviour of judges,

129 Since integrity is the norm that is to account for the trust in public officials, which in turn ensures de facto acceptance and thus democratic legitimacy, one might ask whether integrity is a species of democracy. This objection deserves nuance. The norm of democratic legitimacy does not 'include' integrity, but rather points out that the norm of integrity is a necessary one. Democracy as a norm is better seen as a *ratio cognoscendi* of integrity – it is the basis on which we know that we need the norm of integrity. On the other hand, integrity is the *ratio essendi* of democracy: without officials adhering to the norm of integrity, democratic legitimacy could not exist. The same goes for rule of law legitimacy. The rule of law needs the integrity of officials to exist, whereas we know of this presupposition through the rule of law. Thus, I think that it is safer and more functional to consider integrity a separate norm in respect of the legitimacy of public functions.

the independence of judges and neo-managerialism in the judicial organization. In developing democracies there is also the difficult issue of corruption: bribery, political interference and organizational corruption have a grave impact on the rule of law.

In recent decades the concern to safeguard judicial integrity has grown on both international and national levels. On an international level, safeguarding may for example exist in fashioning principles, laws or guidelines and in the stimulating role of NGOs. On a national level, there may in established democracies be committees to review closed cases, codes or guidelines with respect to judicial conduct and mandates to councils for the judiciary with respect to judicial ethics. In developing democracies, safeguarding may exist in judicial reforms, in codes of conduct and in initiatives by civil society.

I have also looked into factors that may explain the growing attention on integrity in the last decades. These factors are the growing power of judges, the growth of public scrutiny and the resulting call for professionalism. As this professionalism concerns the whole public sector it raises the standard of judicial performance.

These inquiries into the debates on violations, into safeguarding activities and into the growing attention to judicial integrity do not provide an answer to the question whether judicial integrity is, as Simon Lee once put it, merely 'a catch-all for more or less everything that is good in judicial thought'[130] or a norm in its own right. The latter is the suggestion, both in the debates about violations in which judicial integrity seems to be a norm that can be violated, and in the debates on safeguarding integrity where it seems to be a kind of overriding principle that governs professional ethics for judges.

Insight into the normative structure of integrity can be gained by looking at it within the normative framework of democracy and rule of law. The rule of law presupposes the norm of integrity, as the holders of its offices are to be of the right professional character. With regard to democracy, trust in institutions appears to be a condition for democratic legitimacy. To the trust in institutions correlates the norm of trustworthiness. The term of integrity denotes both norms, as it covers both the internal aspect of professional ethics and the external aspect of public accountability of institutions. Integrity thus appears to be a separate norm, besides rule of law and democracy, on which the legitimacy of public offices hinges.

Accordingly, we must view integrity from two perspectives. The first perspective deals with the professional character of the office holder as is presumed by the rule of law. The other perspective to judicial integrity is external – it concerns the external accountability of the institution. In this perspective, the office holder is seen as subsidiary to the office, because public trust is in the first place directed at the institution. The specific domain of integrity concerns the interplay between these two perspectives.

130 Lee (1988:30).

Now that it has been assessed that integrity is a norm in its own right, we should revert to philosophical theory in order to come to a further understanding of what it might entail.

# Chapter 2
# A Theory of Professional Integrity

## 1. Introduction

In the previous chapter it was shown that judicial integrity is a norm. This norm is twofold: the rule of law demands that the holders of public offices are of professional character and democracy demands that the office is worthy of public trust.

In this chapter, the concept of professional integrity of public officials will be explored as to its philosophical merits. For, in order to be able to make integrity as a norm *operative*, we need to know more about the concept than the mere fact that it is a norm. What does it mean to be of professional character? Where is the trust of the public directed? What kind of accountability should be rendered and to whom? What does the precedence of the institution entail? What is the interplay between these two dimensions?

Before proceeding to theory (section 3) I will look at examples in practice (section 2). In order not to base a theory of integrity solely on the problems and nature of judicial integrity, I will first look at examples from three other professions which have had to deal explicitly with integrity problems: accountants, police officers and government ministers.

I will then proceed to a theory of integrity. After discussing the concept of integrity in philosophical literature, I turn to virtue ethical theory to show how the difficulties in the literature can be accounted for. Then I will show how the institutional dimension of the integrity of officials sets about its own problems. I will argue that integrity is to be understood as a generic norm, covering both the norm to be of professional character and the norm to render external accountability with respect to the democratic legitimacy of the institution.

## 2. Three Practice Examples

In order not to be dazzled by the faults of one profession, I will briefly look at three professions other than the judiciary. These are professions which have had to deal explicitly with the concept of integrity in recent years. I will look at the accountant – insofar as the profession has a public dimension – whose integrity is nowadays to a large extent enforced by regulations; at the police officer, whose integrity is largely dependent upon his professional character; and at government ministers, who have had to resign in order to uphold the trust in their office regardless of any fault on their part.

### *2.1 A Strict Compliance Based Approach: The Accountant*

The core value of the accountant is to form his own, objective, qualitative judgment of annual accounts – undistorted by the interests of the controlled party or any other party.[1] The importance of this objective judgment lies – among other things – in a public dimension of accountancy, which concerns the security added to financial accounting. For third parties, the judgment of the accountant must also be seen to be professional and independent. This independence is easily threatened by the fact that for his income, the controller is dependent on the commissioner.[2] After all, accountancy is in many countries a commercial activity.

One has but to remember the scandals of Enron, Worldcom and Ahold to understand that integrity has become a central subject of discussion in the world of accountancy. Fraud scandals have had a severe impact on the trust in accountants. This has, for instance, led Arthur Andersen, Enron's accountant, to be split up and divided among its competitors. In order to secure this trust, strict regulations have been implemented – for instance the Sarbanes-Oxley Act in the United States in 2002.[3] The large accountancy firms have taken rigorous measures and have divested themselves of their consultancy branches.

As a reaction to the aforementioned scandals, in the United States the discretionary space of the individual accountant has been limited. Under the regime of the Sarbanes-Oxley Act a vast number of rules were introduced, to a large extent turning the question of integrity into one of strict compliance with standards that are objective and enforceable. This led to extensive audit trails with huge compliance checklists – managers being personally liable if there were any mistakes.

### *2.2 The Necessity and Limits of Prudence: The Police Officer*

More directly than the work of the accountant, the work of the police officer is done in the public interest. As with the accountant, this is in part regulated on an institutional level where regulations and policies are established with which the police officer must comply. As with the accountant, these measures are primarily focused on preventing violations of integrity.

---

1 See Schilder & Nuijts (2005:77–98, esp. 80–87).

2 The principal–agent relation between the accountant and his client is, of course, an essential difference between the accountant on the one hand and the police officer, minister and judge on the other. This creates integrity problems of its own, which I will not discuss in this chapter as I am concerned with developing a theory of integrity of public officials.

3 It was implemented 'to improve quality and transparency in financial reporting …, to strengthen the independence of firms that audit public companies, to increase corporate responsibility, … to protect the objectivity and independence of securities analysts …'. Ironically, regulations such as these have created a vast amount of work for accountants, whose revenues have subsequently increased.

Such violations can be manifold. Just to give some examples from the Netherlands: a police officer violates his professional integrity when he removes his own fines from the computer system[4] or when he looks into the police information system in regard to a private interest[5] – for instance to look up the criminal record of a business partner of an acquaintance. In another case the judge regarded the mere *suspicion* of a crime committed by a police officer as a serious breach of the legal order.[6]

Not everything can be foreseen by regulation or code. The police officer has to fulfil a multitude of tasks, which are not all foreseeable. Therefore, next to some strict rules with which an officer must comply, many things are left to the professional character of the officer. In his actions, he is not merely to stay away from clear-cut violations of integrity, but he is also to perform his duties in a manner that shows integrity. This is left to his commitment to professional values.

This sheds light on the type of violations of integrity. A violation of a clear integrity standard is a rather clear-cut matter: a standard is violated or it is not. Not living up to standards of professional character, however, is a rather gradual matter, which lies in the difference between performance and aspiration. In practice, the difference between these forms of violations is difficult to tell. It is usually up to the judge or an executive to decide whether integrity with respect to public trust has 'apparently' been violated.

For instance, an officer was given a two-year probational disciplinary discharge for sexual intimidation of a trainee with whom he had a good relationship.[7] They were good company and also met in private, but the fact that he had kissed her, put his arm around her and once delivered a slap on her buttocks was deemed as not permissible, in spite of the fact that she did not say anything about it when the incidents occurred and in spite of the fact that at that time they were in her house on her initiative.[8] Integrity as an integral part of the professional character of police officers thus demands a high level of prudence, and also as regards one's private behaviour.

Thus, compared with the integrity of the accountant, the professional integrity of the police officer is left to a large extent to prudence – to an extent also in his private conduct – and not solely to clear and enforceable standards of strict compliance.

4 *Rechtbank Leeuwarden* 20-06-2005 LJN AT8029.

5 *Centrale Raad van Beroep* 27-10-2005 LJN AU5298.

6 *Rechtbank Maastricht* 21-11-2005 LJN AU6536.

7 That is, until she filed her complaint.

8 *Rechtbank Dordrecht* 9-9-2005 LJN AU2897. The fact that she was a trainee was crucial.

## *2.3 The Precedence of the Office: The Minister*

In many countries, the government apparatus has grown to immense proportions. The constitutional demand that government ministers are responsible for all that is done in their ministries seems therefore to be unrealistic. After all, how can the minister assess vigilantly all of what goes on at the lower levels?

In spite of this, many countries stick to the doctrine of ministerial responsibility. A classic example is the English Crichel Down Affair in 1954. The Minister of Agriculture, Thomas Dugdale, had to resign despite an inquiry suggesting that the mistakes within his department were made without his knowledge. Some mistakes in fact involved deliberate deceit by some civil servants.[9] Another example is the resignation of Lord Carrington in 1982 as Foreign Secretary shortly after the invasion of the Falkland Islands. According to official reviews, there was no responsibility attached to any individual within the government, although there had been some misjudgments within the Foreign Office.

It is even possible that ministers are held accountable for the actions of their predecessors. In 2006 the Dutch ministers Donner and Dekker resigned after a report had shown that responsibility for the death of eleven illegal immigrants, who died in a fire lit by a detainee in a cell block at Schiphol Airport, was to be ascribed to departments that fell under their responsibility. The majority of the policy decisions that led to mistakes on behalf of these departments had been taken under their predecessors but, as Donner said: '... ministerial responsibility is more. In the eyes of the victims, I am responsible for the departments which are understood to have caused their grief'.[10]

Though these examples of government ministers may be unusual, they shed a different light on the phenomenon of integrity. It seems not to be about the integrity of the office holder, but about the integrity of the institution. Discarding an office *holder* 'before' or 'in spite of' the assessment of his true guilt seems therefore to be justified. Speaking from the perspective of public trust, trust in the *office* – not the office holder – takes central stage.

## *2.4 Evaluation*

What do these examples tell us about the concept of integrity? In the previous chapter, we concluded that integrity was a twofold norm: that the holders of offices are of professional character and that the trustworthiness of the office takes precedence over the office holder with respect to public trust.

With the example of the accountant we saw how after grave violations the question of integrity turned into one of strict compliance with objectified standards.

9 However, in papers released 30 years after the affair it was found that Thomas Dugdale had known and approved of his civil servants' actions.

10 '*Donner en Dekker treden af na rapport*', *NRC Handelsblad* 21-09-2006.

The professional character of individual professionals is distrusted to such an extent that the discretionary space is limited to a minimum.

Basic rules of strict compliance establish limits to the discretionary space of office holders, but they do not act as a guide to the ends of discretionary action. The difference between the police officer and the accountant is that more is left to the discretion of the individual police officer and thus to his professional character. This difference between compliance and discretion shows something about the nature of professional character: there are limits on the one hand, but professional autonomy on the other. This also shows in the nature of violations. While a violation of a clear norm is usually understood as binary, not meeting the standards of prudence is a rather gradual matter.

But what about the precedence of the institution over the office holder with respect to public trust? In the example of the ministers, the mistakes of lower officials generated an appearance of a violation of institutional responsibility by their superior – but research still had to be done to find out whether the minister was *actually* responsible. However, as the norm that correlates to public trust, integrity does not merely refer to the character of the office holder. Integrity is also attached to the office itself towards which public trust is directed. When this trust is in danger of being compromised, the office holder himself might have to go – independent of his professional character.

Thus, we have seen three aspects of the phenomenon of integrity. First, the limits of integrity can be enforced by clear and enforceable rules of compliance. Second, these rules set the limits as to how integrity can be understood in a positive sense, namely the professional character of the office holder. Third, the professional character of the office holder may be moved into the background with respect to the external accountability of the institution.

I will now let these examples lie. The three aspects, however, seem to be of vital importance with respect to integrity. The question now is: How do they interrelate? It is up to a theory of integrity to provide an answer.

## 3. Towards a Theory of Integrity

### *3.1 The Concept of Integrity in Philosophical Literature*

In practical philosophy, theoretical deliberation on integrity is fairly new.[11] The literature is impressionistic, differentiated and desultory. I therefore choose to treat the literature by discussing two often-mentioned considerations.

11 To give just an impression, German works such as the *Historisches Wörterbuch der Philosophie*, the *Philosophisches Wörterbuch*, the *Europäische Enzyklopädie zu Philosophie und Wissenschaften*, the *Handbuch philosophischer Grundbegriffe*, Höffe's *Lexikon der Ethik*, the *Metzler Philosophie Lexicon* and the *Meiner Wörterbuch der philosophischen Begriffe* grant no space to the consideration of integrity. Neither do the American *Routledge*

Firstly, speaking about integrity seems to be specifically meaningful with respect to a role in a public or social sphere.[12] For example, questions about the integrity of a cleric are meaningful especially within the framework of his church, questions about the integrity of the police officer in relation to his societal role and questions about the integrity of the accountant in relation to, inter alia, corporate mores. Other forms of integrity, such as personal integrity or moral integrity seem equally tied to roles and not to direct personal relations. For example, it seems less meaningful to require of your partner or a good friend that they should be people of 'integrity' in their direct relation to you. They should rather be loving, honest, faithful, caring and the like.[13] This also suggests that integrity is something other than authenticity. There is, for instance, a difference between whether a policeman who privately holds racist views is authentic or is a person of integrity in the execution of his profession.

Secondly, a distinction is often made between a subjective and an objective dimension of integrity.[14] Subjective integrity denotes the commitment to 'moral principles' or 'ground projects', which constitute one's identity. Therefore it has been labelled as 'wholeness' of the person, as 'harmony with oneself' or as 'unity in moral considerations'.[15] It is associated with terms such as 'authenticity,' 'uprightness' or 'purity', which are to express the consistency, coherence or correspondence between the principles of projects that constitute one's identity

*Encyclopedia of Philosophy* and *MacMillan Encyclopedia of Philosophy*, the French *Encyclopédie Philosophique Universelle*, the Italian *Sansoni's Enciclopedia Filosofica* and the Dutch *Winkler Prins Encyclopedie van de Filosofie*. It is only in the more recent dictionaries that the term occurs with various meanings, such as in the British *Oxford Dictionary of Philosophy* (Blackburn 1994), *Oxford Companion to Philosophy* (Hepburn 1995), *A Dictionary of Philosophy* (Mautner 1996), the Dutch *Woordenboek der Filosofie* (Willemsen 1992), and extensively by Damian Cox, Marguerite La Caze and Michael P. Levine in the online *Stanford Encyclopedia of Philosophy*.

12 Cf. Van Luijk (2002:58–77), Dobel (1999) and Musschenga (2002:169–201).

13 Musschenga (2002:171).

14 Ashford (2000) introduces the terms objective and subjective integrity and places the emphasis on objective integrity. Halfon (1989) bases his book on two similar accounts of integrity, namely 'being true to one's commitments' and the 'commitment to morally justifiable commitments'. According to Halfon, the difficulties between these accounts 'parallel … the difficulty between choosing between an absolutist moral position and ethical relativism' (1989:28–37).

15 See for instance Frankfurt (1971:5–20 and 1987:27–45: 'He who is of integrity is not a "wanton"'), Cox, Caze & Levine (2003:41: 'Integrity is a kind of wholeness, solidity of character or moral purity. It involves a capacity to respond to change in one's values or circumstances, a kind of continual remaking of the self, to take responsibility for one's work and thought') or Pritchard (1972), who treats integrity as moral wholeness within the context of human dignity. See also Musschenga (2002 and 2004:21). Accounts that oscillate between philosophy and – usually Jungian – psychology are occupied with 'subjective' integrity as well: as wholeness, (inner) harmony, uprightness, being untouched, completeness or sincerity (see Storr 1960 and Beebe 1992).

and the actions of the person. In philosophical literature, however, it has also been suggested that integrity has an 'objective' dimension.[16] As McFall says: 'In order to sell one's soul, one must have something to sell'.[17] Here integrity is seen as a collection of core values that are to be followed and duties that one ought not to avoid if one wishes to be a person of integrity.

These notions are problematic and so is their interplay. To start with, the notions of 'oneness', 'purity' or 'uprightness' are unclear. Some writers choose a 'formal' explanation and demand consistency, coherence or correspondence.[18] These terms, however, demand a strictness that is not directly applicable to an ethical discourse. For example, integrity is also understood as a person's capacity to account for the *discrepancy* between his own values and those of others:[19] a judge who rightly withholds his authentic moral judgment about the defendant and delivers a – different – professional verdict can for this reason be a man of integrity.

Then we may ask in respect of *what* someone is upright or consistent. For example, in order to establish the uprightness of someone, we must know in respect to what he acts, thinks or chooses in an upright manner. Not surprisingly, there is disagreement on the specific values and duties which are to be the object of integrity. A recurring problem is that it always seems to be possible to find someone who is called a man of integrity while he is not fully compliant with the established catalogue. For instance, Martin Luther King is often mentioned as an example of a man of integrity,[20] but his lapses in his marital life leave some ethicists puzzled.[21] Lastly, it is unclear how integrity is a collection of values, norms or duties, while it *itself* also seems to be a value or norm. What is the relation between integrity and other values or norms?

A key to understanding integrity may lie in the interrelation of these dimensions. Below, I will argue that virtue ethical theory aptly combines these dimensions.

---

16 See Ashford (2000:421–39). A milder version can be found in McFall (1987:5–20), who limits the object of integrity to that 'which a reasonable man could accept as important' (11).

17 McFall (1987:10).

18 On these three notions see Musschenga (2002). See Halfon (1989:48–52) on consistency. Pritchard concedes reluctantly that although his notion of integrity 'requires that one maintain a somewhat unified moral stance', this 'need not to imply that he has a well-worked-out set of completely consistent principles' (1972:302). From the contrary perspective, Taylor (1985:108–141) argues that 'lack of integrity does not mean lack of overall unity, of sets of identifications which all cohere with each other. It means the mutual undermining of identifications' (129).

19 Critical of notions of integrity as 'sincerity or honesty', Gutmann defends a 'realistic' concept of ethical integrity as wholeness based upon the effort to 'weave' together certain stances or views. He even goes as far as to claim that the 'Faustian sense of inward division and struggle may be the basis of integrity' (1945:211, 214–216).

20 Cf. Halfon (1989:14, 44, 82) and Carter (1996:23, 39, 172, 180–186).

21 Cf. Musschenga (2004:14).

From a virtue ethical perspective, integrity concerns, in the first place, the solid character of the office holder, or the 'subject' of integrity, which comes about in orientation to the values and rules that form the 'object' of integrity, which may differ according to time, to society and to office.

### *3.2 A Virtue Ethical Dimension*

In her essay on Franz Kafka, Hanna Arendt famously warns against the 'natural law of ruin'. The rule of law, she argues, has a tendency to degenerate into a bureaucracy: the rule of laws. In this process, the upholders of the rule of law transform into bureaucrats. It is then not good will, but functionality which characterizes the rule of law.

> One of the main topics of Kafka's stories is the construction of this machinery, the description of its functioning and of the attempts of its heroes to destroy it for the sake of simple human virtues. These nameless heroes are not common men whom one could find and meet in the street, but the model of the 'common man' as an ideal of humanity; thus they are intended to prescribe a norm to society.[22]

In Hannah Arendt's philosophical framework a rule of law requires a notion of an intention on the part of office holders, which is directed at the key values that override the body of rules. For instance, she perceives Kafka's heroes – usually the victims of bureaucracy – as figures to demonstrate how it is 'simple' values that set the rule of law in perspective. These values may be basic notions of well-being or humanity, which are to lie at the base of the rule of law.

When extrapolated to office holders, the rule of law seems to require that office holders are to be of good character in order to preserve its vitality, as has also been made clear in Chapter 1. They ought to act with the key values of the rule of law in view, to prevent it from turning into a rule of laws and to ensure that it serves its overriding ends.

In other words, the good character of the office holder is needed against a framework of rules. But what should constitute such character? As has been shown in Chapter 1, we live in an age of moral heterogeneity. Therefore, an appeal to the conscience of the office holder or a shared conception of well-being is not self-evident.

22 Arendt (1994:76).

It is in this lack of moral homogeneity that virtue ethics has resurged. More than utilitarianism[23] or deontological ethics,[24] virtue ethics[25] focuses on the relation between a complex of ends related to an idea of well-being and the character of an office holder.[26] As to the contents of these ends, these may differ to some extent – thus allowing for different interpretations. Below, I will demonstrate how a virtue ethical approach[27] contributes to the understanding of integrity. Its

23 A utilitarian theory does not look so much at the character of the decision-maker but at the rationale of his decision. Because of its intentional nature, integrity – in its differing meanings – has been put forward as an objection to utilitarianism. It is said that in utilitarianism, one would have a 'boundless obligation' because the distinction between causality and intention has not been made sufficiently clear. As a result, by merely looking at the consequences of an action, the utilitarian pays no attention to individual integrity and conscience (see Smart & Williams 1973:98–118, esp. 116). Bernard Williams (Williams 1985:75) emphasizes that, in contrast with utilitarianism, integrity can only exist when people act on the basis of 'ground projects', which are projects that are determinant for one's identity. This objection is not undisputed. John Harris points out that although utilitarianism as a whole may be at odds with integrity, one does not necessarily act contrary to integrity when one sacrifices some projects to which one is dedicated, to the principle of utility in some circumstances (1974:265–273, esp. 267). To this, Stephen Carr adds that Williams' thesis – that there might be other 'projects' which are of a greater moral value than utilitarian projects – can be disputed in traditional terms without making an appeal to integrity (Carr 1976:241–246, esp. 246). These articles have not prevented Williams' account from becoming a standard objection. It has also been defended against later forms of utilitarianism (cf. Harcourt 1998:189–198).

24 A Kantian approach classically perceives the relation between decision-making and the decision-maker as the adherence to norms. Although 'neo-Kantian and 'Kant' are seldom identical, it is telling that Kant focuses especially on the notion of duty within conscience. Cf. Kant (1902 and 1922). Kant also has a *Tugendlehre*, but in comparison with Aristotle, Kantian virtue ethics concern the development of character towards norms that are tested categorically – not the development of good character as such (for a defence of Kantian virtue see O'Neill 1989:145–162; for a critical analysis of Kantian virtue and an attempt to improve it by means of Aristotle's ethics see Sherman 1997:121–186, 331–361).

25 The *locus classicus* for virtue ethics is Aristotle's *Ethica Nicomachea*. This work was written for the citizens of Athens, who were to fulfil several political functions during their lifetime. Aristotle's *Politica* and *Retorica* were written for this same audience. In the last 50 years, there has been considerable attention to virtue ethics and a number of aspects has been revisited, cf. for instance Anscombe (in Anscombe & Geach 1961), Aubenque (1963), Oksenberg Rorty (1980), MacIntyre (1981), Nussbaum (1994 and 2004) and Höffe (1995).

26 See Von Fritz (1984:69–91).

27 I speak here of a virtue ethical approach in a general sense and not specifically of Aristotle in respect to whose philosophy there is a considerable hermeneutical distance. For example, he does not share the modern understanding of the subject–object distinction. In the next chapters I will go more precisely into Aristotle's philosophy.

main contribution lies in the fact that it is able to focus upon the integral relation between subject and object.

Two preliminary remarks need to be made. First, in this book I am concerned with the *professional* character of an office holder.[28] I am therefore concerned with virtue as a political or professional virtue, not as the moral quality of the private individual. Second, virtue should not be understood in the sense of 'piousness'. As will be made clear in the next chapter, it should be distinguished from later, mostly Christian, associations. It is sometimes downright 'impious' acts that can be virtuous. I will go more specifically into the sources of virtue ethical theory in the next chapters.

*3.2.1 The relation between the subjective and objective dimension*

From a virtue ethical perspective, it is possible to integrate the dimensions of subjective and objective integrity.

The professional character of the office holder lies at the basis of every act or deliberation. If we understand this to be the 'subjective' dimension of integrity, then it would seem that integrity is not a *specific* professional virtue, but seems rather to concern virtuousness *itself*.[29] It concerns the quality of one's character to act optimally with respect to professional values. When speaking about the 'objective' dimension of integrity, we may understand this to be the complex of values, norms, duties or rules that are connected with the profession.

What is the relationship between the professional character of the office holder and the 'object' of the office? The professional character of the office holder comes about by acting prudently[30] on a continuous basis. This means that in his actions,

28 It is not the custom to use virtue ethics in such manner, but it seems to be wholly in line with Aristotle. In fact, the political nature of Aristotle's virtue ethics – on which the focus lies here – has been underexposed. Although Aristotle had the difference between 'normal' and 'political' virtues in view (see Aristotle's *Ethica*, *EN* VI.8:1141b33), some virtue ethicists (e.g. MacIntyre 1981) seek to limit virtue to the private sphere.

29 With respect to the judge Solum has attempted to catalogue judicial virtues. He distinguishes between 'the (mostly) uncontested judicial virtues (and vices)': incorruptibility and sobriety, courage, temperament and impartiality, diligence and carefulness, intelligence and learnedness, craft and skill; and 'the (mostly) contestable judicial virtues': the virtue of justice (as fairness or as lawfulness), equity and practical wisdom (2005b). It is not exactly clear how this catalogue is related to Aristotle as Solum claims. For instance, Aristotle avidly distinguishes craft and skill from virtue (cf. *EN* II.3:1105b7–9). Also, impartiality is not a virtue found with Aristotle. Similarly, the vice of 'sloth' which must be avoided by a diligent judge, is found with Aquinas – not Aristotle. In an earlier work (1988), Solum speaks of the virtue of judicial integrity but here he has not Aristotle but Dworkin in view: 'A good judge should have special fidelity to the law and its coherence. I call the judicial character trait that expresses this fidelity judicial integrity'.

30 On the nature of prudence and prudent decision-making see Aubenque (1963) and Ebert (1995). Prudence is the central virtue of Aristotelian ethics, since it combines the theoretical virtues with practice. One who steadfastly acts in a prudent manner acquires

the office holder aptly assesses the requirements of a specific situation in light of the values, the 'object' of his office.[31] The quality of this assessment determines the measure of excellence in professional character. If he does this continuously, then character will be formed and in turn, when such character is formed, the virtuous will be better able to act prudently. Eventually his character is 'trained' in mediating the specific requirements of the situation with the values of his office. It is important to note that acting virtuously differs from acting skilfully, since skills can be used for both good and bad intentions whereas prudence is intentionally aimed at the right ends.[32]

There is a distinction that is of importance here, namely the distinction between the values and rules of the profession or office.[33] I understand values in an aspiratory or ideal sense.[34] Values are what the prudent professional has as his aim. They give direction to his acts and should become part of his attitude.[35] They are thus important when positively safeguarding professional character. Rules, on

---

excellence of character, by which he is able to act more prudently. In the next chapter, the notion of prudence is elaborated.

31 The rightness of the values and rules, which constitute the object of integrity, cannot be guaranteed by the right attitude (cf. Hepburn 1995:410–411). It is possible, however, to establish some boundaries to the object of integrity, which follow from the virtuous nature of the attitude. Because integrity as professional character demands that an intentional and solid attitude must be kept up against challenges and temptations, 'spinelessness' or 'indifference' will not be the best candidates. They seem to be at odds with the 'right attitude' which integrity demands. On the problem of the 'good' see section 3.4.3 below.

32 In his *Ethica* Aristotle makes clear that it is 'intention' which distinguishes virtue from technical skills, which are usable for both good and bad intentions (*EN* II.3:1105a27–29 and *EN* VI.4:1140a1–24).

33 In this respect, John Kekes distinguishes between 'unconditional' and 'defeasible commitments'. The first form the core of one's personality, 'the fundamental components of his identity' and are indefeasible while the second are a reflection of the social and historical context of the person (Kekes 1983:514). Somewhat analogous is Musschenga's distinction between the defensive and the prescriptive or evaluative function of integrity. The first concerns the boundaries drawn, the second concerns aspirations or ideals (Musschenga 2004:73–76, 90). In the case of these authors, the range of the defensive or unconditional function is too limited, since it concerns merely the well-nigh absolute inviolabilities, such as the inviolability of the body. They thereby lose sight of the deontic aspects of contingent contexts, such as professional contexts.

34 In this respect I follow the characterization that Taekema gives of *ideals*, following Dewey and Selznick, as 'values, of a complex and dynamic nature, which are embedded in social practices. That is, they are desirable states of affairs which are difficult to realize completely, which provide direction in problematic situations' (see Taekema 2004:39).

35 McFall adopts Kekes' distinction but labels them as 'identity-conferring' and 'defeasible' commitments. The distinction remains uncomfortable. It remains difficult to see which values are identity-conferring, without conceptualizing one's intentional orientation. What is identity-conferring for one person, does not have to be so for another. As an example of a 'defeasible commitment', McFall mentions the value of professional

the other hand, mark the boundaries of prudence. Where values provide an aim to prudence, rules limit the scope of virtuous conduct.[36] Values and rules are closely connected: values determine the demarcation of rules and rules mark the limits of a value-oriented assessment.

In this sense it is possible to retake the notions of 'subjective' and 'objective' integrity on a virtue ethical level, while avoiding the problematic aspects. Instead of speaking of 'coherence, consistence or harmony' – terms, which are logically strict, but in practice unclear – we are now able to speak in more concrete terms: of constancy, solidity or 'backbone' in one's attitude.[37] With regard to 'objective' integrity, one is not bound to a search for a general catalogue of values. Instead, there is the freedom to focus in each profession on what the 'object' is of the right professional attitude.

Integrity is in this respect a 'higher order virtue'[38] – it concerns in the first place the character of the office holder, but this character is subsequently made concrete in the 'object', which may differ according to time, to society or to office.[39] It is also a 'master virtue'[40] since it is no virtue next to other virtues, but denotes the virtuousness of the office holder itself.

---

success. It is, however, hard to see why abandoning the value of professional success could not be for some persons 'identity-conferring' (McFall 1987:12f).

36 Integrity concerns both values and rules. I therefore regard treatments of integrity as a Kantian project in the sense of a 'minimally acceptable social life' as too one-sided. See for example Halfon (1989) and the pertinent review by George W. Harris in 1990, *Ethics* 101(1):188f. Ramsay also takes a Kantian approach, pointing out 'several incommensurable basic goods' instead of 'reason' (Ramsay 1997). The other extreme, which rejects a Kantian approach (see for instance Williams 1981:1–19) I regard as equally one-sided.

37 Chesire Calhoun (1995) argues that integrity should be described as 'standing for something'. By putting the emphasis on the attitude, other demands that are connected with integrity can be put into perspective. For instance, from the perspective of a strong attitude it is possible to say that integrity can cope, to a certain extent, with ambivalences and inconsistencies.

38 Cf. McFall (1987:14) following Gabriele Taylor: 'One cannot be solely concerned with one's own integrity, or there would be no object for one's concern. Thus integrity seems to be a higher order virtue. To have moral integrity, then, it is natural to suppose that one must have some lower-order moral commitments; that moral integrity adds a moral requirement to personal integrity'.

39 As the object of integrity acquires its meaning in institutional or social contexts, McFall's notion of personal integrity seems to be too solipsistic (1987:9): 'personal integrity requires that an agent (1) subscribe to some consistent set of principles or commitments and (2), in the face of temptation or challenge, (3) uphold these principles or commitments, (4) for what the agent takes to be the right reasons'. Integrity is not the virtue of perseverance in one's own convictions in light of troubles or temptations. Rather it requires a careful assessment of the social or institutional embedding of these convictions.

40 With some reticence, Calhoun (1995:260) concludes: 'What I have had to say about integrity suggests that integrity may be a master virtue, that is, less a virtue in its own

By means of this virtue ethical approach, we have thus found a mode of relation between subjective and objective integrity. Both ideas are necessary. If the object is simply translated into rules and there is no prudence on the part of office holders, it may lead to Kafkaesque situations. On the other hand, decisions of office holders that are taken in 'uprightness' yet irrespective of the right values or rules are equally discomfiting.

### *3.2.2 A closer look at the object of integrity*

McFall speaks of integrity as 'a personal virtue with social strings attached'.[41] This is certainly true for the integrity of holders of public offices or institutions. The office or institution is embedded in a specific society and an overriding value is that it is to further the well-being in such a society. This means that it is prudent for the office holder to look 'beyond' the office in order to determine the rightness of his actions.

For example, in the Netherlands, a big fraud scandal in the construction sector concerning the violation of competition laws came as a 'surprise' to many. Many of those involved regarded informal agreements as part of the mores of the sector.[42] It was held against them that the mores of the construction sector were not the only mores that they were to uphold. Integrity thus demands a form of *alertness* or *sensitivity* in the attitude towards the normative expectations of the social environment.

This can be extremely demanding. For example, societies are far from homogeneous when it comes to well-being. Also, there can be many levels on which ideals of well-being are expressed: different national, European, international levels et cetera. As will be outlined in the next chapter, the idea of well-being is highly complex – yet still provides guidance in deliberation. This means that judicial deliberation cannot be left to procedure alone: prudence is necessary to assess requirements with respect to well-being, which is the result of a complex of values, ends and norms in a certain place or time and connected with a specific profession. It is exactly this complexity that requires experience, training and careful deliberation.

### *3.2.3 Integrity as professional character*

To summarize, the rule of law demands that the holders of its offices are people of integrity, in the sense that they are to be of professional character. From the viewpoint of virtue ethics, this notion has been concretized.

To be of the right professional character means that the professional rightly takes into account in his actions the values and ideals that are connected with the

---

right than a pressing into service of a host of other virtues – self-knowledge, strength of will, courage, honesty, loyalty, humility, civility, respect and self-respect'.

41 Cf. McFall (1987:11). In the next chapter we will see that this is true for all virtues.

42 See Huberts (2003:11–13).

institution. The selection and assessment of these values and ideals in specific actions is a prudent activity. It is not just about having the right intention or aim, but also about having the ability to mediate professional values and rules with the concrete situation, with an idea of general well-being in view. By continually searching for the optimal way to act, the professional character of the actor increases in quality. He then becomes able to act optimally in future situations.

### *3.3 The Institutional Dimension of Integrity*

Until now, we have spoken of integrity in virtue ethical terms. The institution was understood from the perspective of virtue as it is institutional values and ideals that form the object of virtue. The institution also limits prudence. As competences are stipulated by the institution the discretionary space will be limited to these competences. Yet, the institution or office also provides another dimension to integrity that is independent of virtue.

Integrity bears the connotation that the values and duties that refer to it have the function to give institutions the predicate of 'sacrosanctity' or 'inviolability'[43] in the public domain. Much stronger than in the Greek *polis*, the Roman world empire, or the budding *Rechtsstaat* of the nineteenth century, we have to do with a democratic embedding of public institutions. With respect to democratic legitimacy, integrity is not merely an obligation of the office holder but also of the institution itself.[44] This obligation entails that public trust is upheld, but in a specific manner. I will argue that trust is to be directed at institutional values.

#### *3.3.1 Institutions and trust*

In democratic societies, the legitimacy of public institutions rests in part in the trust that is placed in them. Public trust is not in the first place directed at the individuals holding these institutions, but at the institutions themselves. We expect a judge, a minister or a police officer to act according to his role regardless of who this judge, minister or police officer is. The trust in public institutions is in part dependent on the professional character of these people, as described above. It is not in the first place directed towards professional character, however, but towards the institution *as institution*.

43 These terms reflect the etymological origin of integrity as *non-tangere* or *intangere* (*tangere* meaning 'to touch').

44 See Böckenförde 2002 on the early foundations of public offices. In a recent work, Dobel distinguishes between three traditional models to 'resolve the conflicts between public discretion and liberal, democratic life': the 'legal-institutional model', the 'personal responsibility model' and the 'effectiveness' or 'implementation model'. The last model deals with discretion, the middle one with personal responsibility and the first with the official's subordination to legal and institutional authority (Dobel 1999:2). I do not separate the levels of personal responsibility and discretion, but would suggest that discretion plays a role at both a personal and an institutional level.

In the example of the minister, we saw that there was little room for reproach on the level of professional character. Rather the reproach was directed at the institution. It seems that in some cases, the public is indifferent as to an excuse that a minister might have as an individual, because his *office* is at stake.

Thus, from the perspective of trust, the integrity of the individual professional is ancillary to that of the office. Integrity as professional character is a necessary condition for meeting the norm that correlates to public trust, namely that the institution is trustworthy. It is not a sufficient condition. Trust is primarily directed at the institution and may be indifferent to moral expectations on the part of the individual professional. Institutional values may even be protected against the office holders: procedures about judicial disqualification, for example, protect the value of impartiality against possible mistakes of office holders.

In Chapter 1, the observation has been made that the democratic legitimacy of public institutions rests in the de facto acceptance thereof. This acceptance was, as argued in that chapter, linked to the trust placed in these institutions. But what norm correlates to this? It cannot be to secure de facto acceptance *outright*. For example, what if review polls were to show that the trust in judges would rise significantly if they had no moustaches? This does not correlate directly to the norm that all judges should shave off their moustaches. On the other hand, if the de facto trust in the judiciary is high, this still does not mean that the trust is directed at the right values. The public perception may be far from accurate.[45] So what is to be done about this fluid idea of trust?

The norm to hold the institution accountable with respect to public trust is not simply about upholding good confidence statistics. Rendering external accountability[46] is a *normative* activity: it is to make sure that public trust is directed at the right values, namely the values that are connected with the institution.[47] For example, no risk is taken that the public trust in the value of impartiality of the judiciary is harmed. Therefore procedures about disqualification are fashioned that disqualify judges automatically: with no respect to the question whether they would be able to judge well in the case, according to their professional character. On the other hand, the shaving off of moustaches does not seem to be linked to institutional values – perhaps only if understood as an expression of propriety – and it does therefore not fall under the norm to render external accountability.

---

45 Transparency International (2007:104). Also, a negative image of the judiciary may be self-fulfilling and self-extending.

46 I use the term *external* accountability to refer to a specific relation, namely between the institution and public trust. It is does not, for example, concern internal relations, such as the accountability of the institution towards office holders. I certainly do not rule out the existence of other forms of accountability, but I regard this form of accountability to be of special importance with respect to integrity as it has a bearing upon the democratic legitimacy of institutions.

47 In Chapter 4, I will elaborate further upon the relation between the public institution and the values of which it is 'symbolic'.

Thus, the norm to render external accountability sees to the specific relation between the institution and the public forum. The trust that the public has in the institution correlates to the norm to render external accountability. In this respect, public trust needs to be directed at the right institutional values. As it is hard to distinguish between de facto trust and trust directed at the right institutional values, external accountability is a norm that will remain to sit uncomfortably.

*3.3.2 Violations against an institutional backdrop*

In the examples at the outset of this chapter, we saw that violations of integrity are heavily punished. As mentioned, the accountant firm Arthur Andersen was cut up and divided between its competitors, the police officers were all fired or were given probationary discharges and the ministers had to resign.

What is the justification for such serious retribution? On many occasions the direct harm of such actions is not grave. The justification for the weight of the sanctions lies, however, not merely in the retribution for the lapses, but also in the fact that public trust is harmed as a result of such lapses. It is not merely the direct harm that is punished but also the harm that is done to the trust placed in these offices. Thus, weighty consequences are also to be understood as retribution for the violation of public confidence.

Is, however, retribution fair when there was no intention to harm public confidence, as has been established at the time in the case of the ministers? And how are we to understand the phenomenon of an 'appearance' of a violation of integrity?

This is to be understood from the tension that exists between the institution and the professional. The divergence between institutional and virtue ethical demands may lead to a difficult situation. From a virtue ethical perspective, it may not always be possible to develop an alertness to all the demands of the public sphere. The professional attitude can be very strong and cope with ambivalences in values or rules, but there are limits, as the examples involving government ministers have shown. It is not impossible that an action that is not wrong in virtue ethical terms can cause a violation of integrity in institutional terms. In this sense, the tension between the integrity of the individual in a virtue ethical sense and trust in the integrity of the institution can be tragic for the individual. Trust in an institution is to some extent indifferent to moral quality.

### 3.3.3 Integrity as external accountability

In summary, next to the norm to be of professional character[48] I have now explored the norm of external accountability.[49] This norm entails upholding public confidence with respect to institutional values so as to secure the democratic legitimacy of the institution.

Integrity is a condition for democratic legitimacy, as we saw in the previous chapter. In order to see how integrity correlates to public trust, it should also be viewed from an external perspective. Integrity bears the connotation that the values and duties that it generates have the function to give offices or organizations the predicate of 'sacrosanctity' or 'inviolability' in the public domain. Therefore trust is directed at the office but in a second instance at the office holder.[50]

The importance of this external dimension for the judge is well illustrated in the verdicts of the European Court of Human Rights, following a long-standing tradition of English natural justice.[51] Regardless of the deliberations of the judge, justice should also *be seen to be done*.[52]

---

48 The norm of external accountability is different from a form of accountability that can be understood from the perspective of professional character. We will see in Chapter 3 that the prudent person has to 'take into account' societal mores, emotions or values. This form of 'virtuous' accountability is described in terms of sensitivity, openness or empathy (Schipper 2007:102–104, 114). It differs from external accountability which sees to the relation between the institution and public trust. From this external perspective, accountability implies institutional responsibilities, which are not necessarily equivalent to the responsibilities of the individual office holder.

49 Accountability has also been described in non-normative terms, which are not the focus of this book. In a non-normative sense, the focus lies on accountability as a relation or a mechanism. For example, Bovens defines accountability as 'a relationship between an actor and a forum, in which the actor has an obligation to explain and to justify his or her conduct, the forum can pose questions and pass judgement, and the actor may face consequences' (Bovens 2007:450). In Chapter 5 at section 2.4 I will return to the distinction between accountability as a mechanism and as a norm, when discussing judicial independence.

50 I have not conceptualized the term responsibility in the distinction between professional character and external accountability. That is because responsibility can be understood at both levels. On the level of professional character, it refers to 'objective' integrity: the professional responsibility of the office holder consists in the demands that are stipulated by the profession for the office holder. On the level of external accountability, responsibility concerns the responsibility of the institution with respect to public trust. For instance, since ministries have bureaucratic aspects – they are complex organizations – ministerial responsibility is located with the top office holder so that he may be held accountable with respect to public trust. Responsibility here relates to institutional structures rather than professional character (see also Bovens 1998:85–89).

51 Wade & Forsyth (2004:439–558).

52 ECHR, 1 October 1982, Piersack – Belgium (Series A-53), § 30; ECHR, 24 May 1989, *Hauschildt - Denmark* (Series A-154), § 48.

### *3.4 Integrity as a Generic Norm*

Integrity as a *generic* norm is more than the sum of its parts. Defining integrity as a generic norm does not end the discussion about what integrity is. Instead, it sparks off and catalyzes such discussions. These discussions are part of the concept of integrity, but also point out its inherent difficulties.

#### *3.4.1 The institution as a point of convergence*

Integrity is a generic norm, concerning on the one hand the norm that office holders are to be of professional character and on the other hand the norm to render external accountability. What is the relation between these two norms?

The answer lies within the nature of the institution. Professional character is an institutional virtue. The institution determines the scope of prudence and without virtue, institutions as organizations risk diverting into estrangement from their core values. It is virtuous professionals who act with institutional values in view and who in this manner secure institutional vitality. Equally, external accountability is institutional accountability. It is institutional values at which public trust should be directed and it is because of the importance of these values that the institution takes precedence over the office holder with respect to public trust. Thus, virtue and external accountability converge within the institution.

Both virtue and external accountability need to be furthered in order to enhance the legitimacy of an institution within a democratic rule of law. Virtue furthers the legitimacy within the rule of law, as institutional actions are performed with the institutional values in view. External accountability furthers the democratic legitimacy of the institution, as it is to further the trust placed in the institution.

Within the institution, the relation may be one of reciprocity or one of tension. The virtuous person will have external accountability in view in his deliberations. On the other hand, external accountability may require strict compliance, thus limiting the scope for prudence. External accountability may also force one who has been of professional character to resign as the trust in the office is at stake. External accountability is in turn limited by virtue as some actions cannot be taken other than by careful deliberation.

Although there are many interrelations between virtue and external accountability – which will be shown in the next chapters – for the sake of clarity I will attempt to distinguish them here as much as possible.

#### *3.4.2 A norm that raises awareness of itself*

How do virtue and external accountability relate in concrete situations? In each context, in each legal order, at each time, the configuration between virtue and external accountability can be different. It is in fact part of the nature of integrity that the question as to the relation between virtue and external accountability is then asked.

This question has a specific function: it is a question that raises awareness. Awareness of the difficulty of prudence and the difficulty of rendering external accountability, but also awareness of the precise relation that is to be sought continuously. This may be an explanation for the fact that integrity is sometimes called a 'buzz word'. Although it sounds pejorative, it reveals that integrity is a term that sharpens consciousness and confronts with the question as to the balance between the professional character of office holders and the democratic legitimacy of the office.

### *3.4.3 A second level of prudence*

Finally, when is the relation between virtue and external accountability *good*? This question cannot be answered by a theory of integrity. The normative framework of democracy and rule of law does provide some impetus, as it is not devoid of values or ideas about well-being. Yet still, the final answer to what integrity demands will depend on the concrete legal order at a concrete time. As a consequence, the meaning of integrity will differ in different contexts.

For example, in a time of trust in accountants the limits of discretion may be wide. Yet it is easily understandable that after a fraud scandal – when systems of checks and balances have failed – the integrity of accountants is approached in terms of strict compliance.

The right relationship depends in the end on the configuration of many elements. This requires extreme prudence. This level of prudence is different from prudence on the level of virtue. On the level of virtue, prudence was shown by the individual office holder – as a constituent of professional character.

On the level of configurating both virtue and external accountability it is, however, unclear who the subject of prudence is. For instance, it may be a legislator, it may be a committee, it may be the joint prudence of professionals and policy-makers together or it may be the prudence of individual professionals. The discourse in which such prudence comes about is complex and multifaceted. The question as to who is involved with safeguarding and how one should go about it will be asked in Chapter 5, but not answered – that simply falls outside of the scope of this book.

It is part of a theory of integrity to activate and catalyze such a discourse. And although a final answer to what *judicial* integrity demands precisely in a concrete situation cannot be given in this book, it can certainly be *anticipated*: by sketching carefully the dimensions of virtue and external accountability and articulating their interrelation in a democracy under the rule of law.

## 4. Conclusion

It can be concluded that integrity is a generic norm. It denotes both the norm that office holders are to be of professional character and the norm that external accountability is rendered with respect to the trust placed in the institution. The first I call integrity as virtue, the second integrity as external accountability.

Both perspectives are necessary in a society in which the judiciary is a public institution. To be of the right professional character means that one is able to mediate professional values and rules with the concrete situation. Consequently, if an office holder does not possess the right character, discretion in public functions cannot be exercised properly. The norm to render external accountability entails that effort is made to secure the democratic legitimacy of public institutions. After all, public institutions ought to carry the predicate of 'sacrosanctity' or 'inviolability' in the public domain. Therefore trust is directed at the office and only secondarily at the office holder. Although it corresponds to the de facto acceptance of the judiciary as an institution, it is in itself a norm: trust should be placed in the right institutional values and in the right manner.

Yet the whole is more than the sum of parts. That integrity is a generic norm means that it immediately raises the question as to the relationship between these two norms. This question is a part of the concept of integrity. The concept of integrity raises awareness: not only of the nature of virtue and external accountability, but also about the balance between the two. This dynamism is specific for the norm of integrity. Speaking of integrity implies deliberating about the complex relation between the virtue of office holders and the external accountability of the institution, about its tensions and reciprocities.

A theory of integrity cannot answer the question as to the right relationship between virtue and external accountability. The normative framework of democracy and the rule of law provides some help, but much will depend on the specific demands of a specific society in a specific time. Yet an answer to the question what integrity demands precisely in a specific society can be *anticipated*: by outlining carefully the dimensions of virtue and external accountability and articulating their interrelation in a democracy under the rule of law. In the following chapters, such anticipation will be performed with respect to judicial integrity, by means of a theory of integrity in the judicial decision-making, in judicial conduct and in safeguarding.

# Chapter 3
# Integrity in Judicial Decision-Making

## 1. Introduction

What is it that we speak about when we speak of integrity in judicial decision-making? The theory, developed in Chapter 2, will now be applied: integrity in judicial decision-making is to be understood as a generic norm, covering both virtue and external accountability.

The framework for judicial integrity is, as set out in Chapter 1, a democracy under a rule of law. The rule of law presumes the professional character of judges in judicial decision-making. Not only is the notion of fair trial void without fair judges, but the rule of law is also in need of judges who can interpret the law in light of its ends. As for democratic legitimacy, it has been set out[1] that there is an asymmetry with respect to a judge's deliberations as we find ourselves looking into the black box of the legal system: the minds of the judges. Even if we could see the deliberations – would we understand them? In spite or because of this asymmetry, in an age of individualism and accountability, judiciaries are expected to go the extra mile and account for their actions.

This chapter is not about the integrity of *law*, but of the *judge* in the judicial application of law. In this respect, at the outset of his monumental work on the application of law, Wróblewski distinguishes between the 'material of decision'[2] and the 'psychological material'[3] of decision-making. As my concern is with the latter, I will not speak of the 'judicial application of law' but of 'judicial decision-making'. I will therefore devote little attention to a theory of just law, the validity of rules or the coherence in law. I will also not infer a theory about judicial integrity *from* a theory of law, as is for instance found with Dworkin.[4] Although it is not the focal point of this book, the assumption that our societies are democracies under the rule of law, which encompass fundamental rights, against which laws can be held or even tested, is of great importance: I by no means wish to bestow upon the

1 See Chapter 1 at section 3.2.

2 Wróblewski (1992:11) understands the material of decision to cover the issues of the validity of rules, that of their meaning and that of proven facts and their consequences.

3 See Wróblewski (1992:14–16). To avoid misunderstanding, I am not concerned with empirical knowledge as to the 'material' of judicial decision-making but with normative analysis.

4 Dworkin (1986). For a reworking of the strengths of Dworkin's theory with respect to the application of law, see Claes (2002).

reader the idea that, in modern states, judicial integrity in judicial decision-making is possible without it.

This chapter is set out as follows. In line with the argument developed in the previous chapters, integrity will be viewed from a virtue ethical perspective and from the perspective of safeguarding public trust (section 2). A virtue ethical approach is a *sine qua non* when thinking about the relation between integrity and decision-making. A virtue ethical approach must, however, be supplemented by a theory on external accountability (section 3).

## 2. A Virtue Ethical Approach to Integrity in Judicial Decision-Making

### *2.1 Why Virtue Ethics?*

In the short period that legalism was a general phenomenon, the activity of the judge was – at least formally – restricted to the Montesquian idea that the judge was to be a '*bouche de la loi*'.[5] This idea of a legalistic attitude of judges was fiercely attacked at the beginning of the twentieth century. In the United States we see the 'legal realists',[6] in Germany there is the *Freirechtschule* and in France there are the influential works of Gény.[7] In the Netherlands, there is the 'school of Amsterdam' with Paul Scholten as its most influential exponent.[8] In England, there is Lord Denning who argued for a more liberal interpretation.[9] There are many more examples.

In these debates, the idea that a judge is a '*bouche de la loi*' or a 'logomachist' is rejected. The reactions can be categorized into two groups. In the first, the notion of the 'real reasoning' of judges serves to counterbalance legalism. The interest in 'real reasoning' brings about attention to the role of intuition, sociological elements, psychological processes and moral considerations. Its proponents seek to replicate legalism by looking carefully at the extra-legal elements of the application of law. The other reaction to legalism can be called 'ethical'. Roughly speaking, its proponents argue that the legitimacy of the law does not ultimately rest in the law, but in justice. The judge will have to 'check' his judgment by ethical standards.

5 Montesquieu (1868:XI.6).

6 Cf. Cardozo (1921:167–77); Dewey (1924:17–27); Radin (1925:357–362) and Hutcheson (1929: 274–288).

7 Gény (1922, e.g. 80): 'Dans ce but, la "philosophie nouvelle" prône, sous le nom d'intuition, un mode de connaissance plus subtil que l'intellect pur, qui, s'installant au coeur même de la réalité, la pénétrerait pour ainsi dire du dedans, et, se laissant emporter avec elle, la suivrait dans son incessant mouvement'.

8 See Scholten (1949 and 1974).

9 Cf. Vogenauer (2001) on literal interpretation (780–962) and on the teleological approach (963–1252) that was advocated by Lord Denning.

In both of these reactions, there is much attention to the person of the judge. Even in a legalist scheme, so 'ethicists' say, there is a certain ethos of the judge, namely to subject his personality to his office. And the 'legal realists' will point out that if the judge does so, there must be a good sociological explanation. For instance, in some early eighteenth century European states aristocratic judges had been misbehaving so badly that Montesquieu's ideas about judging were eagerly followed.

This interplay between the character of the judge and the nature of his decision-making is the subject of this section. Various interpretations of this interplay have been proposed – notably by Sherman.[10] With respect to legal theory, Kronman has accentuated this interplay, wishing to revive old values for lawyers from a virtue ethical perspective.[11] As has been argued in the previous chapter, virtue ethics is necessary to understand this interrelation, as it is to articulate the positive relation between the character of the judge and judicial decision-making.

Integrity is the generic term denoting virtuousness itself and the norm to render external accountability. Here, the first aspect is explored by looking at virtue ethics. Its foundational patterns date back to the fourth century BC. I look at virtue ethics with regard to political decision-making from Aristotle's point of view in the Athens of his time, so that not only the specific elements but also the idiosyncrasies of virtue ethics become clear. The focus here lies on *understanding* Aristotle. Thereafter the focus switches to the *usability* of Aristotle's theory for present-day purposes. I will devote special attention to the following subjects: acquiring professional character, the purposiveness of judicial decision-making and the role of intuition in judicial decision-making.

## *2.2 An Aristotelian Introduction*

Aristotle wrote his *Nicomachean Ethics*[12] – the most important work for our understanding of virtue ethics – specifically for citizens who exercised functions in the public sphere, for instance in the assembly, in the council or in courts. This concerned nearly every citizen, since Athenian citizens were expected to occupy several political functions during their life. The *Nicomachean Ethics* should thus be seen as a tutorial for the citizens of Athens who were mature men with

10 See Sherman (1989).

11 He confesses at the beginning of his book that he is not really a fan of contemporary lawyers and therefore seeks to come to an 'ideal' account of a virtuous lawyer, the 'lawyer statesman'. This makes his tone somewhat dramatic. For instance on the decline of the ideal of the lawyer statesman, he says: 'This is the great inward change that has taken over the legal profession in my generation, and its outward manifestations, which are visible in every branch of professional life, all point to a collective identity crisis of immense – if largely unacknowledged – proportions' (Kronman 1993:354).

12 I quote from the Bywater text (*EN*). For English translations, I have used the translations of Ross, Irwin and Rowe as is indicated in the abbreviations.

experience of life. It was to aid them in developing virtues, which were necessary to govern the *polis*.

Given the antiquity of his thoughts there are some elements, which were completely accepted in his days, which are blatantly at odds with contemporary standards. The most notable are Aristotle's rather negative views of women and slaves. These views[13] are so evidently wrong to the modern reader that I will not discuss them here.[14]

The purpose of this section is to clarify the meaning of the basic concepts of Aristotle's virtue ethics and its application to the judge. Many of these concepts have a different meaning today. 'Virtue' for instance, nowadays has a 'soft', 'pious' connotation whereas in Aristotle's philosophy it has the connotation of 'excellence'. As with other central concepts, such as 'well-being', 'prudence', 'character', 'justice' or 'community', it functions within a philosophical framework in which its systematic-philosophical meaning must be understood.

### *2.2.1 The virtue of justice*

Aristotle was critical of the legal system of his day[15] and his virtue ethics, which places a careful, prudent assessment at the heart of political decision-making, should be seen as an attempt to provide a safeguard for good adjudication. In

13 With respect to slavery, the aristocratic nature of Aristotle's ethics is commonly replaced by a meritocracy.

14 Commentators have relentlessly pointed these issues out, cf. Fortenbaugh (1975:53–61).

15 Adjudication in Aristotle's time was very different from that of our time. The courts in Athens in the fourth century BC can be called democratic in the original sense of the word. Justice was administered by citizens in judicial councils of up to 6,000 men. These councils were passive to a large degree. The claimant had chosen the procedure and the potential punishment or measure. The parties would present their cases having exactly the same amount of time. Thereafter the judicial council voted solely on the basis of the presentations made by the parties. The vote was performed by ballots, which these judges threw into urns after the parties' presentations. The actual deliberation of the judges was highly uncontrollable. A case was presented from two sides and a decision had to be made immediately. The walk to the urns in which the ballots were thrown was the only occasion for judges actively to deliberate on the case. This happened on the basis of what they had just heard and on the basis of their personal knowledge. 'Personal knowledge' (Cronin 1936:27–30), however, all too often meant 'personal interest' or 'personal preference'. In this regard, much is said by a telling remark made by Aristotle in his *Retorica*: 'They will often have allowed themselves to be so much influenced by feelings of friendship or hatred or self-interest that they lose any clear vision of the truth and have their judgment obscured by considerations of personal pleasure or pain' (*Ret.* I.I.1:1354b10–12). In this respect, the case of Socrates (see Scholz 2000:157–79 and Todd 1993:310–12) and, earlier, of the Admirals (see Burckhardt 2000:128–143) were – especially in Aristotle's view – notorious miscarriages of justice. On adjudication in ancient Athens see (Pseudo-) Aristotle (1952); Bleicken (1995); Böckenförde (2002); Boegehold (1995); Burckhardt & von Ungern-Sternberg (2000) and Plescia (1970).

securing the virtuous character of the judges, Aristotle hoped to come to grips with the obscurity of judicial decision-making.

The central virtue that judges were to develop, according to Aristotle, is that of justice: the virtue not solely directed at one's own well-being, but also at the well-being of others.[16] 'Well-being' (εὐδαιμονία) is the central concept in Aristotle's practical philosophy. It directs all actions, including actions exercised in a political context.[17] Happiness, or well-being, exists in an evidently successful – i.e. *excellent* – life, which comes about when one continuously directs one's knowledge and actions towards it.

It is in relation to well-being that Aristotle develops his idea of justice.[18] Aristotle distinguishes between a general and a specific concept of justice. As to the first, the law commands that citizens are virtuous. For instance, they ought to be brave in war, modest with regard to adultery and composed in social conduct. Thus, justice in a general sense concerns 'what is lawful'.[19] As a result, justice consists in the fact that all virtues are put into practice for the well-being of oneself and others,[20] just as the law stipulates. It can therefore be labelled 'virtue in its most complete sense'.

Justice in a specific sense denotes a specific realm of justice that cannot easily be reduced to other virtues. For instance, one who commits adultery or abandons a fellow warrior in battle is in the first place inordinate or a coward but not unjust in a specific sense. According to Aristotle, acts can only be specifically unjust when they are committed from the motive 'of a delight to make profit'. It concerns unjust enrichment, whether in connection with esteem, material possession or personal security.[21]

For the purposes of this book, I am solely concerned with the wide sense of justice, which covers much of what we now understand as integrity.[22] In line with the theory as discussed in the previous chapter, this form of justice can be viewed as a cross between 'subjective' and 'objective'. When seen as excellence of character the subjective element is emphasized, but when viewed from a relational perspective[23] the focus lies on 'objective' laws, mores and morals that regulate

16 *EN* V.1:1129b32.

17 *EN* I.1:1094a1–3.

18 *EN* V.1:1129b17–19.

19 This is a wider concept than the concept of positive law used today. It includes traditions, shared values, habits and written law. Aristotle characterizes the law as 'mind without emotions' (*Pol.* III.16:1287a32). See von Fritz (1984:20f) on the wide connotation of 'δικαιοσύνη'.

20 *EN* V.1:1129b15–32.

21 *EN* V.2:1130b1–5.

22 Therefore the reader should not expect a modern reworking of Aristotle's specific concepts of justice – i.e. of corrective and distributive justice.

23 *EN* V.1:1130a11–13. This is true for both general and specific justice (for specific justice e.g. *EN* V.10:1134a2–14). With respect to specific justice it will usually not be a 'law' establishing the right relation but a mathematical or arithmetical principle.

the relation between oneself and another, or between others. In respect of public functions, these two perspectives cross.[24] For example, the right attitude of the judge towards the just regulation of the relations within the *polis* only comes about if the judge has interiorized the laws of the *polis*. Justice as a virtue – a quality of an individual – can be viewed as a necessary condition for the maintenance of just relations within the *polis*.

*2.2.2 A just judge is a prudent judge*

In order to understand the concept of virtue, we must look carefully at the terminology and system of virtue ethics. Two concepts are particularly important: 'attitude' and 'prudence'. In order to be just, the judge must have a consistent and right attitude, which enables him to have the right orientation towards the community in which he delivers his verdicts in a right, prudent, manner.[25]

The 'attitude'[26] (ἕξις) can be described as being orientated to the life-environment to which one stands in relation. This orientation is complex and may concern both cognitive and affective relations to one's life-environment. Like many other ancient Greek thinkers, Aristotle believed that emotions include a rational component.[27] Emotions can be 'modelled' in a specific manner, by means of an interplay of external incentives on the one hand and internal convictions on the other. This modelling determines the attitude that one may have in respect to one's life-environment. Since convictions are partly the result of rational deliberation, one can rationally influence the 'rightness' of this attitude.[28] Emotions and reason are thus intricately related in respect to the attitude. The orientation to the life-environment also implies that the attitude is immediately social. The

24 It must be said that Aristotle is sometimes hesitant in this respect (see *EN* V.2:1130b28 and see section 2.3.5 below), but he can still say that the content of virtue can be found in the law (*EN* V.2:1130b24).

25 See Aubenque (1963); Höffe (1995); Oksenberg Rorty (1980) and Verbrugge (1996) for detailed discussions of prudence.

26 I do not translate ἕξις as 'disposition' (Rowe) or 'state' (Ross/Irwin) since it somewhat 'depersonalizes' the notion. I follow Sherman in her translation with 'attitude' – the emotional and intuitive elements are better expressed in this manner (1997). I use 'orientation' when the 'modelled' relation between the e[xij and something external to it, such as the life-environment, is described.

27 The understanding of emotions of the ancient Greeks was fundamentally different from that which is nowadays commonly held, as is aptly described by Nussbaum (1994:80). Every 'great classic Greek thinker' (1) understood emotions as a form of 'intentional awareness', (2) saw an intimate relation between emotions and beliefs, and (3) could qualify emotions as true or untrue on the basis of the beliefs with which they were connected. These three characteristics are also present in Aristotle's understanding of emotions. For a more detailed analysis see Fortenbaugh (1975:9–12).

28 Note the modal terms. It is not *necessarily* so that one can influence conviction by reason, and consequently emotion by conviction.

attitude does not exist in a vacuum, but it is shaped in its orientation to this social environment.

In exercising 'practical wisdom' or 'prudence' (φρόνεσις) one proceeds from the right attitude to the right decision in the right way and vice versa. The nature of deliberation is determined by the various elements that constitute the situation in which the decision is to be taken: the 'for whom, where, when, by which, why and how' of the act. Reason is used to determine what is demanded in relation to these factors. This deliberation may lead to a decision. A decision may lead to an act, but this is not necessarily the case: the prudent person can reconsider his decision before he acts. Finally, the right decision is a 'middle'[29] in the sense of an optimum – it is doing 'exactly' what the situation demands.[30]

There is interplay between the attitude and practical wisdom. By continuously making right decisions, the prudent person improves his attitude, by which he is able to make better decisions.

We may now move on to see what *judicial* practical wisdom is. Aristotle subsumes judicial activity under the genus of *political* practical wisdom.[31] Political practical wisdom is the practical wisdom that has the interests of the *polis* in view.

Aristotle gives the following definition:

> Justice is the virtue in accord with which the just person is said to do what is just in accord with his decision, distributing good things and bad, both between himself and others and between others. He does not award too much of what is choiceworthy to himself and too little to his neighbor (and the reverse with what is harmful), but awards what is proportionately equal; and he does the same in distributing between others.[32]

29 I follow Ross in this translation because it is literal. Irwin ('mean') and Rowe ('intermediate') rightly express the specific quality of Aristotle's concept, as described in the main text.

30 This middle is an optimum in relation to *us* (*EN* II.6:1106b37–1107a2). It is thus relative to the community. Aristotle is very clear about the relative nature of the middle: whereas the right amount of food for Milo is an ox a day, this might be different for a philosopher who needs less energy (esp. *EN* II.5:1106a28–b5).

31 EN VI.8:1141b33. Cf. Berti (1993:452): 'Ainsi donc, la phrónesis, comme la science politique, mais sans se confrondre avec elle, comprend des espèces, qui, dans le langage commun, s'appellent, respectivement, phrónesis tout court, concernant l'individu, « économie » (οἰκονομία), concernant la maison, « législation » (νομοθεσία), concernant les lois, « politique » tout court, concernant les décrets. Cette dernière, ajoute Aristote, se divise en « déliberative » (βουλευτικη,), lorsque ses décrets sont des déliberations prises dans une assemblée, et « judiciaire » (δικαστική,), lorsque ses décrets sont des sentences de tribunal'.

32 *EN* (*Irwin*) V.5:1134a2–7.

Thus justice can be characterized as a 'middle' between two forms of injustice.[33] Every 'too much' or 'too little' harms the just relation. By this means the judge tries to allot to the parties what is due. Aristotle famously uses the figure of the doctor to illustrate this. When administering medicine, too much or too little can be fatal – he must administer exactly the right amount to cure the patient.

This requires the judge to assume a prudent attitude. In this manner justice is a quality of the individual judge. Finding the 'middle' takes place in deliberation and is an inner process. In a manner of speaking, it can be said that the judge 'embodies' the middle. Not only is he the middle between the parties, but he is also the 'personification' of justice: justice comes about because it happens in the mind of judges.

### *2.2.3 The ends of judicial decision-making*

Aristotle is very explicit about distinguishing judicial practical wisdom from what he calls technical skills or crafts. The essential difference is that prudent deliberation comes about by an inner focus on well-being as an end.[34] This is what makes practical wisdom ethical. It cannot – unlike technical skills – be employed for both good and bad intentions. This inner directedness towards well-being provides practical wisdom with intrinsic value. It is good in itself to deliberate in such a manner. Technical skills, on the other hand, are good only because they 'produce' something. Their purpose is not the skills itself, but the result.

Following from the above, the purpose of virtuous deliberation is well-being. This is fairly unclear: how can we understand well-being as an end of judicial practical wisdom? Aristotle mentions three ways in which this question can be answered.[35]

First, virtue has *itself* as its purpose. This should not be understood in a modern sense, as the autonomous striving for a particular view of happiness. To Aristotle there is no well-being in the abstract, Platonic, sense. The virtuous person does not just *strive* for well-being, but he concretely aims to *be* well: he wants to live a 'life worth living'. In other words, well-being does not *exist* as such, but only in

33 The exact nature of the 'middle' differs – just as in contemporary law – according to the area of law, although it needs to be noted that the Athenian legal system from the fourth century BC does not recognize the basic distinctions such as those between civil and penal law. There is a difference within specific justice between distributive and corrective justice, whereby the middle is found according to mathematical and arithmetical proportion respectively.

34 *EN* II.3:1105a30–35. The actor must know what he is doing, he must choose consciously what he is doing, choose the act for the act itself and he must act from a solid, unchangeable inner attitude.

35 The discussion on the purposes of prudence is by no means unequivocal but it would go beyond the scope of this book to provide an extensive treatment. See for an overview Anagnostopoulos (1994:65–101).

and through ethical action.[36] This is also true at a political level: the judge aims to develop his virtuousness as judge in his judicial activity.

Second, there are the specific goals of ethical deliberation. These will be the most obvious in reality: for instance, punishing a criminal or condemning one to pay a penalty restores or attributes to well-being in a specific situation. These goals are commonly seen as the actual ends of judicial decision-making.

Third, when speaking of *political* virtues, we speak also of the well-being of the *polis*. Virtue is thus not isolated from society. In fact, to act prudently necessarily implies taking into account societal ends. Reducing virtue to an egoistic end fails to recognize the social context, which the prudent person takes into account. Judicial decision-making does not happen in a vacuum but in a concrete *polis* – the interests of which the judge will take into consideration when judging.

Unlike Plato, however, Aristotle does not consider the *polis*[37] to strive after well-being as an entity.[38] Striving after well-being is not a matter of a whole but of actual people.[39] Therefore, Aristotle advocates that citizens take part in the administrative bodies of the *polis*. In this way, the *polis* can become a *forum* for virtue – for individual *excellence*. Thus, the *polis* can only be said to 'have' well-being because its citizens live good lives.

These three ends, the specific purposes, the purpose of the *polis* as a whole and the purpose of individual excellence, cannot be separated. Well-being denotes a complex of ends starting with the well-being of the adjudicator and finishing with ends that belong to the *polis* in general. Crucial to Aristotle's theory is that although the notion of well-being consists in this complex of ends, its *reality* is the optimum with respect to these ends as assessed in a prudent decision. Their relation can be outlined as follows. The deliberation 'about' (περι,) the act is done 'in view of' (πρός) the whole. To be virtuous, acts should not only be excellent in the sense that they meet their specific purpose, they should also meet the ends of the *polis* in which they are performed and be consistent with the other activities that this person undertakes.

Aristotle again makes a comparison with the doctor. The doctor does not act with a general view of 'health' in mind, but he has the health of an individual in view in each specific action.[40] Likewise, a judge does not act from a preconceived

36 Cf. *EN* I.3:1095a5 and *EN* II.2:1103b26. Well-being (εὐδαιμονία) is made *concrete* in well-doing (εὐπραξία). The connection between well-being and ethical action is that ethical action has well-being as its purpose and concretizes it at the same time. Well-being and well-doing are not identical. Well-doing is a necessary condition for well-being but factors such as luck, being of good birth or having friends are equally necessary for well-being within the *polis* (cf. Forschner 1984:5–10).

37 Aristotle defines the *polis* as a 'community of citizens within a constitution' (*Pol.* G 3:1276b2).

38 Cf. Verhaeghe (1980: 124–131) and Becker (1997:100).

39 Cf. Price (1989:204).

40 *EN* I.6:1097a10.

idea of general well-being but tries to do justice in each situation so that one may say that the well-being of the *polis* is furthered. The general well-being of the *polis* is not subject to the power of the judge. As a purpose it does, however, determine the direction of judicial deliberation.

*2.2.4 A theory of judicial deliberation – between intuition and reason*[41]

Now that we have an understanding of the fundamental elements of Aristotle's virtue ethics – and therewith of judicial integrity as virtue – the process of judicial deliberation will be outlined in detail in this section. This section is somewhat more technical than the other sections of this chapter, but then judicial deliberation is a highly complex matter.

The character of the individual judge has a distinct role to play in judicial decision-making, as is pertinent in the notion of intuitive reason.[42] Aristotle makes the somewhat cryptic remark that in relation to prudence,

> intuitive reason is concerned with the ultimates in both directions; for both the first terms and the last are objects of intuitive reason and not of argument.[43]

In other words, prudence – the key virtue – is embedded in intuitive reason. What does Aristotle mean by this? The thesis that the first and last terms of deliberation are intuitive will be used as a framework to construe Aristotle's theory on judicial decision-making.

We will see how intuitive reason as the 'first terms' concerns a 'qualified perception'. I will then proceed to discuss the reasoning process itself, as embedded in intuitive reason. It will become clear in the tension between decision and act how intuitive knowledge is also the 'last terms' of the judicial decision. Special attention will be devoted to the role of emotions in judicial decision-making.

*Intuitive reason as concerned with the first terms of decision-making – a mode of perception* The first part of the thesis is that the first terms of practical wisdom are the objects of intuitive reason.

41 For a more elaborate account see Soeharno (2005).

42 I will not focus on ἐπιβολή, which is usually translated as 'intuition', but on the role of the νους within the process of deliberation, which Ross translates as 'intuitive reason'.

43 *EN* (*Ross*) VI.11:1143b1–9. Sherman is equally intrigued by this passage and understands it as governing the quality of perception (1997:256). I agree with her, yet rather take it to describe the relation between the νους and λογος from the perspective of the φρόνησις (cf. *EN* VI.11:1143a34).

Intuitive reason (νους[44]) is a complex notion with Aristotle.[45] Practical intuitive knowledge has a twofold character. First, the concrete situation is always unique. Therefore the perception of the judge will have to be *attentive*[46] to the simple,[47] the specific 'this or that'. It thus concerns perceiving the uniqueness of the situation.[48] This is an ability that has to be developed by experience.[49] Next to this perception of the essence of the unique situation, intuitive reason perceives a second principle for practical reason. By means of general knowledge, beliefs or ideas, it is capable of articulating the unique situation in a certain way.[50] Intuitive reason, in its perceiving activity, is *mindful* of this general knowledge. Intuitive reason is thus *attentive* to the unique situation and *mindful* of general knowledge by which it can

44 The νους is regarded as one of the more problematic concepts in Aristotle's philosophy. There is a certain consensus that it has a bearing on the understanding activity of the soul in a broad sense, then on immediate consciousness or intuition, and more specifically on intuitive reason. Here, I focus particularly on the working it has within the φρόνησις. Cf. Wedin (1993:128–161) and Urmson (1990:115f).

45 It bears a close connection to concepts such as induction (ἐπαγωγή) and 'sensation/perception' (αἴσθησις, hereafter translated as 'perception'). As with νους the meaning of αἴσθησις is broad, cf. Kahn (1979:23): '… αἴσθησις can indeed cover the whole range of meaning of thought, feeling, and perception, including the affective feelings of pleasure, pain, desire, and the like'. Here too, I am merely concerned with the working of αἴσθησις in prudence.

46 I borrow the designations 'attentive' and 'mindful' from Verbrugge (1996:111f: '*aandachtig*' and '*indachtig*').

47 The principle and the specific act are perceived by perception (αἴσθεσις) and are aligned by intuitive reason (νους) towards well-being, cf. Kuhn (1960:130).

48 *Cat.* 5:2a11–2a18. The expression τοδε τι', functions as a label for primary substance: the essence from which all other can be understood. Primary substance is always individual and unique. Generic specification is possible when secondary substance is predicated from primary substance.

49 *EN* VI.8:1142a15–16.

50 For more on the role of education see Aristotle in *Pol.* III.4:1176b16–1277b33 and *EN* X.9. He talks in the first place about the didactic value of *laws* for adults, *EN* X.9:1180a3–5, cf. Nussbaum (2004:36). If such educational activities 'are neglected on the communal level, then it would seem appropriate for each to contribute towards his own children's and friends' acquisition of excellence, and for him to have the capacity to do so, or at any rate to decide to do it', *EN* (*Rowe*) X.9:1180a31–33. Thus, according to Aristotle there is a role – albeit ancillary – for education within the *family*. Then, there are *teachers* and of course, one can also learn from one's *own experience*. The teachers ideally teach in such a manner that the student sees the principles of ethical action by his own experience. The maieutic activity of the teacher and the personal experience of the student are therefore important ingredients for developing a right intuitive reason, cf. Kenny (1979:152). Lastly, *habituation* and *natural talent* are important conditions.

adequately characterize the situation. This relation between mindful and attentive comes about spontaneously.[51]

When we speak of a spontaneous relation between being attentive to the presented case and the mindful knowledge, which a person has acquired previously, we may speak of a judicial 'mode of perception'.[52] Intuitive reason as concerned with a first term can subsequently be characterized as the power of perception of the prudent person.[53] It qualifies the manner in which the prudent person 'sees' the presented case.

Here is room for the emotions of the prudent person. His emotions can help him to recognize the essence of the specific situation immediately. As Sherman puts it:

> … emotions … are modes of moral response that determine what is morally relevant and, in some cases, what is required.[54]

In this way, the prudent person is capable of perceiving reality in a more adequate way. The prudent person is consistently mindful of general beliefs by which he adequately characterizes the given situation. This is the result of repeated activity, whereby the prudent person becomes increasingly better at perceiving the essence in the specific case. This experience – and also his previous education – will be crucial to the quality of the attitude by which he stands in immediate relation to the situation.

*Intuitive reason and deliberation – finding an optimum* Not everything has been said about both judicial intuitive reason and judicial practical wisdom. Firstly, if practical wisdom were merely to consist of this form of intuitive reason, then judges would be able to administer justice as though by the wave of a magic wand. A careful process of deliberation by which an optimum is sought is then no longer

51 This connection between the general and the specific is expressed by the notion of induction (ἐπαγωγή). Induction makes possible that the knowledge acquired by means of perception is interiorized and may serve as general knowledge by which reality may again be seen. As von Fritz (1964:31) accurately puts it: '*Die* ἐπαγωγη, *steht am Anfang der Überlegungen, die dann erst zu praktischen Entscheidungen führen können*'. Aristotle's notion of induction is broader than contemporary ones. It includes several ways of 'connectedness' between the specific and the whole. For example, induction also denotes a manner of deictic (*Physica*); a competence of the νους to perceive the general in specific cases (*Analytica Posteriora*); or ad hominem claims to truth in the dialectic discussion whereby it does not necessarily concern truth, but that which is sufficient to accept something 'as true' (*Topica*).

52 Cf. Sherman (1997:254–261).

53 *EN* (*Rowe*) VI.9:1142b33–34: 'So if it is characteristic of the wise to deliberate well, deliberative excellence will be that sort of correctness that corresponds to what conduces to the end, of which wisdom is the true grasp' (Rowe reads 'wisdom' for φρόνεσις).

54 Sherman (1989:2).

necessary. Secondly, if this were all there was to be said about intuitive reason, it would remain unclear how judicial intuitive knowledge also functions as a 'last term' in this process of judicial deliberation.

Now that we have seen how intuitive knowledge constitutes the first terms of practical wisdom, we can proceed to view the process of deliberation. The immediate understanding of the situation that is acquired by means of intuitive reason is now considered in light of the purposes of juristic activity.[55] Excellence in deliberation is achieved when the interests 'for who, where, when, by which, why and how' are optimally met. It concerns the 'middle' as an optimum.[56] Here, the judge may also take into account the emotions of others concerning the case.[57] The 'middle' is not just found in relation to the case, but also with respect to the *polis* community – and this is so with respect to the emotions surrounding the case.

This deliberation results in a decision, which may in turn lead to an act. But before the judge leaps from his decision to an act, the process of deliberation may repeat itself. He may ask whether this decision is the right one. The pivotal question is now 'by which criterion can it ultimately be determined that the decision will be made in favour of the right person, from the right motives, in the right proportion, et cetera'? The deliberation is right when the final decision contributes to well-being.[58] This is only the case when the decision adequately meets the complex of the specific demands of the concrete situation, the demands of the *polis* in general and the convictions of the individual judge.[59]

55 In deliberation the right means must be found in relation to an end. Aristotle distinguishes between πραξις and ποίησις, whereby the first refers to the act done for its own sake and the second refers to the act done for its result. Although every act contains the two elements, the emphasis with respect to judicial decision-making lies on πραξις, as the purpose thereof is the deliberation itself with well-being (εὐδαιμονία) in view. Therefore it must not be solely understood in a technical manner – although Aristotle's illustrations are all drawn from this sphere. Cf. Verbrugge (1996) and Kenny (1979:149).

56 *EN* (*Irwin*) VI.9:1142b27–29: 'good deliberation is correctness that accords with what is beneficial, about the right thing, in the right way, and at the right time'.

57 After all, the judge has to find the middle 'in relation to us', not just to himself (see the definition of virtue in *EN* II.6:1106b36–1107a2). It may thus stretch to the broader *polis* community, the parties or others involved with the case.

58 *EN* VI.9:1142b30–34.

59 The process of deliberation does not follow the 'formal syllogism'. Concerning the limited value of the formal syllogism in judicial deliberation, Dewey states that '... it purports to be a logic of rigid demonstration, not of search and discovery. It claims to be a logic of fixed forms, rather than of methods reaching intelligent decisions in concrete situations, or of methods employed in adjusting disputed issues on behalf of the public and enduring interests' (Dewey 1924:21f). At most, we could speak with Kenny of an 'ethical syllogism' (1979:111–124). This is different from the formal syllogism, where there are middle terms that do not appear in the conclusion. Strictly taken, the ethical syllogism does not appear in Aristotle's works, but it can well be used to illustrate the point made

*Intuitive reason as concerned with the last term of practical wisdom* Aristotle seems to leave us with a fair theory on judicial decision-making, which starts with intuitive reason as a power of perception and runs through *deliberation*, *excellence in deliberation*, a *decision* and an *act*.

The character of the judge and the activity of judicial decision-making are intricately related. The judge has attentively viewed the specific situation, mindful of his relevant general beliefs. From there, he has gone into deliberation about the specific demands of the situation in light of the purpose of well-being in the specific situation and the *polis* in general. He has then made a decision, been able to deliberate again from that standpoint and finally has decided to act.

Then what is meant by the thesis that intuitive reason also has the last terms of practical wisdom as its object?

Aristotle points to the fact that the act does not necessarily follow from the judge's decision, because the decision may *itself* function as an intuitive term. Here Aristotle does justice to the dynamics of ethical deliberation. Intuitive reason, as has been said above, is a kind of perception. By means of the decision that is the result of deliberation, the judge again attentively perceives the specific case. Thus, the result of judicial deliberation – i.e. the decision – itself functions as a part of intuitive knowledge. This process is dynamic: it proceeds until the judge 'sees' that this decision leads to a right judgment. This 'final' knowledge cannot be reached by a mere syllogism. It is rather the conviction of the individual judge, wherein the complex of his own knowledge and emotions, of the emotions and interests in the community, of the nature of the case and other factors, is recognized.

In this way, intuitive reason as 'prudent perception of the concrete situation' concerns also the last term of practical wisdom. In this intuitive perception, the decision of the judge is again verified against the demands of the specific situation, so that the judge could possibly deliberate again and come to a new decision. This new decision will then function again as 'mindful knowledge' by which he again views the situation. This process repeats itself until the decision 'fits' the complex of specific demands of the case and the demands of the *polis* in general. The last term is then the intuitive – or knowledge-laden – assessment that the decision that is to be taken is in keeping with the demands of reality.[60]

---

in the main text. With well-being as the purpose of the action, a principle has been found that mediates the *maiores* (what the actor is mindful of) and the *minores* (drawn from the attentive perception of the life-environment) to a right decision – i.e. one with well-being in view, which is the *conclusio*, from which an act might originate.

60 That the decision can 'possibly' lead to an action, can again be illustrated in terms of the ethical syllogism. The decision is the *conclusio* of the syllogism, but functions itself as the *maior* in respect to the final *minor*: a concrete situation in need of a decision, cf. Sorabji (1980:208f).

### *2.3 Integrity in Judicial Decision-Making – A Virtue Ethical Account*

Justice cannot exist without the performance of adjudication. Aristotle's ethics demonstrates how the complexity of reality is taken into account. The notion of prudence is crucial here: not only is it needed to mediate theoretical knowledge and specific demands of a concrete situation, it also demonstrates how the virtuousness of the judge is a constitutive element of decision-making.

Now that we have a better understanding of Aristotle's theory of judicial decision-making, we may ask what the value is of Aristotle's ethics for our theory on integrity. Some hermeneutical problems impede direct applicability. Yet his theory does seem to contribute substantially to the questions relating to integrity.

The ideas that I will consider are the following. First, acquiring excellence of character is vital: the interrelation between character and the nature of decision-making will be discussed and so will the importance of formation of character. Second, the notion of *trifocality* in judicial decision-making will be held up against present-day demands. Third, according to Aristotle, practical wisdom is permeated by intuition, which shows how judicial decision-making is intrinsically linked with the character of the judge.

#### *2.3.1 Hermeneutical problems and the notion of integrity*[61]

With respect to judicial decision-making, three hermeneutical problems prevent direct applicability.

First, Aristotle's theory of justice is rather optimistic by modern-day standards. Defining injustice as a deviation from justice demonstrates a confidence to be able to say what justice is.[62] His optimism is also reflected in the ontological connection between justice and well-being. Although some notions of social justice equally aim to further well-being, present day notions of justice – although by no means homogeneous – have a more stringent character, referring to base norms that provide the final legitimacy of the legal order. The notion of the decision as an

61 As has been said in the preface to this book, I am not here considering Aristotle within the framework of his metaphysics and ontology. Rather than taking a 'top-down' approach, I look at Aristotle's philosophy from a 'bottom-up' angle. As a consequence, the overarching claims – for instance Aristotle's metaphysical claims about men – need only be considered *after* we have seen their plausibility in dealing with a specific problem. I will therefore not deal with ontological or metaphysical problems here.

62 Aristotle's theory of justice, as finding the middle and establishing injustice by deviation, seems insufficiently concrete to work in practice, cf. Cardozo (1921:86). It is also not free from inconsistency. Aristotle puts it as follows, *EN* (*Irwin*) V.5:1133b31–34a1: '… it is clear that doing justice is intermediate between doing injustice and suffering injustice, since doing injustice is having too much and suffering injustice is having too little. Justice is a mean, not as the other virtues are, but because it is about an intermediate condition, whereas injustice is about the extremes'. The concept of justice is problematic, because it fails to explain why someone who chooses to take 'less' than what is due to him – i.e. chooses to be equitable – can still be just.

optimum may also be averse to modern understanding. The 'middle' is more often described as an equilibrium or sometimes even as a dilemma. However, the rationale behind the middle – meeting the specific demands of a concrete situation – still stands.

Another difference lies in the understanding of the law and its function. To the ancient Greeks, the law denoted a wider concept than the concept of positive law used today. It included among other things traditions, shared values, habits, written law and morals. The law was a rather static given, which was far from coherent or consistent and which functioned as a somewhat large and ungainly point of reference for claimants, defendants and judges. Although few agree on the concept and function of law, the modern-day understanding of the law includes at least a notion of positive law. Judicial deliberations aim not only to assess the difficult nature of the specific elements of the case, but also the difficult process of interpreting the legal norm. The decision in turn contributes to the understanding of the law and in some traditions even to law itself. The idea that the law teaches citizens to be virtuous is not per se held anymore, let alone the idea that virtuousness and lawfulness are two sides of the same coin.[63] Instead, we tend to differentiate between law and morals with a rigidity unknown to the Greeks.[64]

The third difference with respect to adjudication is the departure from a solipsistic position with respect to decision-making. The judge in ancient Athens was a silent deliberator who cast his ballot in one urn or the other. Nowadays, a decision in higher courts comes about by deliberation by multiple judges. Even if a judge sits on his own, insight in the case comes about by a process of deliberation where lawyers, prosecutors, parties and ancillary personnel each fulfil distinct

63 This also has to do with a different perception of the *polis*. The purpose of the *polis* is essentially 'ethical-pedagogical', whereas nowadays the state rather has a 'preventive' mission: taking away any obstacle for the individual development of citizens (Verhaeghe 1980:128–130, 163).

64 I agree with Duff (2006:90) in his criticism of virtue ethical theorists who ascribe to law an aim to make citizens virtuous. Whereas society is the realm of moral heterogeneity, the state is 'abstract' with respect to morals: it is impartial, independent and value neutral. Although it can rightly be objected that value neutrality is a value in itself, it certainly differs from particular morality at the level of society. For instance, in modern states formation of character is done within families, in schools or in churches rather than by the state. Since the rise of the modern state and its division between civil society and state, this claim can no longer be made. The concept of civil society has ancient roots, which go back as far as Aristotle's κοινωνια and Cicero's *societas civilis*, cf. Riedel (1976:77–108). The *distinction* between civil society and state, however, is the result of modern revolutions: 'die Entstehung einer entpolitisierten Gesellschaft durch die Zentralisierung der Politik im fürstlichen bzw. Revolutionären Staat und die Verlagerung ihres Schwerpunktes auf die Ökonomie, die eben zur selben Zeit diese Gesellschaft mit der industriellen Revolution, in der "Staats-" bzw. "National-Ökonomie" erfuhr. Erst in diesem Vorgang traten innerhalb der europäischen Gesellschaft ihre "politische" und ihre "bürgerliche" Verfassung auseinander' (99).

roles. The establishment of the right legal norm, its interpretation, the nature of the facts and the interests at stake, come about by an argumentative discourse. In this sense, Habermas speaks of deliberative discourse, of a *Kommunikationsstruktur*, in which the arguments and interests of participants can be met.[65] For example, he may need to enter into communication with lawyers and experts in the courtroom with respect to the parties, and with court staff who prepare case materials. In all this, he has to be aware of asymmetry and differing perspectives. Finding an optimal decision may come about dialectically through a process of such communication.

With respect to these differences, we might wonder whether 'justice' is still viable as a connecting term between public morality and the character of the public official. Clearly, nowadays we do not use the word 'justice' in this wide sense anymore. A judge needs to uphold the law, not morality, is the modern adage, so why bother about his character or his moral views? Today, however, when we seek to rearticulate the connection between public functions, the character of the officials, public morality and law, it might well be worth reconsidering the Aristotelian link between the judge and this wide concept of justice – albeit with modern reservations. Therefore I will focus on the link between the character of the judge and justice, not on substantive notions of justice.[66] By using Aristotle's notion of justice in this way, I follow Bambrough who remarks that 'in modern English', we tend to speak of 'a man of complete *integrity*, who is *fair* in all his dealings'.[67] The focus is on the character of the judge, not on a precise analysis of the notion of the law – let alone an analysis of the integrity of law.[68]

### *2.3.2 Acquiring excellence*

Safeguarding integrity entails more than establishing rules of strict compliance or assuming a competence oriented approach.[69] However important these practices may be, they overlook a significant element of integrity.[70] Integrity is not just about avoiding what is wrong or developing the right skills; it is first and foremost about developing a steady character by acting in view of the ends of deliberation.

The key difference between a virtue ethical and a competence oriented approach lies in the distinction between virtue and skill. Unlike technical skills, prudent acts do not derive their worth simply from what they produce. As has

65 See Habermas' critique on Dworkin and his notion of intersubjectivity with respect to the application of law (Habermas 1994:258–291).

66 As I said in the preface, I presuppose just or nearly just societies.

67 See Bambrough (1965:159), and his treatment of Aristotle's concept of justice.

68 See the preface for my hesitance concerning a theory of integrity of law.

69 These practices are sometimes copied from corporate experiences. See Berenbeim (2004) and Dienhart (2004) for overviews of business ethics approaches. Also within business ethics, however, the need for virtue has been advocated, for instance by Sharp Paine (1994).

70 For example, Freidson emphasizes professional knowledge (which includes the knowledge of rules) and skills. His notion of habituation ('working knowledge') is, however, poorer than the habituation by prudence that is requisite for excellence (2001:17–123).

already been said, they have intrinsic value because they are intentionally directed towards well-being. In the literature, this distinction between an ethical approach and a competence oriented approach is often overlooked.[71] Although a competence oriented approach certainly has its own merits – it is manageable, specific, and seems not to be ideology-laden – a theory about decision-making cannot do without the notions of intentionality, purposes and well-being. Thinking about the *character* of decision-makers, about a notion of the public good and about optimal solutions for the parties is mandatory. Competences do not say anything about the appropriate use thereof, whereas virtue dictates that competences are intentionally employed for the good.

Equally, a theory of decision-making cannot be developed by rules of strict compliance alone. Rules of strict compliance are necessary to mark the bandwidth of deliberation. As deliberation is *professional* deliberation, it is limited in its scope. A judge will not take into account the latest horoscope or use an Ouija board to establish guilt or innocence. The institution stipulates that deliberation is to be reasonable, empirical and argumentative. The prudence that is exercised is thus exercised within institutional limits. Yet it is one thing to embank the limits and another to stimulate for excellence.

Judges acquire excellence of character by formation of character. It seems natural that a judge must know the law and its purposes in order to develop the virtue of justice – but the notion is wider. A typical Aristotelian feature is the emphasis on habituation[72] and natural talent as conditions for the success of professional formation, as 'soil must have been previously tilled if it is to foster the seed'.[73] In this process, the intellect and the emotions are 'educated'[74] and an apt attitude is formed. But the most important condition for virtue is that a judge prudently deliberates on each case. This continuous exercise in acting virtuously is what definitely shapes his character.[75] By learning from others and by judging rightly he will become an apt judge. He is also to be alert to the developments in

71 Hazard & Dondi's (2004:109f) 'virtue of competence' is therefore somewhat of a contradiction in terms.

72 According to Aristotle, common opinion differs on the causes of virtue. Can we be taught to be good? Are we good by nature? Or do we become good by habituation? The last is eliminated as a sufficient condition. Being more subconscious, habituation differs from experience although it is impossible without it. Because this process is largely controlled by intuition and not by reason, it is difficult to become virtuous on the basis of habituation only, cf. Sorabji (1980:216f). For more on the concept and value of habituation see Sherman (1989 and 1999).

73 *EN* (*Ross*) X:9:1179b24–26.

74 On the education of emotions see Fortenbaugh (1975:45–53).

75 According to Aristotle the inclination to virtue is natural. In this context 'natural' does not refer to 'casual' or 'by causality'. Rather, it refers to the capacity of men to actualize their potential *optimally* in virtue. Judges acquire justice as virtue by means of interplay between having the right attitude and acting prudently on a continuous basis.

the community and the interests that are in play, so that his verdicts serve the well-being of society.

It is part of the call for integrity that the difficult notion of the formation of character is professionalized.[76] The judge should not only know the law, have had a good education, have some life experience and possess some natural talent but needs also to be able to assess the elements of the case with respect to *institutional ends*. As we shall see in Chapter 5, these notions are crucial for developing apt selection procedures. With respect to learning programmes, it is important to take into account that excellence can only come about by prudent deliberation on each case.

*2.3.3 The purposiveness of judicial deliberation*[77]

According to Aristotle, judicial decision-making is *trifocal*. What is the relevance of these thoughts for our understanding of judicial decision-making? Let us look at the three ends of judicial decision-making.

With respect to the first end, the professional character of the judge himself,[78] it is important to be reminded of the notion that judicial decision-making is not merely a 'skill' that produces a result, but an activity that is performed for its intrinsic value. The process of deliberation itself is the core of the judicial process, because here all the relevant factors are assessed against the ends of deliberation. Deliberation improves in quality when the professional character improves in quality and vice versa.[79] This 'circle' of virtue characterizes prudent deliberation. It comes therefore as no surprise that the *motivation* of judges to produce good judgments is often *intrinsic*.[80] After all, it is not just the well-being of society or of the case that he has in focus, but his excellence itself is also at stake in every decision. The judge must be able to stand for his decision.

The second end of decision-making is well-being on a case level. Are the interests of the parties being served? Is the right legal norm chosen and is it interpreted correctly according to the specific demands of the case? It should be

76 For a plea for the revision of legal education for lawyers on the basis of virtue ethical theory see Graham (1996).

77 This notion of purposiveness differs from Barak's idea of purposive interpretation. Barak uses purposiveness to describe the relationship between intent of the author of a text in relation to the intent of a reasonable author of a text (2005:xi). I am not talking about purposive interpretation, however, but purposive deliberation.

78 Here I am not concerned with the well-being of the individual person 'behind' the judge, but with well-being on a professional level. On the former issue see section 2.3.5.

79 This opens the possibility of looking at the judicial decision not from the viewpoint of a decision-based theory, but of an agent-centred theory, as Solum (2003) claims. See McDowell (1979) for a meticulous articulation of agent-centred behaviour and decision-making.

80 On Aristotle and the pleasure intrinsic to practice see Sherman (1999:251–257) and more elaborately Sherman (1989). For an assessment of intrinsic motivation amongst present-day judges see Armytage (1996:130).

noted that although a judge has well-being as an end in view in deliberation, this well-being does not become concrete until the judge has found an optimum with respect to the case. Well-being is thus not – as with Plato – an idea according to which reality must be moulded. Well-being comes about as specific demands of a situation are mediated by knowledge that a judge thinks is applicable.

What then does the well-being of society as the third end in decision-making entail? A decision is not taken in a vacuum but in a concrete society. The judge has therefore to look 'over' the case to the demands of society[81] – or to look at the case with society 'in view'. At the present time, where the decision contributes to the understanding of law, this insight is indispensable. Taking into account the purposes of the community implies both being conscious of the law but also knowing the wider scope of the rules and taking into account developments in society.

Purposive deliberation is a matter of great complexity, as the exact interrelation of these ends – especially between the second and third – will differ from case to case. It falls outside the scope of this book to articulate how specific concepts of justice in modern-day democracies under a rule of law are related to these ends. Yet one thing is clear: these three ends must be met in every decision.

Institutional values are to secure the purposiveness in judicial deliberation. The precise content of institutional values, their codification and enforcement may differ according to the legal order, but as to content, the Bangalore Principles – independence, impartiality, integrity,[82] propriety, equality, competence and diligence – may be regarded as generally shared. These institutional values, of which the institution is a symbol,[83] determine and limit the scope of prudence. Prudence cannot be exercised in violation of these values and these values should guide judicial decision-making.

Take for example the institutional value of impartiality. By rightly assessing all elements of the case and abstaining from improper interference, the professional character of the judge will be strengthened in the right manner. Being impartial on a case level ensures that the right decision is taken with respect to the specific demands of the case. Lastly, society benefits from an impartial judiciary as it a cornerstone of the rule of law. The same goes for other values. For example, without the value of constitutional independence, the judge might give precedence to the well-being of society as perceived by the executive over the well-being on a case level.

Meeting the ends with institutional values in view also ensures that the judicial institution does not morph into a bureaucracy. For example, the demand for efficiency – even though legitimate – may affect the quality of decision-making. A judge may think twice before calling upon another witness or allowing another

81 Cf. Hol & Loth (2004:125).

82 On the nature of integrity in the Bangalore Principles see Chapter 5 at section 2.4.

83 I will elaborate on this relation between the institution and institutional values in Chapter 4.

expert analysis, as it may delay the case. Thus, in order for the judicial institution to preserve its vitality, judicial deliberation must be performed with institutional values in view. They provide the backbone of judicial deliberation.

*2.3.4 The role of intuition in judicial deliberation*

In his discussion of the relevance of Aristotelian practical wisdom for today's lawyers, Kronman remarks that 'the concept of intuition is less helpful than might at first appear'.[84] This, however, seems to be coloured by contemporary reservations about intuition. Aristotle's notion of intuition is about spontaneous theory-laden perceptions, a critical assessment thereof in the light of the ends of judicial deliberation[85] and the specific demands of the concrete case, and a repeated theory-laden assessment of the decision before the act is performed.[86]

Judges may optimize their perception by rightly interpreting their emotions. In this manner, the emotions of the judges – when rightly assessed – can serve as an apt guide to perceiving the essence of the case quickly.[87] The emotions surrounding a case can also be taken into account – equally not without reasonable assessment. The better habituated a judge is, the more accurate are his emotions and intuitions to perceive the essence of a case.[88]

The process of deliberation embedded in intuition is not merely an internal one. Voicing intuitions and emotions, deliberating about hunches, suggestions about the right legal norms and their interpretation, all come about in a broader,

84 Kronman (1993:67). Kronman only focuses on intuition as initial perception and asks whether judgment can be characterized as a form of intuition, which he denies (cf. Kronman 1987:848–850).

85 Guthrie, Rachlinski & Wistrich are entirely right to say that 'Intuition is dangerous not because people rely on it but because they rely on it when it is inappropriate to do so'. They then propose 'that, where feasible, judges should use deliberation to check their intuition' (2007:5).

86 In this respect, Aristotle's theory is in keeping with recent insights in psychology. For instance, Pizzaro and Bloom defend the idea that 'fast and automatic moral intuitions are actually shaped and informed by prior reasoning', cf. Pizzaro & Bloom (2003:193); Blair, Ma & Lenton (2001:828–841) and Kawakami, Dovidio, Moll, Hermsen & Russin (2000:871–888). These psychologists claim to support a 'second order control over emotional reactions and automatic judgments' following Aristotle and William James. It is exactly the interplay between emotion, conviction, reason and decision – not the antithesis – that is deemed to be of importance.

87 Cf. Posner, who distinguishes between emotion as a 'cognitive shortcut' and 'emotion as a nonrational influence on belief or behavior'. The first 'is triggered by, and more often than not produces rational responses to, information'. The 'epistemic significance' depends on which emotion is engaged (2008:106).

88 Posner relates intuition to experience and education when he qualifies intuition as a 'subsconscious repository of knowledge acquired from one's education and particularly one's experiences' (2008:107). He pays little attention to intuition as a last term as described in section 2.2.4 (only when discussing the opportunity that writing the opinion affords the judge an occasion to postpone a decision; 2008:111).

communicative, discourse.[89] The judge may check his hunches by asking questions of lawyers or defendants, he may inquire as to what punishment the prosecutor had in mind, he may ask the legal secretary as to the content of the dossier or converse with other judges.

Yet it is not the discourse itself that leads to the decision. The judge has the final responsibility – he is the independent and impartial decision-maker. If necessary, he should be able to distance himself from emotions or intuitions voiced and from legal norms or sentences suggested. If the judge fails to do so, he may risk exposing himself to the dangers of tunnel vision. Of course, a hermeneutical 'circle'[90] cannot be avoided in its entirety: the framework by which the judge perceives the case will limit him in understanding the narratives of the litigants and the specificity of the case – these will remain in some way 'asymmetrical' to the judge.[91] But this does not mean that no effort can be made to avoid hermeneutical 'tunnel vision': by re-evaluating the mindful knowledge of the judge – e.g. reconsidering the framework of interpretation – or by looking closer at the specific elements of the case, or by a re-assessment against institutional values, the judge makes all the effort he can not to be blinded by his foreknowledge.[92]

A notable difference between the deliberation process in ancient Athens and present-day deliberation is the role of the law. Judges have knowledge of a corpus of positive law, by which they first perceive a case. In the process of deliberation, judges might have to make interpretative choices with respect to the norms that constitute this corpus.[93] There is an intricate relation between deliberation and legal norms. The selection of the norm is in part assessed by prudence and in turn the norm co-determines the process of deliberation. When assessing whether the decision is the right one with respect to the case, the judge will also take into account that the outcome of deliberation contributes to the understanding of law.

Another difference lies in the institutional values mentioned in section 2.3.3. Institutional values determine judicial prudence. The initial perception of the case is laden with these values. In the process of deliberation, the judge checks his deliberation against these values and finally, the judge must see to it that the decision meets institutional standards. Institutional values mark the difference

89 Cartuyvels & Van Campenhoudt (2004:43–45) speak of interaction in a micro-social context: 'Ces interactions sont cadrées par les formes institutionelles mises en oeuvre par les décisions et les modes de fonctionnement des agents du système judiciare' (44). See also Hartendorp (2008:186) on the dialogical structure of judicial decision-making.

90 Cf. Gadamer (1986:270–312), who – on the basis of Heidegger's existential philosophy – elaborates the idea of '*Verstehen*' as a historicized notion.

91 Cf. Ricoeur (1995:29–40) on the otherness of someone from the perspective of the institution.

92 See again Gadamer (1986:317–346) who lauds Aristotle's notion of prudence in this respect and applies it to judicial hermeneutics.

93 In fact, legal interpretation is seen by some as the core of judicial decision-making. Dworkin has even defined the law as an 'interpretative process' (1982). For criticism, see Barak (2005:4 note 11).

between different kinds of prudence, say between judicial and legislative prudence. Consequently, they resonate in each stage of the decision-making process.

Finally, although the differences between the practice of adjudication in ancient Athens and the present-day judicial application of law are manifold, there is a resemblance with respect to established democracies. In Aristotle's time, a just judgment had to be found 'quickly' and 'adequately' in the presented materials. In present-day western democracies, where the caseload is growing, judges are ordered to work efficiently – having to decide more quickly on a case. This, however, requires an accurate judicial intuition: a judge must quickly perceive the essence of the case brought before him. Thus, if one wishes for efficiency, then one has to make an effort to guarantee the quality of judges. Aristotle's theory of intuition also marks the limits. A last check is required and a judge should – from a virtue ethical perspective – have the liberty to take the time to reconsider.

## 3. Integrity as External Accountability with Respect to Judicial Decision-Making

Judicial decision-making is performed against the expectations that surround the judicial institution. Therefore integrity in judicial decision-making has not just to do with the virtuous aspects, which form the core of the process of deliberation, but also with decision-making in light of the integrity of the institution itself. For this reason, the theory of virtue must be supplemented with a theory of external accountability.

Aristotle left us with valuable insights concerning integrity as virtue, but his theory leaves us with very little when thinking about external accountability.[94] There are numerous reasons for this. It has for instance to do with the difference in adjudication. Nowadays, judges sit as single judges or in small numbers and they usually give grounds for their judgments as their decisions contribute to the understanding of law. It might be fair to say that the primary legitimacy of judicial work currently lies in the rule of law, whereas in Aristotle's time the legitimacy was the democratic aspect of their work: the high degree of direct participation

94 From the perspective of public trust, external accountability is distinct from virtue. Yet, as has been said in the Chapter 2 at section 3.3.3, there is also accountability from the perspective of professional character as openness or sensitivity – as 'taking into account'. In the virtue ethical theory outlined above, accountability in the judicial decision-making is an integral part of prudent decision-making. The judge has not only to do justice to the case, but must also find the optimum in relation to the well-being of the community. In order to do this, he must be sensitive and open to societal demands and be empathetic to emotions of the parties and others. This form of accountability can be understood as part of the character of the judge. Accountability from the perspective of public trust is substantively different – it concerns the specific relation between the institution and the public forum – and may therefore call for other demands.

provided immediate legitimacy.[95] Separate accountability was not necessary, as the judges *were* the citizens of Athens.

Another reason is that nowadays, human fragility in judicial decision-making is to a large extent recognized in institutional structures. The recognition of this fragility lies at the heart of public reasoning and is reflected in procedures for executive decision-making and modes of parliamentary control. With respect to judicial decision-making, this principle is reflected in for instance the appeal system and the practice of annotations.

### *3.1 The Institutional Nature of External Accountability*

The matter of rendering accountability in order to uphold the trust in the institution goes beyond a virtue ethical approach – it is not only about justice being done but also about demonstrating to the public that every effort is made that it is done. From this perspective, the character of the judge may prove to be insufficient to satisfy the norm that public trust is to be safeguarded to a reasonable extent. This statement rests on the simple notion that, from the perspective of society, confidence is not placed primarily in the individual office holders, but in the judiciary as a public institution. To society it is to some extent immaterial which individual fulfils the judicial role, as long as he acts as a good judge. This differentiation between the judge as an institution and the judge as an individual office holder means that institutional demands exist next to, or may take precedence over virtue ethical demands.

Institutional values may even be protected against office holders. Mixed forms of lay participation, which do not necessarily improve the quality of deliberation but clearly hold judges directly accountable, or an appeal system, in which parties can appeal regardless of the rightness of the decision, are instruments not merely designed to further judicial deliberation, but also to *demonstrate* to the public that effort is made to protect values such as impartiality, independence and diligence in the process of decision-making.

### *3.2 Accountability for Decisions – Bridging the Gap from Deliberation to Public Discourse*

Accountability with respect to decision-making is not to be confused with the demand for transparency. Although some elements of transparency are to aid accountability, such as openness in the courtroom or recording all that happens at trial, accountability with respect to decision-making is essentially different from transparency. There are two problems.

The first is that the demand for transparency may not fit well with integrity in a virtue ethical sense because the latter lacks transparency by nature. The process of deliberation concerns intentionally – and therefore 'inner' – weighing the specific

95 Cf. Cronin (1936:129–140) on the identification between judges and the public.

elements of the case against the purposes of judicial deliberation.[96] This process is not only characterized by rational elements but also by non- or semi-rational elements such as emotion and intuitions. Subsequently, many of the elements of the process of deliberation do not translate easily into the justification of the verdict. Then there is the 'confidentiality of the court' shielding the true deliberations from outsiders. The mind of the judges remains to some extent a closed book. The measure by which transparency can be guaranteed is therefore limited.

Yet the complexity itself may not be an objection to transparency. As doctors are obliged to seek informed consent, so it may well be part of the professionalism of judges to explain in everyday language what they are about to do. Yet this does not mean that the public *understands* what the judge does – as is also often the case with informed consent. This is the second problem connected with transparency vis-à-vis deliberation. Even if the judge explains what he does, the public cannot be presumed to have the capacity to understand the fine implications. These two problems mean that, with regard to deliberation, transparency is necessarily limited. Thus, transparency cannot mend the asymmetry with respect to judicial deliberation – instead it makes it visible.

There is an important difference with the doctor, however. Whereas informed consent is a duty towards the patient, writing a judicial decision is not just a duty to the parties but also to the community. With giving reasons for his decision,[97] the judge enters into a public discourse.[98] It is a means of providing insight into the reasons leading to the decision and thereby of making the decision acceptable and controllable.[99]

---

96 On judicial panels, lay participation and other instruments to safeguard integrity in decision-making, as professional and external accountability, see Chapter 5 at sections 3.2.1 and 3.2.2.

97 For a more elaborate discussion on how giving grounds for the decision can contribute to external accountability see Chapter 5 at section 3.2.2.

98 At common law, the grounds of a decision are also important with respect to the doctrine of precedent. A distinction is made within the judgment between *obiter dictum* and *ratio decidendi*: the former is a statement of law based on facts as found but not forming the basis of the decision, the latter denotes the rationale of the decision, which has precedence value to courts of the same level or lower levels. There is an ongoing debate about how the *ratio decidendi* can be distinguished in judicial decisions – as this is not always clearly indicated by the judges. As Lord Asquith once joked, 'The rule is quite simple, if you agree with the other bloke you say it is part of the ratio; if you don't you say it is obiter dictum, with the implication that he is a congenital idiot' (Cross & Harris 1992:50).

99 Posner is rather sceptical of the justificatory nature of the opinion as there may be confirmation bias: 'the well-documented tendency, once one has made up one's mind, to search harder for evidence that confirms rather than contradicts one's initial judgements' (2008:111). Posner, however, shifts rather directly from the 'intuitive judgment' to the rationalization thereof in the opinion, and thereby underemphasizes the deliberative check of intuitions against the ends of judicial decision-making.

The notion of the 'public' can be differentiated, although the exact differentiation will be different from one legal order to the next. Important examples are the academics who read and comment on cases, those directly affected by judicial decisions, higher level judges who are to review lower level decisions, other state powers which see their laws or executive acts reviewed, an independent press that follows cases with a high level of scrutiny and the public at large, which wants justice to be seen to be done, the Bar and the prosecutor who calculates his chances. To these audiences distinct forms of accountability are correlated, for example constitutional accountability, accountability with respect to the academic quality of decisions and popular accountability. It is quite a task to demonstrate the rationale of the decision on all of these fronts.

As the trust is directed at the institution, the question will be asked whether the judicial decision is a proper *institutional* one. Is the decision – and are its effects – within the boundaries of institutional discretion? Does it reflect institutional values, such as diligence and impartiality? Is it what the public generally *expected* of the institution? The nature of accountability may differ according to the legal order. For example, in civil law systems, criticism by reputable law professors will have a different effect than in the common law tradition.[100]

External accountability should be rendered so that public trust is directed at institutional values. Yet, as has been said in Chapter 2, it is a task of great difficulty to render accountability in a *normative* sense in order to secure de facto acceptance. These notions do not relate smoothly and it requires help from the social sciences to chart whether public trust is in fact directed at institutional values or at other aspects of the judicial imagery.

### *3.3 Integrity as a Generic Norm*

What is the relation between external accountability and judicial deliberation with respect to decision-making? Decision-making is in essence a virtuous activity. It is where the specific elements of the case are assessed with the ends of the institution in view. Yet virtuousness alone is not enough to secure public trust. For one thing, the judge must bridge the gap between deliberation and acceptance and give reasons for his decision by which he *demonstrates* that he has done so. External accountability may also be rendered by other means, for instance an appeal system or by instituting lay participation. These instruments will be discussed in Chapter 5, with respect to safeguarding external accountability.

The demand for external accountability can, however, also suffocate virtue. Deliberation with respect to difficult and complex circumstances does not always sit well with demands for clarity and transparency. Although serving demands in respect of social legitimacy, they do not always serve optimal deliberation. In some way, a line must be demarcated as to where virtue has room to develop and

100 For an historical overview of the relation between academia and the judiciary in the civil law and common law traditions, see van Caenegem (1987).

be exercised and with respect to what one must safeguard public trust. Without taking into account the peculiarities of a legal culture, this balancing act will undoubtedly fail.

It thus requires careful consideration of specific elements of concrete legal orders. For example, let us look at a treatment by Lasser about the legitimacy of French and American judgments.[101] He describes how French judgments, which are formulated in a concise, syllogistic manner, nevertheless seem to spark much trust. Since they are accompanied by scholarly annotations, judgments are directly embedded in the deliberative discourse in which those partake to whom the technical discussion is relevant. In contrast, American judgments aim at direct transparency: the judicial decisions are individually signed, the votes of the panels are disclosed and concurring and dissenting opinions can be published. This changes the nature of deliberation, as judges might be keen to dissent instead of dialectically finding a unified stand. The technical juristic discussion is performed within the judgment itself and the entire discussion – not just the outcome – is to provide legitimacy for the activity of judges. As a result, American judgments are relatively long and may express different stances.

This example shows how multiple factors contribute to determine the specific balance between decision-making and rendering accountability. Is there a system of dissenting and concurring opinions? What is the role of academia? Is there a doctrine of precedence? Are judges connected to their verdict in person or merely as 'the court'? These questions reveal that at a meta-level, policy decisions must be taken with respect to peculiarities of a concrete legal order. This discourse is performed by many actors, as has been argued. For instance, the legislator must make sure that the laws are generally of good quality, academia has to sharpen its knives in annotations and the executive may have to reserve extra money, so that decisions are available to the public via the internet.

A second level of prudence is therefore needed to configure and balance virtue and external accountability with regard to institutional values.

## 4. Conclusion

In this chapter, a theory of the integrity of the judge in judicial decision-making has been developed. As judicial integrity is understood as a generic norm covering both virtue and the norm to safeguard public trust, the theory was developed along both lines. Much attention has been devoted to virtue, as it is concerned with the core of judicial deliberation. This has been supplemented by thoughts on external accountability.

As virtue, a theory of judicial integrity in judicial decision-making has been sketched on the basis of Aristotle's theory. Although the concepts of justice and law have changed significantly, Aristotle's theory offers a unique insight into the

101 Cf. Lasser (2004:299–359).

professional character of the judge in relation to judicial decision-making. Three elements are of special interest with respect to integrity.

First, with respect to professional formation a strict compliance approach or a competence-oriented approach, however important, is not a sufficient condition to develop excellence in professional character. Formation of character is needed – that also takes into account 'soft' knowledge such as the sharing of experience by peers, which culminates in continuous exercise in acting virtuously. Integrity is first and foremost about developing a steady character by acting with the ends of deliberation in view.

Second, judicial deliberation is a purposive activity. It has three aims: establishing professional character itself, establishing well-being on a case level and furthering well-being within society. The relation between these aims can be one of deep complexity, which is articulated in the process of prudent deliberation. Institutional values secure, guide and delimit the purposiveness of judicial deliberation.

Third, the intricate relation between decision-making and character can best be seen in the role of 'intuitive reason'. The process of judicial deliberation is embedded in intuition. The perception of the case is intuition-laden. The initial perception of the case is then checked against questions as to the applicable law and its proper interpretation, against questions about the facts of the case and about the proper assessment against institutional values. This process of deliberation is also characterized by a communicative discourse. In the end, however, the judge must be able to 'see' for himself whether a decision adequately meets the specific demands of the concrete situation or whether it should be reconsidered.

Integrity in judicial decision-making does not merely concern the process of deliberation of the individual judges, but also the integrity of the institution in which the public places its trust. As has repeatedly been said, today's democracies demand more than virtue: justice need not only be done, but must also be *seen* to be done. As public trust is directed at institutional values before it is directed at the office holder, several instruments are employed to give citizens a chance to appeal in spite of the rightness of the deliberation. Sometimes these are even to protect institutional values against office holders. These instruments are not merely designed to further judicial deliberation, but to *demonstrate* to the public that effort is made to protect institutional values such as impartiality, independence and diligence in the process of decision-making.

External accountability with respect to judicial decision-making is not to be confused with transparency. Although transparency may be required in some forms, the nature of judicial deliberation will remain to some extent obscure. Even if the process were to be made transparent, it would not guarantee that citizens would understand judicial deliberations. Thus, transparency cannot mend the asymmetry with respect to judicial deliberation – instead it makes it visible. Rendering accountability for judicial decisions is a norm of a different order, as deliberations are made part of a public discourse in which these are held accountable to many actors, ranging from academia to the parties.

As a generic norm, it requires a meta-level prudence to balance virtue and external accountability. Both are necessary in order to meet the norm of integrity but demands for external accountability may also suffocate virtue. It cannot be said *in abstracto* which instruments better serve public trust or which configuration of institutional values should form the object of judicial deliberations. This discourse is one for many actors, ranging from state powers to university professors. In order for this discourse to be up to the mark, much more research is needed into the underpinnings of the legitimacy of our institutions and the values that lie at the base of a legal order.

# Chapter 4
# Integrity in the Conduct of Judges

## 1. Introduction

This chapter is concerned with integrity in the conduct of judges. I distinguish between two realms of conduct: judicial conduct and non-judicial conduct. Judicial conduct concerns matters such as the equal treatment of the parties or the maintaining of rituals within the courtroom. It may also concern ancillary activities that the judge assumes *as a judge*, such as heading public committees or lecturing at a university. Non-judicial conduct denotes all other forms of behaviour. Note that the distinction is not between judicial tasks and non-judicial tasks. For instance, a judge may – *as judge* – be asked to give a lecture at the university. This is a non-judicial task but part of judicial conduct. When speaking of conduct I except judicial decision-making.

Not all matters are interesting from a philosophical point of view: for instance, the discussions on the exact nature of protocols or the factual effect of the judicial robe in relation to public confidence. These are matters for policy-makers or for sociological research. From a philosophical point of view, integrity is understood along the lines of virtue ethics and external accountability. As in the previous chapter, Aristotle's ethics provides the main point of reference. Yet, since Aristotle's theory of public institutions is rather undeveloped, I will look at other philosophers, notably Hegel, who has conceptualized elements that are needed to arrive at a comprehensive theory of integrity within judicial conduct.

This chapter is set out as follows. I first turn to a theory of integrity in *judicial* conduct (section 2), by looking at the nature of public institutions and the relation between virtue and the institution. The treatment of litigants will be discussed as an example. I will also discuss the role of symbols and rituals and the issue of judicial conduct outside the courtroom. I will then turn to a theory of integrity in *non-judicial* conduct (section 3), by discussing the separation between the individual and his role, the freedom to exercise citizenship and conduct at odds with the judicial role. I will also touch upon the relation between integrity in decision-making and integrity in conduct (section 4). Last, I will look at integrity as a generic norm (section 5).

## 2. Integrity in Judicial Conduct

A serious difficulty in drafting a theory about integrity in judicial conduct lies in the fact that the judicial office is not simply a role but a public institution.

Therefore, a theory of integrity requires an understanding of the nature of the institution. What is the nature of a public institution in present-day democracies under a rule of law?

I will attempt to answer this question by revisiting Hegel, who drafted the ideals of the modern state and its institutions by taking seriously the Enlightenment ideals of rationality and freedom. Although his notion of reason is considered to be too strong by present-day philosophers and his overarching claims too pretentious, his theory on public institutions provides a valuable framework, which has been influential to say the least.[1] It is by means of this framework that I will look at the integrity of judicial conduct.

Next, I will turn to the relation between the institution and integrity. What, for instance, is the relation between virtue and institutional values? How are they to be enacted? As an example, I will look at the treatment of the parties. Then I will look at the symbols and rituals that surround the judicial function. What role do they play? And what is their relation to judicial integrity? Why is it that the judicial office is embedded in rituals, whereas they seem to have disappeared to a large extent with the doctor or the politician? Lastly, I will look at judicial conduct outside the courtroom: denied of symbols and rituals, the conduct of the judge is now a direct focal point of public trust.

These matters are complex and many of these questions cannot be answered *in abstracto*. Yet on a normative level these answers can be anticipated.

### *2.1 Hegel on the 'Second Nature' of Public Institutions*

In modern states, institutions are based upon Enlightenment ideals about human nature. Although not all institutional purposes can be traced back to rights and interests of individuals, anthropological concepts commonly function as guiding principles in shaping political theory.[2] From Plato and Aristotle to Habermas and Rawls, the idea of who an individual is and should be has been decisive in the choices made in institutional theory.

This is the same in Hegel's philosophy of right. I revert to Hegel as, in his institutional theory, the value-ladenness of public institutions is articulated

1 Cf. for example Avinieri (1972:vii–xi, 239–241), Siep (1997:5–10).

2 Cf. Zippelius (2003:121). In this manner, Rousseau and Kant developed ideas about democracy and basic human rights with a specific anthropology in mind. Rousseau posited the general will as a normative concept (not the will of 'all': '*Il y a souvent bien de la différence entre la volonté de tous et la volonté générale*', Rousseau (1963:II.3, cf. I.2)), to ensure his conception of free individuals. Kant formulated the imperative of the absolute worthiness of men, cf. Kant (1902:390ff) and (1917). This led him to be optimistic about the world order (Kant 1912) and led others to consider Kant's deontological ethics as the foundation of universal ideas of justice or human rights theories. Montesquieu also used a distinct anthropological conception. He extended the Hobbesian pessimistic view of men, which resulted in the need for a strong sovereign. Montesquieu took this pessimism to the state power itself – a mistrust that led to the separation thereof (Montesquieu 1868).

thoroughly. From there, we reach a good position to consider what role virtue has with respect to public institutions. In this section, I aim to come to an understanding of Hegel's thoughts, as they will be applied to the question of integrity in the next section.

Writing at the dawn of the Enlightenment, Hegel developed a concept of autonomous personality and used this concept as the starting point for his philosophy of right.[3] In fact, in his classic work, the *Grundlinien der Philosophie des Rechts*, he defends the claim that public institutions should be based on the principle of autonomous personality.

What does this concept of autonomous personality entail?[4] According to Kant the 'person' is to be understood according to his rational nature.[5] As rational, a person is equal to all persons and must therefore always be treated as an end in himself and never as a mere means to an end. The 'autonomy' of the person lies in the fact that the person is his 'own' lawgiver. Autonomy in a Kantian sense is, however, not to be thought of as a modern-day concept of self-expression or pursuance of individual preferences, but instead as a rational activity whereby maxims of the will are held against the demands of rationality. Therefore according to Kant a person is autonomous because he gives himself the law as *any* rational being would do. Hegel now criticizes this concept of person for the simple reason that it does not exist in fact but is only a construct of reason. In order to be *actually* autonomous, the person needs not only to be understood as a rational self, but also as a self that seeks realization in concrete social contexts. His needs for food, love, possessions and happiness must be recognized – albeit in a concrete sphere that guarantees the autonomy of all. According to Hegel, it is up to a philosophy of law to expound on the nature of such a social sphere.

The idea of autonomous personality is thus the basic anthropological concept in the *Grundlinien*. The objective order, its laws, its institutions and its governance, should be an expression of autonomy.[6] Without it, we revert to Tacitus's adage

3 There is a catch, however, in using Hegel's concept of autonomous personality. Not rarely and not wrongly is Hegel perceived as a holistic thinker (Siep 2003:63–77). His monstrous ideas of a *Weltgeist* and of historical empires have raised many eyebrows. The problems concern Hegel's strong concept of reason. His philosophy of right is embedded in a philosophy that seeks to understand the reasonableness of 'all that is'. Taking into account that next to this 'holistic' approach (Quante 1997:69ff.), he also used a rational *method*, this concept of reason may be called strong. This has been the subject of much criticism. Does he leave enough room for contingency? Does he see that coincidence and chance may also be experienced as liberating? (Siep 1997:27f). Does he leave enough room for cultural variety? Does his final emphasis on world history neglect the simple individual? Does his concept of right leave room for love and friendship? (Peperzak 2001:646–656). I therefore take a 'bottom-up' instead of a 'top-down' approach; cf. the preface to this book.

4 For a more extensive overview see Soeharno (2007).

5 See, for instance, Kant (1902:428ff).

6 In Hegel's concept of the state, all the facets of personality are in some way *objectified*. Its desires and needs in the economic sphere, its longing for happiness in

that although we escaped tyranny, we now suffer under laws.[7] In the *Grundlinien*, Hegel is concerned with freedom in the objective sphere and it is the concept of autonomous personality that shows how a subject may understand himself as objectively free. There is an intricate relation between the subject who is an autonomous person and the objective order, which has to guarantee the autonomy of persons. The state expects individuals to meet the standards of autonomous personality. Therefore individuals receive education and formation. It is from this consciousness that they fulfil societal roles.

In this sense institutions should have freedom as their – so Hegel calls it – 'second nature'.[8] Second nature is *objectified* reason. This refers to both the reason that has *brought forth* institutions such as law or a state and the reason that these institutions *impinge* on individuals. To rational individuals, who have received education and formation in the state, the social institutions are on the one hand 'powers' that should be obeyed, but on the other hand – since the institutions of the state are an expression of freedom – institutions in which they recognize their own essence. This should ideally prevent *Verfremdung*.[9] Ideally citizens 'trust' that the state has no other interests than the rational, essential interests of its individuals. The state, for its part is to will nothing but the wills of individuals in so far as they are rational.

This brings about a demand to office holders to 'assume' this 'second nature'. Take for example the freedom of religion. The modern state does not have the interest of a particular religion in view, but the rational interest of a right to religion. The judge for his part, if he is religious, cannot act from his particular interest. He is to have the ideals of his institution as a second nature: he acts according to the ideals of the modern state – of freedom, impartiality and independence – transcending his personal interest. Of course the judge may recognize with himself as a citizen the abstract right to religion, but as a judge he is not entitled to act upon

---

the religious community, its need for love in the family, its need for recognition in the corporation and its desire for freedom in the state – which educates him to freedom and administers his justice. The idea of the state is thus construed upon all facets of the will: upon the subject's basic needs and desires, his longing for happiness, his need for love and recognition, and his will to coexist with others. To Hegel, 'love' is not irrational. Since love enables one to view the unity of two persons (the identity in difference) it is viewed as a mode of reason. That is not to say that the concept of freedom is adequately realized, for it is not willed *as such*. Family relations are a 'given' rather than an effect of rational will.

7 '... *utque antehac flagitiis, ita tunc legibus laborabatur*', Tacitus (1965:III,25,2).

8 'Second nature' alludes to the biblical concept of a second 'Christian nature'. For Hegel, it refers to taking part in a sphere that is brought about by reason, which is here the state. How freedom as a second nature becomes *concrete*, depends on which function the institution has in respect to freedom.

9 German term that is best translated as 'estrangement'. The state with its institutions is therefore, in Hegel's terms, ideally *subjective substance*. The opposition between the common will and the individual will is therein sublated but of course not dissolved (*Grl* § 260).

concrete religious ideas. Thus, the rational essence of religion is recognized in the state, namely the abstract right to religion, but the particular interests of a religion are not acted upon.

*2.2 The Relation Between Virtue and the Institution: Enacting Institutional Values*

In section 2.1, I did not go into the complexities of Hegel's theory of the modern state, but focused on the nature of the public institution. The appeal of the strong claims of Hegel's philosophy have diminished, for instance the strong nature of rationality or his holistic view of philosophy, and many facets of Hegel's state theory are outdated, from the class system[10] to his conception of the *trias*.[11] And although an idea of freedom still lies at the heart of public institutions, the interpretation of freedom might be different from that of Hegel,[12] who linked it to a strong concept of rationality. Yet a basic tenet still stands: public institutions in modern-day democracies under a rule of law reflect and serve values that are fundamental to modern society and that are in some way linked to a wider concept of its well-being.[13] It is these values that provide the democratic legitimacy of the institution. This notion is of crucial importance for the concept of integrity.

Let us look at the role of virtue in public institutions. The notion of a modern public institution, which is based upon core values, was not developed in Aristotle's philosophy. With Aristotle the legitimacy of public institutions is primarily grounded in the virtuousness of the office holders. In contrast, with Hegel the basic legitimacy rests in the institution, as it is an expression of the ideal of freedom. The office holder then represents not his personal interests, but the interests of the institution, as these become a 'second nature'.

But if the office holder's conduct should be in accordance with the ideals of the institution, is he then merely to *conform* to the ideals of the institution? According to Hegel, the idea of civic virtue denotes the citizen in so far as he acts

10 On its outdatedness see Hardimon (1994:130f).

11 The personality of the state is finally reflected in the monarch (*Grl* § 279 *Anmerkung*). Hegel's *trias politica* is construed according to the structure of his logic. It consists of the legislative power (the 'abstract'), the executive power (the 'particular') and the monarch (as the 'singular' power). Acts of the government and the legislator thus appear as *personal* acts. The personality of the state thus exists in the person of the monarch. As such, it also has individuality, which is shown in relation to other states (*Grl* § 331 *Anmerkung*). To Hegel the judiciary is not a state power but an institution in civil society (*Grl* § 219).

12 See for example Rawls (1971:201–205), Allan (1993:109) or Pettit (1997:17–110).

13 As was the case in Chapter 3, the level of abstraction of this book does not allow for a concrete interpretation of these values, but as has been said in the preface, I do assume societies with a democracy under a rule of law that encompasses fundamental rights.

in accordance with the nature of the state.[14] In a state where the institutions are a reflection of the right ideals, the virtuous person is he who is permeated by the ideals of the institution. In other words, one should act 'naturally' according to the nature of these institutions, having internalized their ideals and acting upon them.[15]

In other words, virtue becomes subject to the values of the institution.[16] It should not draw attention to itself, but to the institution it enacts.[17] Yet virtue – even if 'invisible'[18] – is needed to make institutional ideals and values *concrete*. These values can only be concretized when office holders act upon them. Without prudence, specific acts cannot be performed with the overarching values in view. This is also true for the values tied to the judicial role. Impartiality, independence and propriety require integrity as virtue to become concrete. Without prudent assessment, they are void of reality. For instance, impartiality comes about when the judge transcends to the 'second nature' of the institution, from his direct inclinations and preferences, and from the interests of the parties. By means of

14 A general outline of concrete civic virtues is the following. 'As citizens of the state, individuals must subordinate the whole sphere of their private lives (including private rights and well-being, those of the family, their corporation and their class) to the final purpose of politics (§ 261) and obey the laws in a patriotic spirit (§ 268). They should loyally take part in political life and fulfil political tasks that might be entrusted to them (§§ 257–319 & 337). If unfortunate situations such as war make it necessary, they must also sacrifice their possessions, including their life, for the state (§§ 324–328)', Peperzak (2001:405).

15 According to Hegel, civic virtue is two-sided. On the one hand, it has a *political* side, which is characterized by 'duty'. The ethicality of the state is laid down in the constitution and it is the duty of citizens to obey these laws. On the other hand, it has a *personal* side. The citizen is not only to obey the laws and fulfill his political duties, but also to develop his character according to the nature of freedom. The unity of political duty and personal character is the ethos of the citizen.

16 Hegel states that 'ethical geniality' has its place only in extraordinary circumstances, for instance in the situation of moral collisions, cf. *Grl* § 150, see also Peperzak (1997:167–191).

17 In this respect, Hegel has been accused of a state-centred philosophy, where contingency and individuality are sacrificed to the state. This is certainly true for the *Grundlinien*, though it must be said in Hegel's defence that this book deals with what he calls 'objective philosophy' and therefore naturally gives precedence to public institutions, cf. Peperzak (2001:43–45), Heyde (1987:255).

18 This departs from the assumption of a just or a nearly just state. If, on the contrary, a state has defective public institutions, then virtue may assume a different – more visible – role. For legitimacy may then come to rest in the ethical character of office holders itself. Virtue is then not just necessary for good deliberation but needs also to uphold public confidence directly. Integrity and virtue can then become synonymous, yet virtue fulfils two distinguished roles: the role of the professional character of the office holder and the role of external accountability with respect to public trust. Virtue assumes the second function as institutional values – towards which public trust is directed – are not displayed by institutional structures, but solely by the virtuousness of the office holder.

his assessment he actively does justice to both parties, which is a prudent activity. In his conduct, the judge can make this value concrete, for instance by making sure that both parties have equal time to present their cases, by not looking at one party with disquiet and at the other with friendliness and by taking into account procedural guarantees.[19] It is here that virtue is needed. Virtue in the conduct of the judge ascertains that, in his actions, institutional values are mediated aptly with the demands of the specific situation. Thus, without an office holder who is a person of integrity, the institution does not *exist* as an expression of institutional values. And when an institution is not an expression of institutional values, it lacks democratic legitimacy.

Institutions reflect core values and ideals but they have an organizational side as well. As such, they are susceptible to flaws that organizations might develop: for example bureaucratic flaws or vices of neo-managerialism, such as an over-emphasis on efficiency. It is up to virtue to act with the core values and ideals in view, and thus secure the vitality of public institutions.

Let us now turn to external accountability. The fact that the institution reflects and serves core values is what provides basic legitimacy to its authority. The citizens of the state 'trust' that the state ideally has these values in view. It is by this conception of the institution that we may understand the precedence that the institution has over the office holder with respect to legitimacy. For the basic legitimacy of the institution rests not primarily in the virtue of its office holders, as with Aristotle, but in the institution as it is an expression of values. The conduct of the judge should therefore be in line with the values that the institution symbolizes. His misconduct can corrode these values and thereby the basic democratic legitimacy of the authority of the judiciary. In modern societies, institutions are protected from their own office holders: even the *appearance* of a corroding act may lead to disqualification or dismissal. This institutionalization of the distrust in public officials serves to uphold the trust that society places in the institution. Therefore external accountability measures are needed, as are strategies to further the professional virtue of office holders.

Thus, with Hegel, we gain a better understanding of the value-ladenness of the public institution and its relation to virtue. The institution is a symbol of the values it serves to uphold. But these values are void without the virtuous activity of the office holder. The values are even protected against the office holder himself by a range of means to ensure external accountability.

### *2.3 Example – The Treatment of Persons*

The idea of a value-laden institution deserves further thought. What would the idea that institutions are symbolic of values imply for the treatment of litigants?

19 See Kelly (2004) who treats impartiality as a judicial virtue, while not separating the value from its virtuous connotation.

First, this would require that citizens involved with a trial are treated not in the first place as litigant, party, suspect, witness, victim or claimant – but as *persons*,[20] if we speak in Hegelian vocabulary,[21] or 'according to *equality*', to speak in the terms of the Bangalore Principles of Judicial Conduct. The recognition as persons or as equals entails the norm that parties are not treated according to social status, gender, tribal identity or race. The enactment of institutional values implies that the judge treats the parties according to these values. This means that the judge transcends specific characteristics such as race, ethnicity et cetera. This transcendence is not always easy and education is needed to perform it.

Second, the recognition of the parties as persons or as equals implies that their individuality is considered *from* the viewpoint of 'abstract personality' or of 'equality'. In other words, not only has the judge in his perception to 'transcend' the individuality of the litigant to his status as equal, but he has from there to 'descend' and consider the individuality of the litigant from that viewpoint.[22]

In this sense, it is about empathy and accommodation. It is about empathy, because the judge has to be attentive to the concrete individual before him.[23] Yet, the judge tries to understand the individuality of the litigant without prejudice and consider only the relevant elements for the case. In other words, the judge is empathetic on a professional level, giving expression to the ideal that he acts according to the second nature of the institution. It is about accommodation, because the judge has to accommodate his treatment so that the parties *understand* that he treated them as persons and not according to their race or tribe – but as

20 Cf. Siep (1979:224–234) on the relevance of Hegel's concept of recognition for social institutions. Cf. Honneth (1992:174–225) on Hegel's theory of the recognition of legal personality and its place in the wider pattern of social recognition.

21 In his first paragraph on the administration of justice, Hegel emphasizes the importance of education, so that it may be recognized: 'It is part of education, of *thinking* as consciousness of the individual [*des Einzelnen*] in the form of universality, that I am apprehended as a *universal* person, in which [respect] all are identical. A *human being counts as such because he is a human being*, not because he is a Jew, Catholic, Protestant, German, Italian, etc. This consciousness … is of infinite importance', *GrlE* § 209 A.

22 Integrity in the recognition of persons thus goes beyond neutrality, as Haarscher argues (2004:44 and 65–67): 'A judge, for instance, is neutral *up to a certain point* – but he or she must always be *impartial* … Integrity is broader than neutrality: *integrity can exist without neutrality … but neutrality cannot exist without integrity*'.

23 It falls outside the scope of this book to go more deeply into the difficulties that surround the concept of empathy. On cognitive, affective and distant forms of empathy see Mackor (2001:35–43). On hermeneutical problems relating to the narrative of the 'other' see Ricoeur (1995). As Ricoeur says: the other for friendship is 'you', but the other for the institution is 'anyone' (1995:29–40). How can the institutional other then be recognized in his specific individuality? It remains a difficult question as to the relation of these emotions and other 'asymmetries' and the law. Is the decision to be different as different emotions are in play? Is adjudication to reckon with affections? I would say that there is more room to adjust and accommodate conduct than decision-making.

persons or as equals vis-à-vis the law. How this treatment is done concretely is determined by the specific legal culture.[24]

Thus in the treatment of persons, acting according to the second nature of the institution entails that the judge transcends to institutional values, such as 'abstract personality' or 'equality', and then descends with empathy and accommodation in recognition of their individuality.

### *2.4 Symbols and Rituals*

The institution of the judge is a symbol, meaning that it 'collects' a number of values, that it 'represents' these values and that it 'enacts' them.[25] Its symbolic nature can be expressed in specific symbols, for instance the judicial robes as a symbol for the neutrality of the judge, the glass ceiling in the courtroom for the transcendence of law, the location of the benches for the parties for the adversarial nature of the trial or the steps leading into the court building for the authority of law. Institutional values are also surrounded by rituals:[26] standing up when the judge enters, the oath to speak the truth or the formulas whereby the lawyers address the judge. Rituals may also serve to canalize public anger or feelings of revenge.[27]

It seems that symbols and rituals are especially important with public functions that represent abstract values – as with judges, appointed mayors or royalty. These

24 For a defence of impartiality against allegations that 'reasonable' notions such as impartiality are also context bound and are thus not neutral to minorities, see Kelly (2004:28–42). He argues that impartiality is a regulative ideal by which one aspires for minimal recognition.

25 Although there is no clear consensus on the meaning of the concept of 'symbol' (Scholz 1998:724, 735), its etymology (σύμβολον is derived from συμβάλλειν – 'to collect, to throw together, to represent, to put together, to come together, to meet, to converge' etc. – see Müri 1976:1–44 for an elaborate study) unveils some of its semantic constituents, which have allowed several uses: from signs to passwords to confessions of faith, to images that are to make present the transcendent, to laws, to mythical and abstract – mathematical – knowledge (Meier-Oeser 1998, Berner 2004, Cancik-Lindemaier 2004 and Recki 2004). I understand 'symbol' in relation to the institution in the following sense: the institution signifies a number of values or ideals in that it 'collects', 'represents' and 'makes present or enacts' these values or ideals.

26 Where symbols are significant of higher values or ideals, rituals are their '*Gestensprache*' (Sigrist 1992:1053). I take rituals to refer to actions that are performed in relation to higher values or ideals (Glei & Natzel 1992).

27 With more nuance, Garapon says that 'Le premier geste de la justice n'est ni intellectual ni moral, mais architectural et symbolique: delimiter un espace sensible qui tienne à distance l'indignation moral et la colère publique, dégager un temps pour cela, arrêter un règle du jeu, convenir d'un objectif et instituer des acteurs' (Garapon 1997:19). Although this is more true for penal law trials than for civil law trials, this does show how the legal ritual can have a cathartic function with respect to public emotions.

become more important as the 'public good' for which they stand becomes more abstract, for instance military who fight for the cause of the country, a king or queen acting on behalf of the people, a police officer who must uphold the law or a priest acting on behalf of a higher power. Uniforms, formal codes, rules of conduct and other symbols and rituals serve to make concrete the 'second nature' of these officials. They stand for the public good and it is in this value that their legitimacy rests. Symbols and rituals are thus to make concrete what is otherwise abstract: the whole, the public, the good.

Sometimes symbols or rituals lose their referential function. This can happen when the symbol itself is no longer understood to refer to that specific value or when the value that the symbol refers to is no longer shared. Therefore symbols and rituals need revalidation now and then. When symbols or rituals are not understood to refer to institutional values, they may estrange people from the institution instead of providing democratic legitimacy to the institution. It is not relevant whether symbols or rituals are old or odd; what is relevant is whether they lead to estrangement or understanding of institutional values. I will come back to this point in section 2.5.

What is the role of integrity with respect to symbols and rituals? It is clear that symbols and rituals should serve external accountability. They are to demonstrate to the public the values that are connected with the institution. They should also show that office holders are subservient to these values. No matter who the judge is, he wears the same robes and adheres to the same procedures.

The importance of virtue with respect to symbols and rituals can also not be overestimated. Garapon illustrates by reference to the Stalinist trial and the 'sacrificial trial' how rituals can become an instrument for the wrong motives.[28] The Stalinist trial serves to demonstrate the guilt *to* the accused. Here, power corrupts right and the trial is used as its instrument. It violates the virtuousness of the judge in that his conduct is not performed with the values of impartiality and independence in view. The 'sacrificial trial' serves to soothe the emotions of the people, irrespective of the guilt of the accused. The accused is sacrificed for the greater good. This position equally corrupts right. It violates the virtuousness of the judge for not considering institutional values at a case level as described in the previous chapter. It also fails to take into account the *risk* that the truth will become known. Then public confidence is harmed in a graver manner.

There is another position, which is more difficult to answer for judicial integrity, namely considering the legal ritual as a game with its own rules of play.[29] The process then becomes the purpose of law. The law has come about to transform,

28 Cf. Garapon (1997:249–256) who discusses '*les cérémonies dégradantes*' and '*la crise sacrificielle*'.

29 Cf. Huizinga (1938:75–86) who bases his claim that adjudication is a form of play on the basis of archaic forms of judging. One may consider naive procedural justice as a modern variant, where procedures are regarded as sufficient condition for a right outcome. But see Bayles (1990) for a more nuanced approach on procedural justice, which comes

ritualize, disputes into a legal matter, thus being able to channel emotions by means of fair rules of play. The judge sees to it that the right procedures are followed. If there is a dispute about them, he has the last word. This position overlooks the nature of the judicial institution. The judge is not merely a referee, seeing to it that the rules of the game are followed. The judge is more than that. He is a decision-maker. This he does with the ends of law in view. The ritualization is not a purpose in itself as the right outcome is not the result of the right procedure. Rituals are rather an instrument of justice and the right outcome is found after deliberation, which cannot be fully accounted for by procedure – as was seen in the previous chapter.

This also has implications for judicial conduct other than decision-making. The judge should not uphold the rituals of the office merely for the rituals themselves. His office does not exist because of these rituals, nor does it exist to uphold these rituals. Rituals have come about to express the values on which the institution is based. The judge upholds and enacts these rituals so that the values that they express are adequately communicated to the litigant and society. It is for this reason that judges in civil juvenile cases sometimes take off their judicial robes or that formulas are adapted according to the jurisdiction. Rituals have a communicative and referential function, whereas integrity is the virtue that enacts values that are expressed in these rituals. Integrity as virtue means that the judge can be critical towards rituals – after all, as one who is to incorporate and enact the values that lie at the basis of rituals, he is to understand their nature and use.

Thus, the judicial office is a public institution, which is symbolic of the values therein expressed. The institution is encircled with concrete symbols and rituals. Although these have a function with respect to external accountability, these should not become the sole focal point. As they are referential to the values that lie at the heart of the institution, it is the judge who should make the meaning of the rituals concrete by virtuous conduct.

### *2.5 The Question of Informality – The Judge as a Symbolic Personality*

We now come to the question of *informality*. In many countries, there are debates about 'old fashioned' rituals and procedures. Do people still accept the 'fiction' of an impersonal judge who is disguised by robe and mores? These debates may be wholly justified when symbols and rituals do not adequately refer to the values they are to represent.

There are a number of ways to deal with this matter. One extreme is a *traditionalist* position: when symbols and rituals are adhered to, the public will in the end be better off.[30] This position is rather paternalistic and assumes the primacy of wisdom on the part of the judicial elite. The other extreme is obstreperous: away

about only when in line with procedural principles. Procedural justice then requires prudent judges.

30 For a discussion on this position with respect to judges see C. Bell (1997:145f).

with the symbols – the judge is a human being as we are. Legitimacy should rather rest in the human face of the judge, not in symbols or rituals. This position overlooks the fact that we have attributed the power to adjudicate to an institution – not to a specific person. Between these extremes there are more nuanced options. One could opt for a *restorative* one, which holds on to symbols and rituals but invests at the same time in the communication of the underlying meaning of these symbols and rituals.[31] Or one could do away with most of the symbols while keeping a bare minimum to refer to the authority of law.

From the viewpoint of integrity, these approaches are all concerned with the question as to what extent informality can be allowed on the basis of formality. Yet they tend to overlook the fact that the judicial institution is *by nature* symbolic. It is therefore expected that it be ritualized to some extent. For instance, the judge can show institutional emotions that may not be on a par with his private emotions.[32] In this manner he can *personalize* the institution. This personalization happens on the level of the institution. It is no strict informality, but an informality that rests in the symbols and rituals of the institution. He may have no feelings of compassion for a murder victim, but acting as an institution he may find it appropriate to express sympathy for the victim in court.[33]

31 Cf. Hol (2006:816, 817).

32 There is a difference between integrity, authenticity and sincerity. Authenticity refers to an immediacy whereby personal views, affections or emotions are expressed. It is highly debatable whether the professional actor should show his authentic emotions and thoughts (cf. Leest 2007:37–62 for an apt discussion on the problem of authenticity in penal law and its relation to legitimacy). Whereas integrity provides a link between legitimacy and the character of the professional, authenticity does not necessarily do so. In fact, one can think of many cases in which we do not even *want* the public official to be authentic (the thoughts of Ferrara, who sees an intimate link between authenticity and validity (1998:1–21) are inapplicable here: the validity that he is concerned with is about identity and self-consciousness, not professional character). For instance, we do not want a judge to be authentic in respect to his personal feelings about the culprit and we do not want a police officer to be authentic to what he thinks about the suspect. It is in fact part of their integrity that they are not authentic to these convictions and rather stick to their professional standards. If a judge displays traits of 'authentic' emotions, he does so as a professional judge. Authenticity is to be distinguished from sincerity, which in this context denotes the proper intentionality towards institutional values. Sincerity in this respect is about a professional uprightness, a professional truthfulness to an institutional mandate. Such a demand can be found with Ricoer (1995) who derives from this a 'rule of sincerity' and with Aristotle (*EN* IV.13:1127a13–1127b33) who speaks of veracity or good faith in negotiations. Sincerity is an integral part of virtue, authenticity is not.

33 Mandeville once called pity the source of the corruption of judicial integrity, yet here I am not necessarily talking about 'authentic' pity but about 'institutional' pity (see Mandeville 1924:56).

To the reader, this may seem Machiavellian.[34] In fact, such notions stem from Aristotle's *Retorica*. Together with the demonstration of *pathos* and *logos*, *ethos* is an aspect by which others can become convinced.[35] This personalization is, however, also a virtuous activity in itself, performed with institutional values in view. In other words, whether a judge wears a robe or decides to take it off: these are both symbolic acts.

This concept of a personalized institution combines Hegel's institutional theory and Aristotle's virtue ethics. Whereas Hegel articulates the institution on the basis of the values that lie at its heart, Aristotle's virtue ethics provides a possibility to insert personal behaviour, yet on this institutional level. It is part of the symbolism of the judge that the adjudication of law has a human face. The individual behind the judge is blindfolded, whereas the judge has his eyes open as an institutional personality.

Thus, the judge should first assume the 'second nature' of the institution. From his particular interests, he transcends to values such as impartiality, independence, propriety and equality. These institutional values become concrete in integrity. They become real in the *character* of the judge and they are upheld by means of external accountability. Impartiality, for instance, is a value in the discretion of the judge and is demonstrated in his conduct within the courtroom. Impartiality then assumes a human face, and it may even assume human emotions: empathetic remarks are not necessarily at odds with impartiality or neutrality, but may be an expression thereof.[36] The judge must, however, always keep in mind that trust is not directed at his person but at the institution that he personalizes.

The relation between virtue and external accountability that is characteristic of the theory of integrity is thus visible when it comes to judicial conduct within the courtroom. Virtue is needed to enact the values of the institution while external accountability serves to uphold the democratic legitimacy of the institution. The personality of the office holder is thus both crucial and limited. Without it, institutional values cannot become concrete. Of course, if the judge acts virtuously, this may directly enhance the confidence in the judiciary. Yet the institution can

34 As Machiavelli (2006:57, 58) advises the prince: 'A prince, therefore, need not necessarily have all the good qualities … but he should certainly appear to have them … To those seeing and hearing him, he should appear a man of compassion, a man of good faith, a man of integrity, a kind and religious man … Everyone sees what you appear to be, few experience what you really are'.

35 *Ret.* 1356a21–25. See for an example of a display of virtue 1361a1–1363b4. See Frost (1994) for a reworking of the rhetoric of Aristotle and Quintilian for lawyers. See Solum (2003:186–194) for a list of virtues that a judge is to display and a list of vices that a judge is to avoid. See Garapon, Allard & Gros (2008) for a more extensive list of judicial virtues, drawn not only from Aristotle but from a wide array of authors.

36 When a judge overdoes such an emotion, however, it may lose all trustworthiness. For example, many eyebrows were raised when Judge Seidlin was seen to cry in the trial about the burial of the body of Anna Nicole Smith (cf. 'Fla. Judge Mocked Over Anna Nicole Case', *Washington Post*, 23 February 2007).

also be perturbed and corroded by the office holder. To what extent the personality of the judge may become visible will depend on the level of trust that exists in society.

### *2.6 Judicial Conduct Outside the Courtroom*

Thus far, the argument has been outlined as to how judicial integrity in conduct is to be understood when a judge acts in his official capacity in the courtroom.

First, it was determined that judicial conduct should be understood both in virtue ethical terms and in terms of external accountability. Then, I showed how the institution is a symbol of the values therein expressed. The symbolic nature of the institution is assumed by the judge as a 'second nature'. Enacting the values that the institution symbolizes requires prudent assessment. Society places its trust primarily in the institution, however, and not in the person of the judge. Hegel therefore prescribes a reticence on the part of the office holder: virtue does not have to become visible; it is to be subject to the institution. I took it one step further than this position. On the level of the institution, the judge may well show human traits: professional emotions, professional empathy or professional distance. In other words: his *professional* virtue may be shown. It is he who decides how the implementation of rituals serves to communicate the ideals expressed in the institution. In his conduct, he makes these values concrete. This prudence takes into account external accountability – conduct must serve to uphold the trust in the judicial office.

To what extent is this argument applicable to *judicial* conduct *outside* the courtroom? Take for instance a judge who is to give a lecture about his activities as a judge, or a judge who has a cup of coffee in a public café with the head of the police service to discuss cooperation between the police organization and the courts. Here, judicial conduct is not linked to rituals – he is not wearing his robes, there are no procedures to safeguard impartiality and there are no lawyers to translate his legal language to ordinary citizens.

There is no *fundamental* difference with the judge in the courtroom. The institution is presumed but it is not made visible in rituals or symbols. Instead, the conduct of the judge becomes a direct focal point for public trust. It becomes in itself the symbol for the values of the institution. It differs according to the situation as to whether this means that judges are to be extra careful in displaying these values or that they can be more relaxed.

Take for instance the Belgian judge Connerotte who, as an investigative judge, 'rescued' two girls from Dutroux, a heinous paedophile. During the investigations, he attended a gathering of a non-profit organization, in part arranged by the parents of the rescued girls. There he ate a plate of spaghetti, received a pen and some ink cartridges and his wife accepted flowers. By the acceptance of these gifts, he was deemed by the Belgian *Cour de Cassation* to have raised doubts about his independence and impartiality and he was removed from the case.[37] One could say that here the judge should have been extremely careful to act according to the 'second nature' of the institution. Sensitive situations may require the judge to raise his standards. If the judge is to avoid any appearance of impartiality in court, he may be obliged to avoid it outside court as well.

But there are also situations in which a judge can take a more relaxed approach. For example, in many countries it is accepted that when a judge lectures to academia, he can take more freedom to state his views than he would have when judging. Judges may publish in legal journals and take stances in scholarly works that are opposite to their decisions in court. This, of course, requires that the public recognize that the judge here accommodates to the academic discourse to which he wishes to contribute.

The rationale whereby the judge acts thus depends on both prudent deliberation and external accountability as required in a specific society.

## 3. Integrity in Non-Judicial Conduct

With Aristotle we find no conceptualization of the private individual. It was in fact part of the definition of the citizen to assume political roles. The *polis* provided the forum where the citizen could develop his virtues. Acting contrary to the interests of the *polis* meant acting contrary to one's own well-being.

In modern-day societies, the distinction between political roles and private interests is a basic tenet. This can for instance be seen in classic human rights such as the freedom of religion, the freedom of speech or the right to privacy. These rights are to be enjoyed freely by citizens. When they act as public officials, however, the exercise of these rights may be constrained, which demonstrates a differentiation between the office holder and the citizen. As we see with Hegel, the office holder has to transcend his private interests in order to enact the institution as a 'second nature'. He must for example transcend the right to say freely what he wants or transcend his specific religious beliefs. He may profess the rights as such, but not their material content. As a judge, he must enact values such as impartiality, independence and propriety – not the values of a private citizen, but the values of the state, which should give room to the rights of all citizens.

Then what happens when the judge takes off his judicial robes? Can he then assume the right to believe and volunteer in his church? May he partake in public debates on societal issues? Can he be active within a political party? May he affiliate himself with the ideology of an NGO? Can he walk through a red pedestrian light?

The extent to which these questions deserve to be answered within a philosophical inquiry varies. Most questions require a careful analysis of the

37 This caused an immense public stir. On the case see Adams & Tanghe (2008) who focus on the legitimacy of the *Cour de Cassation* ruling.

mores and morals within a concrete legal culture and cannot be answered within the scope of this book. It is not without reason that, in the literature, extremely little attention is paid to non-judicial conduct. I will look – in a rather general manner – at the nature of citizenship and conduct at odds with the judicial role.

### *3.1 The Separation Between the Individual and his Role*

In section 3.2 I will turn to citizenship which is more concretely concerned with non-judicial conduct. Before doing so I would like to pay attention to the separation between the individual and his role. Strictly speaking, this does not concern non-judicial conduct, but rather covers the fringes between judicial and non-judicial conduct.

Situations must be avoided whereby basic relationships of the judge, such as family relationships or relationships with friends, force the judge to make tragic choices. After all, judges are human beings: they have family, friends or in some countries perhaps tribal relationships.

In pre-modern societies, there are infamous examples of judges who were tragically forced to judge friends or relatives. Take for example the Persian account of a son who had to judge his father, Sisamnes,[38] who – also in the capacity of a judge – had accepted money from one of the parties. The son could not do otherwise than let his societal duties prevail and order the flaying of his father.[39] The dried skin was used to make a judicial chair, which served as a warning for others not to follow Sisamnes's example. This tragic choice came about as the difference between the office and the individual was not yet conceptualized as contingent. In this case, the judge had necessarily to choose between two 'bad' options: either to violate his duties as a judge or to violate the family relationship with his father. As happens often in Greek tragedy, he let his societal duties prevail and sacrificed his family interest.[40]

38 See Herodotus (1997:14f [V 25]).

39 For a jurisprudential discussion about Gerard David's painting of the flaying of Sisamnes see Hol & Loth (2004:91).

40 This is not to say that such measures were in fact taken in ancient Greece, as Greek tragedies should not be seen as a reflection of the social reality of the time: 'Athenian institutions and social relations are distorted by the genre. The tragic universe, an imaginative reconstruction of the mythical past, simultaneously idealised and dysfunctional, attempts to archaise but is often anachronistic' (Hall 1997:99).

Typical of modern societies[41] is the separation of the individual from his social roles.[42] In 'tragic' cases, the judge can disqualify himself from the case. When a judge disqualifies himself over an interest that stems from a direct personal relationship, this does not harm his trustworthiness but rather enhances it. The instrument of disqualification is to ensure that neither the judicial office nor the human relationships of the individual are harmed. Individuality is never to be at odds with the judicial *office*. It can only be at odds with the interests in a specific *case*.

Is the tragedy with respect to basic relationships and the judicial office hereby fully eliminated? If integrity was limited to virtue, this might be the case. Integrity, however, also concerns external accountability. From this point of view a malicious newspaper article may be enough to harm public trust. It may be that, even though the judge rightly stayed on the case from a virtue ethical perspective, he has been or should be disqualified from the perspective of external accountability. Tragic *choice* may therefore be eliminated, but this does not necessarily eliminate tragic situations.

### *3.2 The Judge as Citizen: Between Reticence and Participation*

The judiciary has been endowed with the task to protect fundamental rights such as freedom of religion, freedom of speech and universal suffrage. It would therefore be at odds with the very nature of the office if judges as private citizens should not be able to enjoy these rights freely. Moreover, by being actively engaged in society, judges acquaint themselves with current sentiments, morals and considerations. It seems therefore that active participation in society should not be prohibited: it even seems to be desirable. This is not to say that there are no restraints on the free enjoyment of citizenship that stem from the judicial role. After all, the judicial role still resonates in non-judicial conduct. Whereas too much reticence may lead to estrangement, too much involvement may lead to doubts about the impartiality of

41 This is not to say that these situations do not occur anymore. See for example Transparency International (2007:105), where the 2006 case of the Chief Justice of Trinidad and Tobago, Satnarine Sharma, is discussed as an example of one who let political views and ethnic relations override his judicial responsibilities – and where this appeared to be accepted by a large part of the population (i.e. the ethnic group to which he belonged).

42 Or as Kierkegaard, who wrote extensively on the nature of Greek tragedy, says: 'A feature in which our age certainly excels that age in Greece is that our age is more depressed and therefore deeper in despair. Thus, our age is sufficiently depressed to know that there is something called responsibility and that this means something' (1987:142). The point he is making is that the ancient Greeks did not fully conceptualize subjectivity: 'Even if the individual moved freely, he nevertheless rested in substantial determinants, in the state, the family, in fate. This substantial determinant is the essential fateful factor in Greek tragedy and its essential characteristic. The hero's downfall, therefore, is not a result solely of his action but is also a suffering, whereas in modern tragedy the hero's downfall is not really a suffering but is a deed' (143).

judges. Such restraints may have to do with two reasons: avoiding doubts about the ability of judges to transcend to judicial values and avoiding doubts about the quality of judicial decision-making.

Doubts about whether judges can transcend to institutional values such as impartiality or independence may explain the reticence that judges are to show with respect to the full enjoyments of their civil rights. Take for example the problem of colliding fundamental rights in democratic societies; say between freedom of religion and freedom of speech. It is then up to the judge to deliver a verdict. The trust that is placed in the judiciary is vested in the institution that is symbolic of fundamental values such as equality, impartiality and independence. If the judge as a citizen affiliates himself with a secretive organization or an organization that holds viewpoints that often collide with other values, the trust that the judge can transcend to the values of the institution might decrease. This in turn harms the democratic legitimacy of the judiciary.

Similarly, political activity of judges may be questioned. Modern-day conceptions about the rule of law include the idea of the separation of powers or at least a theory about checks and balances.[43] The judiciary itself is viewed as a state power or is at least to provide an impartial check to other powers at work in the rule of law. It is therefore a matter of course that when the judge as citizen assumes political roles that he as judge is to check, he reconciles in himself functions that are to be separated. This may harm the transcendence to his role.

Doubts about the ability to transcend to judicial values may easily affect the trust in the quality of judicial decisions. In the previous chapter, it was shown how the attitude is a constituent in judicial decision-making. Yet at the same time, the attitude is in part obscure to the public. The care expressed to set limits to the enjoyment of civil rights of judges is grounded in the fact that such behaviour may affect the attitude of the judge. Doubts about the character of the judge may lead to doubts about judicial decision-making and thereby undermine the authority of the judicial decision.

### *3.3 Conduct at Odds with the Judicial Role*

The issue of conduct at odds with the judicial role is of great importance in practice. In fact, most of the safeguarding instruments are devised with this issue in view. When one hears of the 'integrity of judges', one may be inclined to think directly of preventing conduct at odds with the judicial role. However, the importance of the issue in practice outshines its treatment in theory. This is for the simple reason that, in practice, it is an issue of high scrutiny, of weighing and balancing character and accountability. Yet in theory, it is difficult to progress beyond some general remarks.

The behaviour that may be at odds with the judicial role may concern a wide range of activities and it may depend on the legal order as to which choices are

43 See Soeharno (2006).

prudent and to what extent external accountability is to be secured. Here I discuss the misuse of the judicial function, criminal behaviour, immoral behaviour and 'bad' citizenship. The misuse of the judicial function for private ends is strictly taken to mean not an issue that falls into the sphere of non-judicial conduct but rather as covering the borderline between judicial and non-judicial conduct.

The misuse of the judicial function for private ends is obviously at odds with judicial integrity. It shows that the judge has not transcended to the values of the institution. He did not assume a 'second nature', but placed his private interests over institutional values. It also violates the trust in the judiciary as the pursuance of private interests is at odds with the value of impartiality that the institution is to uphold. Fraud and corruption therefore necessarily disqualify a person from acting as a judge. With respect to external accountability, fraud and corruption violate the high standards of the judicial office, thus harming trust in institutional values.

Equally, it is not hard to see why criminal behaviour is at odds with the judicial role. Apart from the fact that it may well be assumed that there is a serious lack of virtue, it will also affect the public confidence in the judiciary as an institution. After all, criminal actions seriously undermine the trust in an institution that is to uphold justice. Does being a *suspect* violate judicial integrity? This depends on the nature of the case, but sometimes the demand of external accountability will be considered to have been violated. With respect to minor misdemeanours or acts of civil disobedience – for instance a judge who knowingly participates in a demonstration without permission – it will depend on the legal culture and the level of public acceptance as to whether judicial integrity is violated.

Yet what about immoral behaviour which is not illegal? Judges need to be aware of the fact that their private conduct is a direct object of external accountability as there are no institutional symbols to mediate. Again, the role still resonates in private actions. Therefore, immoral behaviour, when exposed, can lead to a violation of judicial integrity. Whether this is the case will depend on the type of norm violated and the acceptance in society. This does not concern de facto acceptance of certain behaviour. It is about the normative question whether this behaviour affects the acceptance of an institutional value. In this sense it is even possible that an illegal act, which is not immoral, underscores a judicial value. For instance, a judge who provides shelter for an illegal refugee might in some legal cultures be seen to underscore his commitment to the well-being of society, while in other cultures he might be seen to be acting highly inappropriately, while in yet others, he may be perceived to be doing both.

The category of 'bad' citizenship is a debatable one. This concerns behaviour which is neither immoral nor illegal. Take for instance a judge who goes bankrupt. In some countries this is seen as a defect in prudence and therefore he is seen as unfit to be a judge.[44] Sometimes the rationale is that judges who have gone bankrupt are in a state of dependence, which may compromise their independence.

44 On the rationale see Shetreet (1976:64–65, 335–337).

It depends on the legal order which choices are prudent and which measures with respect to external accountability need to be taken.

## 4. The Relation Between Integrity in Judicial Decision-Making and Integrity in Conduct

I regard integrity in conduct as a separate condition for judicial integrity, next to integrity in judicial decision-making: judicial integrity involves both integrity in decision-making and integrity in conduct. That is not to say, however, that there is no relation between these two scopes of judicial integrity. I will first look at the relation between judicial integrity in conduct and integrity in decision-making, then at the relation between decision-making and non-judicial conduct. I will not look at all the cross connections – only the most relevant will be considered.

### *4.1 Relation Between Judicial Conduct and Judicial Decision-Making*

Procedures surrounding fair trial are to make sure that the parties have equal rights with respect to presenting their case. This is to ensure that the judge will commence his deliberations on the basis of the viewpoints of both parties. As has been said, virtue in conduct is needed to enact institutional values. Take for instance the value of a fair hearing. The conduct of the judge ensures that the positions of the parties are presented in a fair manner: both parties are given the opportunity to have their say and they are treated with equal respect. We have seen in the previous chapter how important it is that a judge is attentive to all the specific elements of the case. But if the case is not heard fairly, how can the judge render a sound judgment?

Procedures with respect to conduct are not just important with respect to virtue, but to external accountability as well. External accountability with respect to conduct is to deliver a signal to society that judges are also persons of integrity in deliberation. To this end, symbols and rituals can be valuable. If adequate, they communicate to the parties that the judge is bound by law: no matter who the judge is, he adheres to these symbols and rituals because they reflect the values of the institution. As the decision-making process is to some extent obscure, these procedures are an objective – but of course not a sufficient – guarantee to the parties that the judge takes his task to deliver just verdicts seriously.

With respect to judicial conduct outside the courtroom, the same rationale applies to the link with decision-making, but here the rituals and symbols are lacking. No doubts must arise about the ability of the judge to transcend to institutional values when delivering decisions. At times, this may require that the judge is extra careful to express the values of the institution in his conduct as we have seen in the case of Connerotte. At other times, it may spark confidence if the judge, in an academic lecture, loosens the reins and speaks more freely, showing that he is aware of other opinions. Deciding on how to act may not simply be a matter of prudence. Measures of external accountability, for instance procedures about remuneration, may be needed to secure the limits as to judicial conduct outside the courtroom, so as to avoid the appearance of partiality or impropriety.

### *4.2 Relation Between Non-Judicial Conduct and Judicial Decision-Making*

Occasions for tragic *decision-making* are eliminated as much as is possible in modern states. The instrument of disqualification serves to accentuate the contingency of the relation between the official and his role.

If the judge wishes to do justice in his decision-making – to the narratives of the parties and the ends of society – he must know something of society and of the lives of those living in it. If the judge is too reticent and estranged from society, then so is his intuition. On the other hand, the judge must not be too involved as it may raise questions to his ability to transcend 'ordinary' life and enact judicial values. Virtue and external accountability can also determine the scope and nature of ancillary functions. On the one hand, ancillary functions can ensure societal involvement; on the other they can hamper the appearance and reality of impartiality. Thus, also with respect to decision-making, virtuous conduct is needed to find an optimum between reticence and participation when it comes to the exercise of citizenship.

Obviously, conduct at odds with the judicial office undermines the trust in the judiciary and therefore it will also affect the authority of the judicial decision.

## 5. Integrity in Conduct as a Generic Norm

In conduct, virtue and external accountability are more intricately related than in decision-making. Conduct itself is both the result of virtue and the direct object of public trust. There is no clear separation between the process of deliberation and rendering accountability on rational grounds, as with decision-making. Even when 'virtue' is displayed on top of the institutional enactment – when the judge acts as a symbolic personality – the convergence of virtue and external accountability in the institution is enhanced rather than rescinded.

This does not undo the fact that here questions may also arise about the relation between virtue and external accountability. On a general note, measures to secure external accountability may limit the discretionary space of the judge with respect to enacting values in conduct.

There is thus the need for a second level of prudence by which the relation between virtue and external accountability is configured with respect to institutional values. This is performed in a discourse in which many actors may partake: judges, the court administration, a council for the judiciary, academia, the legislator, et cetera. For example, there is the prudence with respect to institutional symbols and rituals. Are they still valid? Do they refer to the right institutional values? Are they properly enacted? Procedures may be fashioned which govern the conduct of judges in court and outside court – regardless of the prudence of judges, while other matters may be left to the discretion of individual judges.

This second level of prudence is not just performed with respect to virtue and external accountability in conduct, nor is it merely performed with respect to virtue and external accountability in judicial decision-making. It also concerns weighing the interests of both scopes of judicial integrity. As integrity is a holistic norm, so the prudence concerned with configuring the possibilities of virtue and external accountability in conduct and decision-making seeks to meet all elements optimally with respect to institutional values.

## 6. Conclusion

Integrity in conduct other than judicial decision-making is an essential element of judicial integrity. Judicial integrity in conduct is needed – from an accountability perspective – to secure confidence in the judicial institution. Therefore its dignity must be upheld by conduct as it can be corroded by it. From a virtue ethical perspective, conduct enacts the values that are connected with the institution.

The judicial office is not simply a role but a public institution. According to Hegel, public institutions in modern states are to be based upon fundamental values. Office holders are to enact these, having the institution as a 'second nature'. This means for instance that a judge does not act upon his religious or tribal values, but transcends them to act according to the 'second nature' of freedom, impartiality and independence: the values of which the judicial office is symbolic.

These values become concrete in virtue. At the same time, the institution is protected from the office holder by means of securing external accountability: judges are to disqualify themselves when a personal interest is or appears to be at stake and they may be subject to removal when they misuse the office for private interests. The fact that institutions are symbolic of values also reflects in the treatment of litigants.

The symbolic nature of the institution shows in rituals and procedures. These rituals have an external accountability function. They demonstrate the values connected with the institution and show that the person of the judge is subjected to these values. Virtue, however, is needed to ensure that these rituals and procedures are upheld according to the values to which they refer.

Can the judge do without these rituals? The judicial office is by nature symbolic and therefore there is no point in denying to society rituals or procedures that refer to this symbolism. Yet informality is possible, but on the basis of formality. The judge can show emotion, yet on an institutional level. He may act informally, but this remains an institutional, a symbolic informality. This means that the judge who is a person of integrity is not 'authentic' in the ordinary sense of the word. He is in fact to transcend his 'authentic' emotions and thoughts and act as a symbolic personality.

Outside the courtroom the judge – when acting in a judicial capacity – is the same symbolic personality, yet devoid of rituals and procedures. The conduct of the judge is now the direct point of reference. Sometimes, extra care is needed to ensure that conduct enacts and demonstrates institutional values. Sometimes, the judge can assume a more relaxed approach.

With respect to non-judicial conduct, first, tragic choices are to be avoided. Family relationships or friendships are not to be at odds with the exercise of the judicial role. Second, with respect to exercising the rights of citizenship, the judge prudently has to find an optimum between reticence and participation. Too much reticence may estrange him from society; too much participation may harm his institutional impartiality. Also, from the perspective of external accountability, this may be of influence on societal trust. Third, conduct that is at odds with the judicial role must be avoided.

How are integrity in judicial decision-making and integrity in conduct related? Judicial integrity in judicial conduct ensures that cases are presented fairly, so that decision-making starts from the right understanding of the case. With respect to external accountability, since decision-making itself is obscure, parties may trust the judiciary more when they have the perception that their case has been heard without partiality by the judge. Integrity in non-judicial conduct is also needed for the intuition of the judges to develop so that they adequately take into account societal views. It also has an external accountability function: knowing that judges understand society may be an important ingredient for public confidence.

As a generic norm, a second level prudence is required to configure not only the relation between virtue and external accountability in conduct, but also with respect to virtue and accountability in judicial decision-making.

# Chapter 5
# Safeguarding Judicial Integrity – Parameters

## 1. Introduction

In the previous chapters a theory of judicial integrity has been drafted and concretized with respect to judicial decision-making and the conduct of the judge. The aim of this book, however, is not only to draft a theory of integrity, but also to elucidate how such a theory can contribute to safeguarding integrity in established and in developing democracies.

Safeguarding the integrity of the judge is a complex activity that revolves around the following questions. What is the object of safeguarding? Who should be assigned the task of safeguarding judicial integrity? Which parameters should be met when safeguarding integrity in practice? How do these parameters relate? What is the role of institutional values? Does judicial independence stand in the way of safeguarding judicial integrity? What adds to this complexity is that integrity has been conceptualized as a holistic norm. It concerns virtue, external accountability and a generic discourse on their exact configuration. Safeguarding judicial integrity is to be a holistic activity. This approach is different from an approach where safeguarding integrity concerns a *specific* domain of judicial conduct, for instance combating fraud, corruption or sexual intimidation. In such an approach, specific practices are *excepted* from the whole and put under the label of 'integrity'. According to the theory of integrity developed in this book, fixation of integrity to such a subset is of limited meaning. The professional aim is to have a bearing on all values and rules and not just the rules that cannot be categorized otherwise in terms of competences or professional ethics.

A philosophical theory of safeguarding integrity has significant limitations. As a theory of integrity cannot give a conclusive answer to the question of balancing professional character and external accountability but can only indicate how to activate and catalyze the prudence concerned with it, so a theory of safeguarding only sets the parameters but does not give conclusive answers about their concrete configuration. Consequently, this chapter sets the parameters for safeguarding and shows their interconnectedness and their relation to institutional values. Yet the exact implementation of these parameters takes shape in a discourse, which lies beyond the scope of this book. Thus, the parameters function as points of orientation, but their concretization remains variable:[1] it requires the prudence

1 The reader should therefore not expect a concrete governance discussion on the conditions for a well-working judicial organization. This chapter is not about the height of salary, the presence of court buildings or the availability of judicial robes. Although I by no

of those who have experience in practice to configure these parameters against institutional values.

Therefore, this chapter is to be read as an *invitation* to engage in this level of prudence. This prudence is performed in a discourse in which many may partake: the judges in the field, representatives of the judicial organization, academia, the press, the legislator, NGOs and others. It is up to their prudent assessment of safeguarding instruments against institutional values as to which choices are made in a specific legal culture. For this reason, all the instruments treated in this chapter are mere illustrations. They are not 'best practices'. What is 'best' can only be determined by the prudence of those who are experienced and acquainted with the specific demands in a concrete legal culture.

The parameters and their relation to institutional values will be discussed in the next section (section 2). Then I will look at safeguarding judicial integrity in practice (section 3): at entry (section 3.1), in judicial decision-making (section 3.2) and in conduct (section 3.3). Each time, I will briefly discuss the parameters and then look at examples of safeguarding. Lastly, I will look at the interplay between safeguarding instruments and touch upon the subject of configuration against institutional values (section 3.4).

## 2. Parameters for Safeguarding

In this section, the concept of parameters for safeguarding is developed. Parameters are points of orientation to safeguard virtue and external accountability. Their exact implementation is variable, depending on the demands of concrete legal cultures. I will first consider parameters for safeguarding virtue and then for external accountability. Thereafter I will move to a discussion of safeguarding integrity as a generic norm. Finally, I will discuss the relation between parameters and institutional values.

### *2.1 Safeguarding Integrity as Professional Character*

There are two deviations from virtue which can be distinguished but cannot always be separated. The first type of deviation from virtuous behaviour is a gradual one: the attitude is good, effort has been made to assess all the variables prudently and it is done with well-being in view, but the deliberation does not reach the desired optimum – it could have been done better. The second is behaviour that goes against virtue: behaviour that has no ethical intention, that lacks any form of prudence or, what is worse, decision-making that springs from wrong intentions

means want to underestimate the necessity of the structural conditioning of a sound judicial organization, the exact implementation of it simply goes beyond the scope of this book, as it requires empirical data about its effectiveness.

or knowingly takes into account the wrong values. This is behaviour *at odds* with virtuous behaviour.

Accordingly, there are two ways of safeguarding virtue. The first aims to further excellence of character. This cannot be done *directly*, as the formation of character is dependent on the intention of the actor. The intention, which is a condition for excellence, lies within the power of the judge himself and not with a body assigned with safeguarding. We may then ask how the internal dimension of virtue – the difficult weighing of ends against the specific demands of the concrete situation – can be safeguarded. This can be done *indirectly* by creating conditions that stimulate excellence.[2] Next, the persons who are best able to guide and stimulate the virtuousness of others are those who know from experience what it is to act virtuously.[3] Subsequently, peer review, training by other judges, visitation or an informal *esprit de corps* are good examples of means by which integrity as virtue may be safeguarded. Thus, while it is the judge himself who finally safeguards the excellence of his character, an environment should be created that stimulates excellence. In this regard, peers especially have the knowledge and the experience to guide others in a unique manner.

Safeguarding integrity as virtue also has to prevent non-virtuous behaviour. This form of safeguarding aims specifically at the boundaries of behaviour. These boundaries – I will also refer to them as the 'bandwidth' of virtue – are mainly but not exclusively concerned with 'minimum norms'.[4] Boundaries may benchmark grave misconduct, as for instance fraud, corruption or overt bias, they may stipulate minimum requirements, as for instance the presence of legal knowledge, some social skills and a representative attitude, and they may concern the limits set to

2 On the difference of teaching ethics or teaching virtue, Davis comments that teaching the latter 'seems to require considerably more control over the whole environment than does teaching ethics' (Davis 2002:244). Although speaking with regard to corporate ethics, Solomon speaks of creating a 'culture' for excellence (1993:125–135). Factors that stimulate excellence are, among others, having enough time, a good salary and conditions and room for self-reflection.

3 Davis remarks that when it comes to virtue, 'Shaping someone else's character seems to require the would-be shaper to claim a very good character. The teacher should not only know more, as required to teach ethics, but be good enough to be trusted with so much power. The teacher also probably needs to have the relevant virtue' (Davis 2002:244). Similarly, Aristotle's definition of virtue shows that the virtuous person acts according to reason or how a *prudent* person would act in a similar situation (see *EN* II.6:1106b36–1107a2). Virtue is acquired either by one's own experience or by acting in accordance with how one who has developed virtue would act. This does not, of course, exclude the option of learning from others than peers.

4 In this respect, van Oostrum distinguishes between an 'integrity strategy' and a 'minimalist integrity strategy'. The first aims to facilitate responsible conduct while the second aims at preventing illegal conduct (2002:214f). I do not agree with this distinction, as safeguarding the boundaries of conduct concerns more than safeguarding against illegal conduct or safeguarding 'minimum norms'.

prudence by institutional values. For instance, a judge who reaches a decision by means of an Ouija board and thereafter writes a perfectly good opinion may not necessarily violate 'minimum norms' but he may very well act against the nature of institutional values. The safeguarding of boundaries can in many cases be performed more directly, since it is often easier to benchmark non-virtuous behaviour than virtuous behaviour. As conduct that goes against institutional values has a harmful effect on public confidence, this form of safeguarding has a strong external accountability function as well. Even in democracies where non-virtuous behaviour seldom occurs, the presence of such a direct safeguarding system will be of value with respect to safeguarding public confidence.

Thus, when it comes to safeguarding professional character, there are two parameters. Professional character must be safeguarded in a negative sense by establishing the boundaries of professional character and preventing non-virtuous behaviour. Professional character must also be safeguarded in a positive sense by stimulating excellence.

### *2.2 Safeguarding Integrity as External Accountability*

Integrity as external accountability is a norm that concerns upholding public confidence with respect to institutional values so as to secure the democratic legitimacy of the judiciary. These institutional values provide the judiciary with the predicate of 'sacrosanctity' or 'inviolability' in the public domain. External accountability is important, as the key elements of virtue – the attitude of the professional and the prudence with which he deliberates – are to large extent invisible to the public.

Since trust is directed at institutional values and only secondarily at the office holder, the institution needs to be 'protected' against the possible non-virtuousness of the office holder. For example, independence and impartiality must not only be upheld, they must also be *seen* to be upheld. Therefore, from an external accountability point of view, the prevention against non-virtuous conduct is taken one step further than the mere safeguarding against behaviour *at odds* with virtue. For in the eyes of the public not only must non-virtuous behaviour be avoided, but so must the *appearance* of non-virtuous behaviour. It is the epistemic asymmetry[5] with regard to the true deliberations of the judge that means that appearances are taken very seriously.

Safeguarding external accountability is not just a matter of defensive strategies – as preventing non-virtuous character or the appearance of it – but it also concerns the *active* demonstration of the values enacted.[6] With regard to decision-making, efforts can be made to publish the grounds on which the decision is based in understandable language or to involve citizens in the process of adjudication.

5 On this notion see Chapter 1 at section 3.2.

6 Similarly, van Lent (2008:225–228) speaks of structural 'responsiveness' as the link between the criminal process and the democratic legitimacy of it.

With regard to conduct, one can ensure that rituals are explained or that a list of ancillary functions is published. Here, it is about actively demonstrating that the judicial tasks are performed with institutional values in view. For example, when a suspected criminal is acquitted on procedural grounds, a judge may explain which values are served by these procedures, so as actively to meet the demands of public confidence.

Just as the main difficulty with safeguarding professional character lies with the intention of the actor, so the main difficulty with safeguarding external accountability lies with the difficult notion of public trust. I have emphasized before that safeguarding external accountability is not about securing trust per se, but should consist in a reasonable effort to ensure that public confidence is directed at the values of which the institution is symbolic. Safeguarding integrity as external accountability does not aim at soothing public opinion or boosting confidence statistics. Instead, safeguarding integrity as external accountability needs to be performed with a high level of scrutiny, ensuring that confidence is placed in the right values and in the right manner. This is, of course, much more easily said than done. How can one establish if trust is directed at the right values? How does one deal with the contingent nature of trust?

There are thus two parameters for safeguarding external accountability. The first is defensive: non-virtuous behaviour and also the appearance of it should be prevented and dealt with. The second is active: public trust can be actively enhanced by, for instance, pro-active communication, by elucidating judicial decisions or by the good treatment of litigants in court. It should be noted that the line between defensive and active safeguarding is not always easy to draw, as they are rather at the opposite ends of a scale.

## *2.3 Safeguarding Integrity as a Generic Norm*

The parameters to safeguard virtue and external accountability can thus be outlined as follows. Professional character must be safeguarded in a positive and a negative sense. In a positive sense, it is about achieving excellence in deliberation and character. In a negative sense, it is about preventing and dealing with non-virtuous behaviour. External accountability can be safeguarded in a defensive and an active manner. In a defensive manner it is about dealing with unbecoming behaviour. This concerns dealing with non-virtuous behaviour and also with appearances of violations. In an active manner, it is about a demonstration of institutional values and about efforts made to further the trust in it.

Considering which instruments safeguard which parameters concerns only the *first level* of safeguarding. After having pinpointed the parameters and viewing which instruments can be used to safeguard them, the more difficult activity of configuring these instruments against institutional values starts. This is the *second level* of safeguarding. It concerns safeguarding judicial integrity at a generic level.

At a generic level, it is about finding the proper relation between safeguarding virtue and external accountability against institutional values. As integrity has a bearing on both professional character and external accountability, safeguarding measures should always have this dual aim in view. For instance, a strict, compliance-based approach may stipulate what not to do and thus enhance public confidence, but it fails to stimulate excellence of character. Prudence is required on this second level to look 'through' strategies, regulations or other safeguarding mechanisms and assess these in the light of institutional values.

The prudence of balancing virtue and external accountability is different from the prudence on a virtue-ethical level, where it is a necessary constituent of professional character. The deliberation on this 'meta-level' is not left to the judge alone, but can be exercised on different levels and by different actors.[7] On a micro-level, there is the deliberative discourse within the courtroom in which lawyers, prosecutors, litigants, experts, legal secretaries or witnesses may take part. On meso-levels, there is the discourse within the court organization,[8] where '... integrity and impartiality are no longer only the domain of the conscientious judge, but become at least a shared responsibility of judges and (judicial) managers'.[9] There is also the discourse within civil society in which academics, the media or NGOs may be involved. On a macro-level, there is the constitutional discourse. For instance, parliament might have a role in checking judges. Or, more remotely, a minister of education may be responsible for ensuring that sufficient knowledge about the judicial system is taught in schools, as it is difficult to render effective accountability when public understanding is marred.

The discourse about safeguarding judicial integrity is not only performed on multiple levels in a *vertical* sense, but also requires raising awareness of integrity in many fields in a *horizontal* sense. In some developing democracies judicial reforms fail not because they do not take into account all the factors having to do with the judiciary, but because they fail to take into account the wider scope of public life. Judicial integrity is not merely safeguarded by looking at the judiciary, but also by taking into account other relevant players and factors in the public sector. If corruption is widespread, a total approach may be needed that aims at

---

7 For instance, see Shetreet (1976:161–267) for an intriguing treatment of mechanisms for checking judges in England. He discusses the role of parliament, the press, appellate courts and the Bar and ends with a list of informal checks. For a similar but more concise overview of checks within the Dutch system see de Groot-van Leeuwen (2003:272).

8 For an excellent study about checks and balances in the judicial organization see Ng (2007).

9 As Langbroek remarks (2007:129) with respect to the allocation of cases. As early as 1982, Resnik argued for a broad-based investigation as to the rules that govern judicial behaviour – so that 'managerial judges' do not lose sight of the core values of adjudication. With respect to neo-managerialist reforms in the Netherlands within the court organizations, van de Klift (2003) warns against introducing hierarchical lines of accountability. The cost may be that the individual judge loses his professional autonomy and changes from a magistrate to a civil servant.

strengthening all institutions – not just the judiciary.[10] For example, in some former Eastern European countries, such a total approach has had relative success[11] while isolated attempts have failed in some Latin American countries.[12] Another positive example is provided by Nigeria, where a United Nations' approach has yielded positive results. Two factors were crucial: the fact that the approach aimed at 'self-help' and consequently activated and involved the local judiciary, and the fact that the approach was an integral one – it aimed at a reform of all aspects of the judiciary while there was also cooperation with integrity programmes in other sectors.[13] The 'success' of this form of safeguarding illustrates that there has to be a broader discourse in order to safeguard judicial integrity as a generic norm. There is no 'one size fits all' solution.

It simply falls outside the scope of this book to take this second level – which includes civil society, other state powers and the whole of public life – into account when discussing safeguarding instruments. That is up to those responsible for configuring the complex of safeguarding instruments. In this chapter, I limit myself to a discussion on the first level of safeguarding judicial integrity: at entry, in decision-making and in conduct. In section 3.4 I go generally into a discussion of how to configure these instruments on a more generic level.

---

10 The understanding of integrity is often similar in all sectors of public life. Shetreet (1976:388) quotes Devlin who explains that 'The integrity of the English judge that we now take for granted is not a virtue that belongs exclusively to them. We take for granted integrity in every branch of our public life and judges are not now, neither have been in the past, much better or worse than other servants of their time'. This also explains Soetjipto's (2002) pessimism about fighting corruption in Indonesia. If on all levels of society corruption is experienced as a part of everyday life, then who can be assigned the task to combat it? Ironically, in 2008 Irawady Joenoes, the coordinator of the division for the integrity of judges, was sentenced to eight years in prison for taking bribes (*Jakarta Post*, 15 March 2008).

11 For an overview of the developments see Bárd (2004), who emphasizes that it is still 'work in progress'. The same conclusion is drawn after a broader account of public institutions in post-communist societies (see Elster, Offe & Preuss 1998). In this respect, especially Bulgaria and Romania are struggling.

12 See Transparency International (2007:138–146) and Chapter 1 at section 2.2.2 on judicial reforms.

13 See Langseth & Stolpe (2002:309–334) for an overview. They emphasize the necessity of local involvement as it is the only guarantee for long-term success and for obtaining crucial soft information. For instance, a priority list was established in cooperation with the local judges: creating a court records management system, making available judicial training, strengthening public confidence in the judiciary, increased control over delays created by lawyers, merit based appointments, a credible and effective complaints system, combating court delays, setting up case management, enforcement of the code of conduct, providing adequate and fair remuneration, fighting abuses of procedural discretion, creating sentencing guidelines, generation of reliable court statistics and active communication with court users. A plan was made to meet these priorities step by step.

### *2.4 The Relation to Institutional Values*

As has been said above, the second level of safeguarding judicial integrity, which concerns the configuration of parameters, should be guided by institutional values. These institutional values govern the choices made in respect of which instruments are used, by which force and in which relation. As a matter of fact, it is the purpose of safeguarding instruments to effect the realization of these values on both the level of virtue and external accountability. Virtue should consist in prudent enactment of institutional values and external accountability should ensure that public trust is directed at institutional values. After all, the democratic legitimacy of the judicial institution is grounded in these values and therefore public trust is to be directed at these values.

What are these institutional values? It has been said before that the nature and the interpretation of these institutional values may vary from one legal culture to another.[14] Here I take the Bangalore Principles – impartiality, independence, integrity, competence, diligence, equality and propriety – as being exemplary of institutional values. Of these values, independence and impartiality are the most characteristic of the judicial office.

Values must be seen in connection with each other. For instance, judicial independence is classically seen as a fundamental tenet of the rule of law as it enables judges to uphold the law *impartially* against the legislative and executive powers, while being bound merely by law and conscience.[15] Judicial independence thus aims primarily at securing the conditions for impartiality at case level, while this independence should also enable judges to uphold the law in a manner that reflects the values of diligence and competence.[16] Judicial independence may be understood at multiple levels: constitutional independence vis-à-vis the executive or the legislative power, organizational independence vis-à-vis the court organization, which sets efficiency demands that limit discretion, or personal independence vis-à-vis family members, associations of which one is a member,

14 For instance, ten Berge (2006:48–50) has drafted a catalogue of institutional values for the Dutch judiciary: impartiality, careful determination of facts, consistent and transparent development of law, propriety in work processes and the organization, and effectiveness. Independence is missing, but he does refer to Bangalore Principles and other, Dutch, catalogues for public administration.

15 Thomas (2005:78) stresses the instrumental relation of independence to impartiality: 'Independence without impartiality is a wayward beast. It is when judicial independence is exercised objectively, without prejudice or favour, that it achieves its real value in a democratic society'.

16 A judge has not necessarily to be independent in an organizational sense in order to judge impartially in a specific case (cf. Moliterno & Harris 2007:184). In fact, independence may at times even be given up (see below in this section).

against the media that throw impediments in the way of establishing guilt of the accused or against organized crime.[17]

Judicial independence may well be limited. For example, on a level of the separation of powers, the executive may stipulate demands with respect to the financing of courts. In an organizational respect, judges may have to account for expenditure or for the hours they have put in. It may even be that one value is put aside to serve other values. A well-known instance is post-apartheid South Africa, where judicial independence was put aside temporarily so that judges could be held accountable for their decisions during apartheid times.[18] This shows that judicial independence should not revert to an excuse for complacency, but must be seen in connection with other values as, in this case, impartiality and equality.

Complaints that judicial independence stands in the way of accountability mechanisms[19] seldom take into account this connection to other values. Some even go as far as to demand civil liability for judges.[20] This is one of the instruments

17 Cf. Kuijer (2004:207–209) or Franken (1997) for different divisions, for example between factual, personal, functional, organizational or constitutional independence. Sometimes personal independence is understood as the independence that is secured by tenure; sometimes constitutional independence is referred to as institutional independence (see Bovend'Eert 2008:17–32).

18 Cf. Dyzenhaus (1998). It must be said that this was part of a fundamental shift in the rule of law and thus of the normative framework, which caused a reiteration of legal and moral parameters, just as had been the case after the Nazi regime in Germany at the Nuremberg trials. This, however, does raise the question as to the limits of judicial independence with respect to other values. For example, in some judicial reforms in Latin America, the safeguarding of judicial independence has had a counter-effect as organizational corruption could not be dealt with because of judicial immunity and the lack of impeachment procedures (cf. Santiso 2004:170–174). This question is equally relevant for established democracies, as judicial power has grown and as public scrutiny has increased.

19 There is a difference between the *norm* to render external accountability and accountability *mechanisms*. Judicial independence cannot stand in the way of the norm to render external accountability, for as an institutional value it forms a focal point for public trust. Judicial independence can, however, stand in the way of accountability mechanisms. On the difference between accountability as a norm and as a mechanism see Bovens (2007). With respect to mechanisms, Malleson (1999) distinguishes between 'hard' and 'soft' accountability. The idea of soft accountability 'deals with openness, and representation and demands procedural transparency at the same time as sensitivity towards different interests and a changing social environment'. Hard accountability, on the other hand, 'deals with removal from office, accountability towards the legislative body, and civil and criminal liability for damage done as a result of a decision', Malleson (1999:38f). The 'definitions' pertaining to this distinction are by Ng (2007:381f). This distinction covers accountability from the perspective of virtue (the prudent person must be sensitive, open et cetera – see Chapter 2 at section 3.3.3 and Chapter 3 at section 3) and accountability mechanisms, but not the *norm* of external accountability.

20 Cf. Janssen (2008) & van Bogaert (2005).

most strongly at odds with judicial independence, as in most legal cultures a system of immunity[21] against civil liability is based upon the argument of judicial independence.[22] From the perspective of integrity, however, it is well understood that in many countries judicial independence can block civil liability.[23] Civil liability seems to be stranded on integrity as professional character: that it is essential that judges operate as independent and impartial representatives of the law and that they do not refrain from publishing their honest opinions of the law if subject to suits from disgruntled participants.[24] The instrument of civil liability is also stranded on rendering external accountability. Who guarantees that civil action is only undertaken for faults in professional character and not when a decision is *perceived* to be bad – as with appeal?[25] The absence of a system of liability may also serve to safeguard external accountability in a defensive manner: leaving no middle way between immunity and dismissal demonstrates to the public the rigidness by which institutional values are protected. This seems fitting for the high standards for judges regarding the institutional values of propriety and diligence – on the condition that the absence of a system of liability then implies a well-working disciplinary system.

Thus, institutional values are to guide the whole practice of safeguarding judicial integrity. It is up to the meta-level discourse to interpret these values for

21 In many legal orders immunity is granted for individual judges on the condition that the conduct of the judge is not criminal, adverse to his core duties – for example if he refuses to take a decision – and within his range of competence.

22 The reason for immunity is twofold: to safeguard judicial independence (see Malleson 1999:211) and to maintain a closed appeal system according to the principle *lites finiri oportet*. As the second reason deals with the integrity of the *system* – it protects the value of legal certainty – I focus on the first reason.

23 For example in Germany, England and the Netherlands judges are granted civil immunity for costs that result from a wrong adjudication. In Germany, this is laid down in § 839 BGB. The first limb covers liability for public officials, the second limb excludes officials in the capacity of judging; it is referred to as the '*Spruchrichterprivileg*' (Mincke 1998:67). For the UK, in *Sirros v Moore* (1974) 3 WLR 459 CA, it was decided no civil action could be taken against the judge. This immunity was extended to magistrates by the Courts and Legal Services Act 1990. In the Netherlands, at the time when judges could be held liable, this happened only once (HR 08-04-1929, *NJ* 1929, 874). In HR 03-12-1971 (NJ 1972, 137) a system of state liability was introduced and since 1 January 2002 civil immunity for individual judges has become complete in the new civil procedure code. The state assumes liability – if at all.

24 Or as the Consultative Council of European Judges expressed it: judges should not have to work 'under the threat of penalty, still less imprisonment' (*Consultative Council of European Judges*, 2nd and 3rd meetings of the working party of the Consultative Council of European Judges, 19–21 June 2002; 16–18 September 2002).

25 The appeal system is designed to meet the norm of external accountability as – in most states – it gives litigants another chance *regardless* of the quality of the decision – thus compensating for the asymmetry with respect to judicial deliberations. For more on appeal see section 3.2.2 below.

present-day demands and to configure the instruments needed to safeguard virtue and external accountability against these values.

## 3. Safeguarding Judicial Integrity in Practice

Now that the parameters have been set, I will look at how they work in practice and will do so in the following way. I will consider safeguarding with respect to entry, judicial decision-making and the conduct of judges. Each time I will review the parameters of safeguarding. Then I will examine a number of examples of safeguarding mechanisms to illustrate how these parameters are used in practice.

Sometimes I will go into concrete examples in specific states but, as I said before, these examples are not meant to be prescriptive and the treatment of instruments is nowhere near exhaustive. It may well be that in some legal cultures some practices may not be at all appropriate. The selection of these examples is done by the criteria that they come from both common and civil law traditions and from both established and developing democracies, yet primarily that they are an apt illustration of how these parameters are met by safeguarding mechanisms.

These illustrations deal with the *first level* of safeguarding judicial integrity: it looks at which instruments could be suitable to safeguard which parameters at entry, in judicial decision-making and in conduct. In the last subsection of each treatment I will touch upon the *second level* and consider the relation between safeguarding instruments. Again, this second level lies to a large extent outside of the scope of this book: it is up to the prudence of those concerned with safeguarding judicial integrity in practice.

It should be made clear from the outset that this chapter is not about safeguarding the integrity of law, but about safeguarding the integrity of judges. Much of the safeguarding activity that is performed with respect to judges is actually about safeguarding the integrity of law, for instance a committee for the review of criminal cases, the appeal system or judicial panels. These measures have, however, an effect on the integrity of judges. For instance, the appeal system may put pressure on judges in courts of lower instance to express themselves prudently, while it is also important with respect to external accountability as it gives citizens a chance of another decision, regardless of the rightness of the former decision. It may be evident that I am focusing only on how these mechanisms meet the parameters for integrity.

## *3.1 Safeguarding Integrity at Entry*[26]

### *3.1.1 Professional character*

The aim of selection should be to find judges who are of professional character.[27] This means judges who are mindful of the right legal knowledge, who are aware of developments in society, who are attentive, who are constant in character, who can transcend to institutional values, who are able to mediate knowledge with the specific demands of the case, who know how to enact institutional values appropriately and who have shown proper behaviour over time.

Virtue is thus a quality that is to be positively looked for. It depends on the system of selection how this is done.[28] Systems or traditions that select judges after a legal career have the advantage of also looking at habituation as character has already been tried over time.[29] However, in a process which selects judges at the

---

26 In all democracies under a rule of law, the norm prevails that judges are to be selected upon merit. There are roughly four systems of selection which can be interchangeable: nomination by the executive, election, co-option by the judiciary or appointment by a committee consisting of judges and academics following a competitive process (Bell 2006:17). Traditionally in civil law systems judges are selected upon graduation whereas in the common law tradition selection is done informally on the basis of legal experience (see Guarnieri & Pederzoli 2002:23, 29, 32, 36, 38, 41, 43 & 44 on the appointment and career structures in England and Wales, federal court judges in the United States, state court judges in the United States, French magistrates, German judges, Italian magistrates, Portuguese judges and Spanish judges respectively). Nowadays the traditions have grown closer together. In civil law systems some judges are recruited from practitioners as well, while in the common law system the procedures are becoming more formalized. Entry within the judicial office is commonly marked by the taking of an oath.

27 Bell distinguishes between judging as a job and as a public office (2006:16) and argues that selection should aim for both qualities. As a job, one has to select for the right skills and routine, while as a public office, one has to select for the quality 'to engage in debates that have more social and even political dimensions'. In line with Kronman (2000) I understand professional virtue to cover both aspects.

28 As to which training or experience is necessary to qualify as judge, opinions differ. Traditionally, a notable difference has been assumed between the civil and common law perspectives on preliminary training. Whereas civil law judges are trained to be judges in a legal system, common law judges are not trained to be judges but are rather recognized as highly experienced legal practitioners (for examples, notably that of Lord Justice MacKinnon, see Vogenauer 2001:927). It must be noted that in legal cultures that are traditionally informal, such as the English, there are developments towards proceduralism. As the result of a 1992 recommendation by Justice, the British section of the International Commission of Jurists, an Independent Judicial Appointments Commission was set up in April 2006. In 2005, the Constitutional Reform Act was passed which prescribes that two judicial appointment commissions are to be responsible for the appointment of judges in England and Wales and the members of the future Supreme Court.

29 On this, see Armytage (1996:65) with respect to the selection of Australian judges.

start of their judicial career, the degree of formalization of selection procedures will obviously be higher. Formalized procedures may involve interviews and psychological tests, which address intelligence, analytical capacity, communication qualities, mental stability, social conduct and decision-making qualities. As it is excellent judges who recognize excellent judges, this requires a high level of input from practitioners.

Safeguarding for professional character also demands that the bandwidth of professional character is determined. When it comes to selection, this is usually about minimum requirements: adequate knowledge of the law, a certain level of intelligence and relevant social skills. Above all, the absence of non-virtuousness is an important criterion. A judge with a criminal record or a judge who has engaged in acts of impropriety may be unsuitable.[30]

Many countries use the taking of an oath to guarantee in some way that judges are also committed to virtue after selection. Oaths are formulated to safeguard professional character in a positive and in a negative sense.[31] In a positive sense, the judge affirms institutional values and commits himself to them. In a negative sense, the judge promises to abstain from non-virtuous conduct: he will not take bribes nor let personal interests override the value of justice.[32]

---

30 Many systems show some equity. In the Netherlands, for example, minor exceptions can be made from the main principle that someone with a criminal record is not suitable for the judicial office, for instance with respect to small misdemeanours or smaller crimes, committed a long time ago. The following guidelines have, for instance, been agreed by the prosecutor-general of the Hoge Raad: a traffic violation settled with a transaction must have occurred at least three years before, a traffic violation with a judicial verdict must have occurred at least five years before and for slightly exceeding the permitted level of alcohol while driving, six years must have passed in case of a settlement and ten years in case of a verdict. See the interview with Savornin Lohman, the departing chairman of the committee responsible for attracting non-career judges (van der Horst 2006:195). These guidelines aim to prevent non-virtuousness but also have a very important function with respect to external accountability in a defensive manner, as one can be virtuous irrespective of the time limits observed.

31 These features are present in every judicial oath. Take for instance the judicial oath for English and Welsh judges: 'I, (*name*), do swear by Almighty God that I will well and truly serve our Sovereign Lady Queen Elizabeth the Second in the office of …, and I will do right to all manner of people after the laws and usages of this realm, without fear or favour, affection or ill will. So help me God'. As in many other countries, other forms of the oath are deemed to be acceptable with respect to cultural diversity. One may, for instance, choose not to swear the oath but to affirm – the sections that refer to God are then taken out – or use other designations of God, depending on one's religion (see www.judiciary.gov.uk on the judicial oath and its variations).

32 In some countries, much attention is given in the oath to safeguarding the boundaries of judicial conduct. For instance, the Finnish oath – affirmation is also possible here – reads: 'I, (*name*), do promise and swear by God and His Holy Gospels that to the best of my understanding and conscience I wish to and shall in all judgments render justice to poor and rich alike and render judgment in accordance with the laws and lawful rules

As the meaning of the judicial oath has come to denote the internal binding of conscience before a public authority, the oath is not only important with respect to virtue – the internal binding of conscience – but also with respect to external accountability – as it is a public commitment.[33] This also reflects in violations of the oath: the judge then violates not only his conscience but also the trust placed in the institution.

*3.1.2 External accountability*

I now turn to the nature of external accountability at entry level. The process of selection and appointment of judges must demonstrably be fashioned according to institutional values. In a defensive manner, some demands in selection may not so much have to do with the professional character of the candidate but with a requirement that is taken a step *further* than mere non-virtuousness. For example, a judge who has used drugs during his youth might in some countries be seen as unfit to assume the judicial office not because of his professional character but because it is a minimum requirement with respect to upholding public trust.

Public trust can also be actively safeguarded. For example, some countries aim for a 'representative' or 'reflective' composition of the judicial corps. This is on the one hand to 'defend' the judiciary against allegations of bias, while on the other it aims to further actively the trust in a judiciary as an impartial corps, thereby seeking to concretize the institutional value of impartiality on the level of corporal composition.[34] Another matter, linked to corporate bias, is political

---

of God and country: I shall never, under any pretext, pervert the law nor promote injustice because of kinship, relationship, friendship, envy, hatred or fear, or for the sake of gifts or presents or other reasons, nor shall I find an innocent person guilty or a guilty person innocent. Furthermore, I shall not, before pronouncing a judgment or thereafter, reveal to the parties or to anyone else anything about the deliberations that the Court has held behind closed doors. All of this I wish to and shall fulfill faithfully, honestly and as an earnest judge, without deceit and intrigue, so help me God, in body and mind' (section 7, Code of Judicial Procedure. Unofficial translation by the Finnish Ministry of Justice).

33 The function and meaning of the oath have changed over time. For judges in ancient Athens, to whom was referred earlier in this book, the oath was an outward pledge by the oath taker that his attestation or promise was made under an immediate sense of responsibility to a god or gods (Plescia 1970:3). With respect to judges, the promissory oath to do justice was performed before each trial to attest that the citizen now acted as an impartial judge. On the oath of the Athenian *dikast* see Cronin (1936:18 and Mirhady 2007:49–53). Nowadays, the oath has come to serve two purposes: internally, to bind conscience and externally, to confirm the political obligation towards the public (cf. Prodi 1992:29).

34 Some authors argue that there is a relevant link between corporate bias and judicial decision-making (cf. Griffith 1997 and Malleson 1999:106–114). The strongest argument is provided by Posner, who argues that 'the broader the range of experiences found in an appellate panel, the less likely it is that relevant considerations will be overlooked' (2008:116). It is especially with respect to tacit elements, such as intuitions, emotions

preference or membership of a political party. In many countries this is in principle no obstacle to a judicial appointment but in fact is seen as a positive sign of societal involvement. Yet criticism that the judges are all left-wing or right-wing is at times taken seriously and the desire for a more balanced corps is reflected in the selection procedures. It has been argued that political ideology should play no role in the selection process of judges. For example, Lawrence Solum argues that US judges should not be selected according to ideology, but according to character.[35] Although it clearly follows from the above that virtue should take centre stage in selection, it should also be acknowledged that in some legal cultures ideology may serve external accountability purposes.

It is, however, difficult to understand what representation or reflection exactly is and how it should be safeguarded. Notions that are to specify representation or reflection are accordingly often unclear. For instance, the 'Fair Reflection' doctrine requires that the judiciary should reflect through its composition the interests of the community it serves.[36] But what is meant by 'reflect', 'through composition' or 'community'?

Usually, reflection is regarded as less stringent than representation.[37] Following reflection, the strategy of many countries is to pay special attention to the recruitment of women[38] and minorities, while stressing that it does not seek

or cultural specific knowledge that diversity with respect to decision-making can be of value. The causal relation between composition and decision-making is, however, difficult to prove. The issue can therefore best be seen as an external matter, dealing with trust and acceptance – and mending to some extent the asymmetry with respect to cultural or gender specific elements within the process of decision-making. It is important to note that representation in *deliberation* is not a matter of numbers, as it does not follow from the proportional representation of the masses in the judicial corps, or from agency, whereby judges from different groups or ideologies decide according to the interests of these groups or ideologies. It is rather about the mindful representation of relevant interests of different spheres of society. Although it can certainly be helpful if judges have first-hand experience of these differing discourses, deliberation is a virtuous activity that involves not only spontaneous intuitions and emotions – which may be context bound – but also rational assessment against institutional ends.

35 Solum (2005a).

36 Cf. Armytage (1996:56, 57). In this respect, Armytage quotes Meagher who is rather cynical about the idea of representation: 'An ideal legal profession should obviously be composed of 5% convicted criminals, 5% drug addicts, 5% dole bludgers and 30% cretins – just like the rest of the community' (Armytage 1996:57).

37 For example, in Israel, which deals with specific problems surrounding pluralism, the notion of representation has been rejected as one seeks for *reflection*. By reflection is meant that effort should be made to recruit actively from different ethnic or religious backgrounds while not striving to copy the composition of the Knesset (Salzberger 2006:253).

38 Some countries set up special 'task forces'. For instance, in the US there is the National Association of Women Judges, one of whose objectives is to 'increase the numbers and advancement of women judges at all levels to more accurately reflect their full

positive discrimination.[39] Even then, however, the matter is not easily resolved. In what sense is a black judge, who graduated from a good university, a representative from or reflective of the black community in the United States? And in what sense does the use of quota aid confidence in the judiciary when the judges who were selected by favourable quota judge disappointingly?

Let us look at the example of South Africa, where Nelson Mandela's famous objection to being tried by a white judge in 1962 'has been echoed more than once' since the abolishment of apartheid in 1994.[40] As the legitimacy of judges has suffered a significant crisis due to the racial composition of the judicial corps, there no longer seemed to remain the luxury of distinguishing between promoting diversity and pursuing representation. Therefore 'hard choices have to be made between diversity and representation, between lawyerly excellence and social legitimacy'.[41] The Judicial Service Commission, which conducts the selection process, aims at maximal transparency: well-publicized open interviews, widely distributed vacancies, published lists of candidates inviting comments, making available transcripts of its discussions concerning the general approach and priorities in making selections.[42] This transparency is to enhance the trust not only in the Judicial Service Commission, but also in the selected judges. After selection, the executive makes the appointments in an undisclosed procedure. These practices have not gone without criticism, as concern about the appointees has been expressed in the newspapers, while others complain about the slow pace of transformation. A chairman of the General Council of the Bar, who was an early advocate of a judicial appointments commission, objected that the Constitution is undermined 'when demographics – and these with broad, selective and inexact brushstrokes – are used to overpaint the core values of the Constitution', of which

participation in a democratic society' (see www.nawj.com). It helped set up the 'National Judicial Education Program to Promote Equality of Women and Men in the Courts' (NJEP). See also Hensler & Resnik (2000:243).

39 For instance in Canada, England, Germany, France and the Netherlands (Böcker & de Groot-van Leeuwen 2006). The fact that no concessions are made to entry standards, including mastering the language, has been an obstacle to many of these candidates. The choice to make no concessions to professionalism when dealing with external accountability is justified: mastering the language is deemed necessary for the right understanding of the case and for a fair hearing. Yet it may be asked which kind of understanding is necessary. In the Netherlands it has been proposed that allochthonous candidates can take a more detailed language test in which they can prove that they have mastered the language even though they do not know all the specific proverbs or idioms (van der Horst 2006:197). I have no information about whether this test has already been used.

40 See Du Bois (2006:280–312) for a critical account of the selection and appointment process in South Africa. The quotations are taken from Du Bois.

41 Du Bois (2006:283).

42 The list of candidates for top functions is even made public prior to the appointments and after the interviews, see 'Judging the Judges. Candidates are lining up for a host of top jobs around the country', *Mail & Guardian* (South Africa), 12–18 October 2007.

one 'is explicitly "non-racialism" ... and which together are the very antithesis of a mere numbers game'.[43]

In light of its history, South Africa is a rather unusual example. Yet it reminds us that while accountability with respect to some factors relating to composition might be inevitable with respect to democratic legitimacy, it should be demonstrated that the process is first and foremost about *meritocratic* aspects. In this sense, we can retake Solum's argument that judges are to be selected according to character, yet on the level of external accountability. Professional character is not only to be looked for, it is also to be *demonstrably* looked for with respect to public trust in the selection process. It must be demonstrated that one seeks to select virtuous judges, who possess the right competences and knowledge, whose character has been tried over time and who are able to transcend to institutional values in all cases.

Thus, policies with respect to composition should be made with the highest level of scrutiny. It must be shown to the public that the selection processes are about finding independent and impartial judges who are competent, diligent and whose conduct is undisputed, lest those processes effect exactly what they aim to prevent: suspicions of bias.

### *3.1.3 Evaluation*

At entry, virtue may thus be safeguarded in a positive and a negative manner. In selection, virtue is safeguarded in a positive manner when the focus lies on excellence of character. It is safeguarded in a negative sense when hard criteria are used to decline applications. In the oath, the commitment to institutional values is positively affirmed, while the judge promises to refrain from non-virtuous conduct.

Instruments for selection should equally serve defensively to safeguard external accountability as they also reckon with societal demands apart from the actual virtuousness of the applicant. With respect to actively safeguarding external accountability, measures as to the composition of the judicial corps might be legitimate as one seeks to have a judicial corps that reflects values like impartiality and equality. Yet the main concern should lie with demonstrating to the public that virtuous judges are selected.

With respect to this *first level* of safeguarding the parameters of integrity at entry, there are many more instruments which could be considered, from psychological tests to specific standards for the level of education. Yet when it comes to final decisions about these instruments, one needs to transfer to the *second level*. This second level of prudence finds its concretization in a broader discourse: Who fashions the procedures? Who conducts the interviews? When is the judicial corps representative? What does the history of a specific legal culture tell? Answering these questions in the light of present-day demands may require a joint effort of – among others – judges, legislators, policy-makers or academia.

43 Du Bois (2006:291).

In order to secure the vitality of the selection process, prudence is required at a meta-level to look 'through' the safeguarding instruments and assess if they meet the standard of integrity: that virtuous judges are selected in a manner that serves the democratic legitimacy of the judicial office.

### *3.2 Safeguarding Integrity in Judicial Decision-Making*

#### *3.2.1 Professional character*

Much of the safeguarding against non-virtuousness can be done at entry. By using high entry standards, judges are expected not to act contrary to institutional values in decision-making. Still, there need to be ways to deal with a judge who makes a mockery of the deliberation process or who repeatedly makes decisions with insufficient knowledge of the law.

Of equal importance is the parameter to safeguard virtue in a positive sense. How does one make sure that judges achieve excellence in deliberation: that they do not waver according to public opinion, that they have self-knowledge, that they are able to interpret their emotions, that they acquire an apt professional intuition? Here too, much can be done at entry, so that one may presume that judges have potential, habituation and education. Of course, the professional character of judges who are selected after a legal career will be substantially better developed. When safeguarding integrity in judicial deliberation, one has to learn specific skills. One has to learn to ask the right questions of suspects, to know how to evaluate certain pieces of evidence or how to calculate fines. Yet prudent adjudication is more than a technical skill: it is deliberation performed with institutional values in view.

There are a number of instruments available to safeguard virtue in a positive or negative sense. I have selected two widely used examples to discuss here: continuing education and judging in judicial panels. Although the focus lies on professional character, these safeguard for aspects of external accountability as well.

*Continuing education* With respect to the parameter positively to safeguard professional character, up until a few decades ago an esprit de corps was believed to be strong enough to ensure the quality of decision-making. Advice, information and mores were informally passed from older to newer judges and judging itself was seen as the most important form of training. Things, however, have changed. In many countries, the judicial corps has grown, there are more deputy judges, specialization has evolved, societies have become more complex and public scrutiny has grown. Therefore, these countries are setting up training facilities for permanent education.[44] This does not just concern knowledge of the law, but also

44 For a review of the rise of permanent education for judges in the Netherlands, France, Germany, Sweden and the United States see Baas (2000). For a broader perspective on the quality checks see Baas & Niemeijer (1999).

the wider array of ethical and managerial knowledge.[45]

As one can best learn about excellence in professional character from those who have developed such excellence, there is much to say for continuing learning with respect to integrity being judge-led,[46] although I do not wish to underestimate the role that other experts or professionals may have in continuing education. Peer education can take on many forms, such as visitation or having judgments checked by more experienced judges. Especially with regard to moral education, formal or informal training by peers is a strong factor in ensuring the integrity of judges.[47] With respect to the development of character, it is also important that an environment is created where judges feel free to pursue and expand knowledge. Creating the right environment for the furtherance of virtue may require practical conditions, such as time reserved for training by the judicial organization, the presence of training facilities, the variety of courses offered, the quality of teachers and individual learning or development plans for judges.

That professional character benefits from education is obvious, but must external accountability be rendered in respect of continuing education? An important factor in this respect is the notion of intrinsic motivation on behalf of the judges.[48] In some established democracies, where a neo-managerial wind is blowing through judicial organizations, this aspect of intrinsic motivation is sometimes overlooked.[49] Dealing with the issue of accountability needs to take into account the importance of the fact that intrinsic motivation must not be suffocated by the demands of accountability – while on the other hand it may be stimulated and canalized by some objective demands with regard to continuing education. If, however, selection is poor or if doubts arise about the intrinsic motivation of judges, accountability mechanisms may have to become more rigid. In some

45 A question linked to the issue of permanent education is that of specialization. This can be understood as a means of safeguarding integrity in judicial decision-making, as it allows judges to develop a certain expertise. At the same time, it may also be harmful for judicial integrity. Specialized judges may be too mindful of their expertise and too little attentive to the specific elements of a case. See for examples Flood, Whyte, Banakar & Webb (2007:137, 138).

46 Armytage (1996:152). See also Graham (1996:10, 49) who emphasizes the notion of imitation, along with the notions of experience and reflection for the development of virtue by lawyers.

47 On the value of this form of socialization see section 3.3.1 below.

48 On the necessity of intrinsic motivation with respect to prudence and the development of virtue see Chapter 3, section 2.3.3.

49 Armytage sketches the learning profile of judges thus: 'Judges as learners are characteristic as being rigorously autonomous, having an intensely short-term problem-orientation, and being exceptionally motivated to pursue competence for its own sake rather than for promotion or material gain; those appointed within a merit system may also generally represent a professional elite possessing extraordinary levels of pre-existing professional competence' (Armytage 1996:130). The importance of selection cannot be overestimated: the motivation of judges should be sought after in selection procedures.

developing democracies, it can be the case that legal education at universities is in its infancy or that there are not enough qualified candidates.[50] Continuing learning may then serve not only to stimulate for excellence, but also to keep a check on the parameter to safeguard the bandwidth of virtuous conduct. Grades or diplomas then serve as objective indicators of what may at least be expected.

The specific demands of a legal culture will thus be crucial as to how a system of continuing education is implemented to meet the parameters for virtue and external accountability.

*More than one decision-maker* One of the strongest forms of safeguarding professional character in a positive sense is judging in judicial panels or en banc.[51] There is also an external accountability aspect as it may heighten the trust in judges when the subjectivity of an individual judge is alleviated by the subjectivity of other judges. Yet the furtherance of sound decision-making seems to be the primary focus.[52]

With respect to judicial deliberation, the sharing of knowledge, intuitions, emotions and perceptions can be seen as an important contribution to the parameter to safeguard professional character positively. The subjective elements of character such as intuition, emotions or moral views, can be checked and mediated with professional standards. The courtroom is also a place where experience is passed from older to younger judges.

The courtroom provides the setting to safeguard against non-virtuousness as well. Judges can speak directly to one another about the manner of deliberation, in a setting of trust and without public humiliation. A sitting in judicial panels or en banc is, however, no guarantee against 'tunnel vision'.[53] This concept is commonly used in penal law to describe the situation where judges – affected by a certain atmosphere surrounding the case – collectively lose sight of the presumption of innocence and convince each other about the guilt of the accused. Other safeguarding measures are therefore needed as well, such as an appeal system or in some states even review committees. Sometimes the process of deliberation is structured in

50 This is a problem in for instance Cambodia, Laos and Vietnam (O'Brien 2006:369). As there is an educational lag, one seeks 'qualified amateurs' to fill vacancies in the short term.

51 A common principle is that the number of judges who sit on a case increases as one ascends the appeals ladder although countries with a system of lay participation usually have a higher number of magistrates, lay judges or jury members at first instance.

52 Since Murphy's call for more research on group dynamics within courts (1966), little research has been done into judicial decision-making by judges sitting together as differing from individual decision-making. Research has been done into decision-making in groups but it is insufficiently clear whether the results may be extrapolated to judges. Research has been done into jury trials, using shadow juries to reconstruct the reasoning process. No conclusive connection has, however, been found between all the variables (see Malsch 2007; see Posner 2008:34 fn 31 for an overview of the literature).

53 See Rassin (2005:159–180).

such a manner as to avoid peer manipulation. The practice that the most recently appointed judge voices his opinion first and the presiding judge last, might be seen an example of this.[54] Equally, procedures surrounding the composition of the bench may contribute to safeguarding the soundness of deliberation.

### *3.2.2 External accountability*

I now turn to safeguarding external accountability with respect to judicial decision-making. I discuss three instruments[55] that are often used to safeguard external accountability: the appeal system, lay participation and stating the grounds of the decisions. The selected examples safeguard virtue as well.

*The appeal system* The appeal system is an important safeguarding instrument for professional character. The appeal system is a form of peer review[56] as judges correct the work of their peers.[57] Judges in higher courts are usually more experienced and are therefore qualified to review earlier decisions. In this way the appeal system may have an important pre-emptive function as well: judges, eager not to be overturned by peers and conscious of climbing up through the judicial ranks, will be extra sharp.[58] An appeal may also cause reflection on one's own work and thereby improve the quality of deliberation. It thus safeguards both parameters of virtue.

Yet in many countries, the primary function of the appeal system lies in meeting the norm of external accountability.[59] The rationale behind this is the asymmetry with respect to understanding judicial deliberations. An appeal is not instigated by a judge but by a *party*. The asymmetry with respect to knowing the true deliberations of a judge and with respect to understanding the legal quality of the decision deprives the litigant of a well-assessed idea of the actual quality

54 This has a pedagogical function for recently appointed judges as well, as it encourages independent judging.

55 Some of these instruments are primarily designed to further the quality of law. For instance, in the appeal system legal errors, doubts or new facts can be taken into account in a court of higher instance. Usually, the highest court decides only on matters of law, seeking to further the development of law and its coherence. Again, I will only focus on these instruments as they safeguard integrity.

56 To say that it is a form of peer 'control' would be overstated, since the number of appeals is limited and appeals are often decided upon new facts. This is even truer in systems where an appeal requires leave. Spitzer and Tally (2000) even speak of judicial 'auditing' and have developed a micro-economical model to look for imprecision and ideological bias. Although clarifying the relation between players, policies and incentives, they do not answer substantive questions surrounding bias and imprecision.

57 For empirical data on the function of error correction in the United States see Hettinger, Lindquist & Martinek (2006:89–90).

58 On the motive of fear of reversal see Klein & Hume (2003).

59 There are nuances. For instance, in England appeal requires leave and in the United States one needs to state legal grounds.

of the decision. Thus the appeal system has an important function with respect to external accountability. It provides an opportunity to litigants to appeal not only against bad decisions, but also against decisions that are *experienced* as bad. Regardless of the rightness of the verdict, the right to appeal is an important factor in retaining the acceptance of judicial power. Thus, the appeal system is primarily to be understood as an instrument that safeguards external accountability as it aims to compensate to some extent for the asymmetry with respect to deliberation.

In the eyes of the public, the appeal system may seem insufficient, especially if miscarriages of justice occur right the way up the appeals ladder. The shock that such miscarriages have upon trust in the rule of law is immense. Therefore some established democracies have embraced the challenge and set up extra committees to re-evaluate closed cases.[60] As far as miscarriages are the result of inadequate deliberation, these committees focus heavily on the soundness of the presentation of evidence and the conclusions that might be drawn from it. They focus on safeguarding external accountability as well, as they provide a possibility of requesting a review to parties or actors within civil society. In some developing democracies, review of closed cases is done by NGOs. Although the results have no legal effect, it is hoped to have an influence on the professional character of judges.[61]

*Lay participation* A very direct form of democratic accountability is when citizens participate in judicial decision-making.[62] This has an influence on both external accountability and the process of sound deliberation. As it is to a large extent a question of external accountability, the discussion on the participation of laymen in the adjudication of law revolves around the question of trust.[63] As dealing with the question of trust, the mechanism of lay participation oscillates

60 For instance the *Commissie Evaluatie Afgesloten Strafzaken* in the Netherlands (www.om.nl/onderwerpen/commissie_evaluatie) and the Criminal Cases Review Commission in the United Kingdom (www.ccrc.gov.uk). For an extensive treatment see Chapter 1 at section 2.2.2.

61 It can, however, have an adverse effect. Case reviews, which receive much attention in the media, have more than once been dismissed by judges on the rationale that these infringe their independence (see Transparency International 2007:117, 118). For the connection between independence and other institutional values see section 2.4 above.

62 A system of near full participation, as existed in ancient Athens, is now nowhere to be found but systems where all forms of lay participation are excluded are rare. There are multiple variants, from the English magistrates to the German *Schöffen*, and from the American jury trial to the Belgian *Hof van Assissen*. The Netherlands is a rare exception, as there is no tradition of lay participation – with only few exceptions in highly specialized fields of law, where experts sit jointly with judges (Malsch 2007:71).

63 See de Hert (2004) for an analysis of the democratic legitimacy of lay participation and an overview of the differences between continental and common law stances on the issue. He concludes that legitimacy is based upon trust, which may differ according to the legal culture.

between meeting both parameters: it may serve trust in a defensive manner, so that citizens keep a 'check' on the judiciary, or in an active manner, so that citizens actively participate and deliberate in the judicial process.

With respect to external accountability it should be noted that trust is intricately connected with the legal culture. This means that different choices can be made on equally good grounds. Proponents of a system of lay participation say that the trust in the judiciary will increase when citizens participate,[64] although it is not helpful that in some countries the opinions of lay judges or juries are undisclosed[65] and the juries fulfil a rather passive role.[66] Also, as the legal system has to lower its threshold and explain its mechanisms, citizens will become acquainted with the law, read newspaper articles about law differently and might become prone to respecting judgments of judges.[67] Those against lay participation argue that this is important with respect to public trust as well, as trust is directed at the knowledgeable professionals,[68] who know judicial values and who are trained to act upon them.

---

64 On this standpoint in a number of European countries see Bell (2006:14).

65 This may be seen to be stranded on the notion of *deliberative* democracy (De Hert 2004:482). In England jury secrecy is protected by section 8 of the Contempt of Court Act 1981. Its legality was confirmed in light of Art. 6 European Convention on Human Rights in the European Court of Human Rights, 25 February 1997, *Gregory – United Kingdom* (Reports 1997, 296) and later in *R v Mirza* [2004] UKHL 2; [2004] 1 All ER 925. See also the report by Michael Zander QC, *Jury Research and Impropriety. A Response to the Department of Constitutional Affairs' Consultation Paper* (CP 04/05) (March 2005). This is not the case in all jury systems. For example, in Spain the jury has to produce a written justification of its decisions, which may include giving detailed reasons (Bell 2006:214).

66 De Hert comments that the rather passive role of juries does not fit very well with a democratic ethos of participation, while the notion of democratic representation can be questioned as the 'will of the people' is at that point the 'will of one who is coincidentally selected' (2004:482). De Hert finally lauds lay participation on the basis that it activates citizenship (2004:487–490).

67 In a 2002 Swedish review committee report, it was regarded as a contribution of lay judges that they guaranteed effectiveness by keeping judicial decisions in line with social values, maintained the confidence of citizens in the effectiveness of the courts and kept the interest of the public in the effectiveness of justice by their collaboration (see Bell 2006:284).

68 Recently, there has been a widely held debate on lay participation in the Netherlands, resulting in a letter from the Minister of Justice to the government saying that no form of lay adjudication will be put into effect (Letter from the Minister of Justice to the President of the Second Chamber of the States-General July 12th 2007). This decision was taken on grounds of professionalism, existing public trust in the present state of affairs and the costs of implementation. Prior to that, the then president of the Dutch Council for the Judiciary had pointed out that in the Netherlands the trust in the judiciary was no lower than in countries where some form of lay participation was employed (see van Delden 2006). See for an overview of the Dutch discussion Bovend'Eert (2008:114–122).

With respect to professional character it has been said that lay participation would force the judges to explain themselves better in the case of a mixed system of lay adjudication. This argument is contested by saying that although the reasoning would be clearer, it might not necessarily be better. Yet the sharing of intuitions and emotions might certainly be beneficial for the virtuousness of judges as it would keep them in touch with society. With regard to evidence at criminal trials, it is argued that although judges are trained in law, they are not trained in the assessment of facts and lay persons would be equally fit for the task – especially as they sit in larger numbers.[69] This argument does not take into account the fact that judges are repeat players and can build up expertise. This argument is countered by saying that juries are a safeguard against judges being set in their ways – failing to start each new case with a fresh outlook.[70] Another argument is that lay participation allows for local justice: who knows better about the background of the defendant than his local peers? After all, a judge will scarcely possess the soft information on local difficulties and practices. This argument is countered by the rhetorical question as to whether one would really want local peers to judge on guilt or innocence.[71]

With respect to safeguarding judicial integrity in decision-making, lay participation may thus be an important instrument to safeguard external accountability if it is what trust requires, while its influence on the professional character of judges is contested. Therefore, the implementation of parameters is highly dependent on the specific demands of the concrete legal culture.

*Stating the grounds on which the decision is based* The grounds are an intrinsic part of the judicial decision, as they bridge the gap between deliberation and accountability.

With respect to external accountability, part of the function of judicial opinions is that they serve to make the verdict understandable to citizens. Whether this is truly the case is heavily contested. The group of readers of opinions is often confined to legal professionals and at times journalists. It has been argued that 'ordinary' citizens, even the parties, hardly seem to read judgments.[72] In accordance with this, in some states it had been the practice that decisions 'should

---

69 Gobert (1997:79–93) attaches great value to the 'mathematical advantage of the Jury'. Greater numbers, he believes, lead to better fact-finding and to more dialectic in deliberation.

70 In mixed systems, one seeks to combine these strengths of a fresh outlook by lay persons based on life experience and the habituated experience of professional judges – as in Sweden (Bell 2006:284) and Germany (Robbers 2002:30).

71 See Robertshaw (1995) for empirical research on decision-making by English criminal judges and juries. See Bell (2006:157 and 287) on empirical research in Germany and Sweden. See Keijser, van Koppen & Elffers (2006) for empirical research on the difference as to how judges and citizens would judge criminal cases.

72 See Schauer (1995).

not be written for the archives'. As a result, they were concise and formulated in technical legal language. In many established democracies it is felt, however, that this practice does not meet present-day demands of suspects, lawyers, prosecutors, citizens, victims and judges. In some countries, this has led to active safeguarding of external accountability by reformulating judgments into clearer language or by using court spokesmen or – in some states – specially appointed press judges who elucidate a judicial verdict.[73] For instance, in the Netherlands a model – called Promis – has been proposed for the writing of penal law decisions that meets the demands of clarity, transparency, comprehension and controllability.[74]

One may doubt, however, whether written judgments contribute to transparency about deliberation. As has been said in Chapter 3, the practice of *justifying* a decision to the public differs from the *process* by which a decision is taken. For example, intuitive elements may be crucial in deliberation, but cannot be used to justify a decision unless they are articulated in acceptable terms. Stating the grounds is therefore not about transparency, but about rationalization of the decision and thereby entering into legal and public discourse. Efforts to clarify judgments by means of stating grounds should be done in the light of this maxim.

This brings us to the question of how professional character and opinions relate. As the Promis-example shows, judges find in opinion writing a tool for guidance and (self-) control in deliberation. This may be so in a positive or a negative sense.

73 In England, Lord Kilmuir was keen to discourage contact between judges and the media on the basis that 'so long as a Judge keeps silent his reputation for wisdom and impartiality remains unassailable'. There is truth in that argument, but as Lord Bingham refutes: 'If judges are fit to judge they should be able to exercise a reasonable judgement on whether to speak to the media and what to say if they do' (Bingham 1995:44, 45).

74 In the Netherlands the projects Promis I and II were conducted in 2004–2005 (I) and in November 2006–April 2007 (II). These projects were a reaction from the judiciary to the quality that society – read: actors in civil society such as academics and the press – demands from judicial penal law decisions. With respect to evidence, the Promis-model is used when there is debate about the evidence at trial. The court presents the arguments as put forward by the prosecution and the defence and argues why it finds some convincing and others not, and also argues which connection it sees between the pieces of evidence. With respect to punishment, it came to light by means of the Promis-model on evidence that similar strands of evidence led to substantially different punishments. The Promis-chambers have now formulated points of departure for discussions on punishment, based on a number of variables, into a Promis-model for punishments. The aim is not to formalize the discussion, but to enhance the level of debate. The reactions were positive. Judges found it to be a tool for self-control, the group of experts who read the decisions unanimously found that the decisions provided better insight into the judgments, lawyers say it is now easier to explain the decision to their clients, citizens find the punishments more acceptable and judges in lower courts find it clearer why appeal courts deviate from earlier judgments. The only problem is that it costs more time and therefore money, as the time to write a Promis-judgment is about a third longer. See Sterk & Ficq (2008) and Raad voor de Rechtspraak, *Eindrapport Promis II. Project motiveringsverbetering in strafvonnissen* (2007) (see www.rechtspraak.nl).

The opinions may safeguard virtue in a negative sense as bad deliberation or lack of deliberation can be unmasked and – if necessary – corrected. The act of writing may also safeguard deliberation in a positive sense, as it may cause reflection and further the quality of the deliberation.[75] The opinion also provides a platform for the demonstration of professional character. For example, deliberation may be different when dissenting and concurring opinions can be issued, as is the practice in higher common law courts, some civil law courts and the European Court of Human Rights. This might make the deliberation process more focused. When outnumbered, a judge might not become complacent but instead work hard to formulate his own opinion.[76] A contrasting tradition is the French, where there is a tradition to 'speak with one voice'. This is seen as an important incentive for dialectic in judicial deliberation: judges are forced to overcome their differences and dialectically come to a unified stand.

Thus the grounds cover all parameters. They are to safeguard against non-virtuousness but also provide a platform for virtue. And they safeguard accountability in a defensive manner by following institutional standards while accountability can also be actively rendered if, for instance, opinions are rewritten in clear language.

*3.2.3 Evaluation*

These instruments show how the parameters of professional character and external accountability can be safeguarded. Excellence in character can be furthered by means of continuing education and when judging in judicial panels, as it allows for the sharing of experience, of intuitions, emotions and deliberations. In a mixed system, the intuitions of lay people may be beneficial to the professional character of judges. The act of writing the verdict might provide a check for deliberation as it stimulates self-reflection and offers an opportunity to correct mistakes. Peer education, judging in judicial panels and opinions are to safeguard against non-virtuousness in judicial deliberation as well.

External accountability is safeguarded by means of the appeal system, as it is not merely a tool against bad deliberation but also against deliberation that is *experienced* as bad. Sitting in judicial panels or en banc may also enhance public confidence, as the judgment is seen not to be dependent solely on one judge. The instrument of giving reasons for one's decisions is important with respect

75 Guthrie, Rachlinski & Wistrich argue that 'the discipline of opinion writing might enable well-meaning judges to overcome their intuitive, impressionistic reactions' (2007:37). Posner argues that the opinion 'is a check on the errors to which intuitive reasoning is prone because of its compressed, inarticulate character' (2008:110). Thus, with respect to intuition, opinion writing may function as an incentive to rational deliberation.

76 For an inventory of the reasons of judges for writing separate opinions in the United States see Hettinger, Lindquist & Martinek (2006:36–41, 47–72). They have looked at ideology, institutional roles, judicial experience, judicial prestige, case factors and circuit characteristics. See also a classic 'defence of dissent' by Brennan (1999).

to external accountability as it subjects judicial deliberation to public discourse. Accountability may be safeguarded more actively as a court spokesman elucidates opinions or if these are rewritten in clearer language. Public confidence may be enhanced when lay people participate, but this depends very much on the legal culture.

This list of instruments that deal with the *first level* of safeguarding is far from exhaustive, as there are other mechanisms that range from randomizing the allocation of cases[77] to providing incentives through a transparent system of promotions.[78] Safeguarding integrity in judicial decision-making is not, however, about one or two instruments. The *second level* of safeguarding should be taken into account, as safeguarding is a holistic activity that concerns a full configuration. In this respect, it is important to note that the instruments are interrelated. There is, for instance, a clear relation between the instruments of opinion writing and judging in judicial panels, lay participation and appeal. These interrelations also stretch to instruments used at entry, as will be discussed in section 3.4.

The configuration that happens on the second level of safeguarding requires a meta-level prudence to ensure that all instruments are used in the proper manner – i.e. with institutional values in view. These institutional values secure the vitality of safeguarding mechanisms.

### *3.3 Safeguarding Integrity in the Conduct of Judges*

#### *3.3.1 Professional character*

Safeguarding for professional character should aim to prevent downright *non-virtuous* conduct. This may concern fraud and corruption but also deviant or unfit behaviour in court. In a positive sense, safeguarding should ensure that professional character is not about the mere internalization of institutional values but about the *enactment* of them. The judge is to 'personalize' the institution, to give the institution a 'human face'. This means that he should not only understand the symbols and rituals that surround the institution but also know in which matter, with what intensity and with what strictness symbols and rituals ought to be upheld.

When not acting as a judge, the judge has to assess prudently between reticence and participation. Participation in society keeps him in touch with current trends, feelings and convictions but it may also compromise his impartiality. Reticence serves his independence and impartiality, but may also have as an effect that the judge is estranged from society. When safeguarding integrity in conduct outside

77 For instance, in Italy the *ius de non evocando* is strictly applied – in part a result of the clean hands operation (cf. Contini & Fabri 2007:243–253), whereas in other countries there is more room for efficiency arguments.

78 A good working system of promotions also has the advantage that it stimulates mobility among judges – so that judges in one court do not become too set in their ways (Bell 2006:23).

court, one oscillates between rules of strict compliance, limiting involvement, or leaving things to the discretion of individual judges.

I will deal with two instruments. The first concerns sharing mores through professional organizations and training. The second concerns codes of conduct or guidelines that ought to secure the bandwidth of professional character while also stipulating institutional values. Both instruments have an external accountability function as well.

*Sharing mores in professional organizations and by means of training* The sharing of mores within professional organizations meets the parameters to safeguard professional character in both a positive and a negative sense. Professional organizations, such as judicial associations or unions, stimulate the informal sharing of mores and the tacit discipline by peers.[79] This offers an important contribution to professional development as peers can guide judges towards excellence while warning them about pitfalls. When formalized to a higher extent, mentoring programmes may ensure that judges come under the scrutiny of reputable seniors. Professional organizations offer the opportunity for socialization – including socialization in respect of ethical conduct.

Socialization is also achieved by training. Training at the outset of the judicial career 'moulds recruits into the judicial or legal community'.[80] Thereafter, the professional character of judges in conduct is for instance enhanced by the experience of peers, courses in rhetoric, video monitoring of their own conduct, instruction about the nature of rituals and symbols or a course about the pronunciation of names of minority groups. Codes or guidelines of judicial conduct may also be a helpful tool in training[81] as these spark discussion and as these are often built upon previous experiences.

Training may also safeguard professional character in a negative sense. Some courses are specifically designed to address integrity violations. Take for instance a course in moral dilemmas: Can a judge use the database to see if his daughter's boyfriend has a criminal record? Can the notepaper of the court be used for ancillary purposes? Courses like this stimulate the sharing of experiences, provide examples of prudence, clarify the bandwidth of professional character and create an awareness of the external accountability of the institution.[82] Anti-corruption education in law faculties or in graduate schools may also alert future judges to integrity issues.[83]

79 On these associations in Europe see Bell (2006:24–26).

80 Bell (2006:24). See for empirical research on the issue Köhne-Hoegen (2006).

81 See van de Burg (1995:27). See also the subsection below.

82 See Hooft Graafland (2005) and Vrieze (2005a & 2005b) on the function of these courses and also on the developments concerning codes of conduct for judges.

83 See Transparency International (2007:98).

*Codes or guidelines of judicial conduct* Codes or guidelines aim at covering a large spectrum of judicial conduct. As is commonly understood, with 'guidelines' the aim for self-regulation is high, while a 'code' leaves less space for discretion and suggests the possibility of enforcement – either within the organization or externally if third parties can enforce their complaints.[84] In terms of integrity, guidelines or 'principles' aim rather at summarizing institutional values, so as to guide prudence positively within deliberation or enactment, whereas 'codes' tend to safeguard virtue in a negative sense by setting rules of strict compliance.[85] For instance, the Bangalore 'principles' cover the institutional values of independence, impartiality, integrity, propriety, equality, and competence and diligence. As a symbolic document, it functions as a blueprint for more concrete 'codes'.

Codes and guidelines have an external accountability function as well. They improve the public perception of the courts by clarifying the conduct expected of judges. They set rules that do not necessarily prescribe limits to professional character, but a breach of which might lead to a violation of public trust. For example, they may be of aid when answering a question where fear of bias is legitimate.

The choice between 'codes' or 'principles' depends on a number of factors. Codes may be experienced as being too rigid, as not being 'living documents', as limiting the discretionary space of judges, as proceduralizing ethical matters and as a cause for bureaucracy. If professional character is suffocated by over-regulation, then these regulations will lose their axiological vitality. On the other hand, codes may provide clarity with respect to the bandwidth of virtue, create opportunities for enforcement, contribute to the preservation of values and stimulate awareness. Codes make a system of accountability possible, but may be limited due to judicial independence. Guidelines or principles share the advantages of codes but lack their rigidity. They may, however, be experienced as too 'unclear' or as a form of mere window dressing.

The choice between codes or principles depends very much on the specific demands of a concrete legal culture – especially on the level of corruption. In democracies where the trust in judges is generally high – for instance because judges have been carefully selected and because the quality of their decisions is good – the need for accountability might be low and therefore the aspiratory function may more often be used to safeguard professional character in a positive sense. In some developing democracies, however, the use of the regulatory function

---

84 With respect to the external effect of a code, the proposed revised Code of Conduct for United States Judges (29 February 2008, see www.uscourts.gov) contains clauses that are common to many codes: 'it is not designed or intended as a basis for civil liability or criminal prosecution' and it 'is not intended to be used to obtain tactical advantage'.

85 See Chapter 2 at section 3.2.1 on the distinction between values and rules. Next to these aspiratory and regulating functions, codes have an educational function (see van de Burg 1995:27 on these three functions).

is more prevalent as the danger of corruption and fraud – or the suspicion of it – needs to be countered by clear and enforceable standards of ethical conduct.[86]

The distinction between codes and guidelines is not as clear in practice as it is in theory. In practice, documents that are labelled 'code' or 'guidelines' often combine aspiratory and regulatory functions. These catalogue values that function as a point of reference for the individual judge and contain rules that delimit professional conduct. For instance, in the American ABA Code of Judicial Conduct,[87] values are concretized with rules by means of glosses and commentaries.[88] In some countries, it is left to individual courts to furnish their own codes of integrity, thus giving practical guidance in ethical matters.[89] As these documents combine regulatory and aspiratory functions, they require prudence with respect to their appliance. As Moats says, present-day codes or guidelines 'should be considered a floor, not a ceiling'.[90]

In codes or guidelines the use of 'integrity' may be somewhat confusing. For instance, in the Basic Principles on the Independence of the Judiciary and the Bangalore Principles of Judicial Conduct the principle of integrity is mentioned after core judicial principles such as impartiality and independence. Does this use of integrity undo the understanding of integrity as the professional character that is to enact *all* these values? I would argue that this is not the case as integrity must be seen in its conjunction with other values. As a 'higher order virtue' integrity provides the impetus to other values. For example, independence and impartiality are negatively formulated, as 'not being dependent' or as 'not being partial'. Yet, integrity as virtue looks at these values from a positive perspective, as how to enact them so that they contribute to well-being in concrete situations. As external accountability, integrity is also a 'higher order norm' in that it governs the relation between the institution and the public forum with respect to all other institutional values.

As may be apparent, the value of codes and guidelines to safeguard integrity is limited: codes and guidelines are part of a holistic approach to safeguarding. Integrity does not concern a specific domain of misconduct which can be

86 For instance, after of a string of cases of judicial misconduct in South Africa there is a call to shift from an informal code of conduct to a formal one, so that disciplinary actions have a formal basis (Transparency International 2007:273).

87 See the website of the ABA: www.abanet.org/cpr/mcjc/toc.html.

88 The same is true for the codes in India (*Restatement of Values of Judicial Life*) and Israel (which came about in 2006). These cover some general values and rules for disqualification (see Transparency International (2007:217, 220)).

89 For instance, the code of conduct of the Dutch Appeal Court in 's-Hertogenbosch deals with very concrete manners, such as confidentiality of files, ancillary functions, extra-judicial activities, the use of internet and e-mail, the acceptance of gifts and procedures for purchases by the court. The code ends with the wise saying that it is a starting point for ethical deliberation, not the end.

90 For developments with respect to general codes of conduct see Moats (2004:177–185, quote from 180).

regulated by codes or guidelines. These are mere facets in the whole pattern of configuration.

*3.3.2 External accountability*

The necessity to render external accountability has become more acute in countries where judges are subjected to public scrutiny. Their actions are public actions, as there is public access to trial or as in some countries trials are broadcast by television. These actions therefore fulfil a direct function with respect to external accountability.

In their appearance, judges are to *demonstrate* good qualities so that the trust placed in institutional values is not violated. Herein the demonstration of virtue may also play an important role. For instance, the judge must seek an optimum while neither appearing too involved, nor too distant; neither being too emphatic nor too indifferent; neither too humorous not too dull. He must uphold the decorum of the court, yet not as if speaking from an ivory tower and he must uphold the standing of the judiciary also in private life, but not to such an extent that it prevents the judge from living a normal life. This optimum in the display of virtue can be developed by experience or be taught by experienced judges. Some of these elements may even extend to the private sphere as the judicial role still resonates in the private conduct of the judge.[91]

In a defensive manner, institutional values are protected against the conduct of judges. Even if aberrations seldom occur, the presence of a system of discipline or of complaint procedures may still enhance public trust. Also, judges can be disqualified, or should disqualify themselves, when doubts arise about their professional impartiality – sometimes regardless of whether this was actually the case. When it comes to conduct that is at odds with the values of the judicial office, such as fraudulent or corrupt conduct, strict procedures may become necessary – accompanied by a system of enforcement. External accountability with respect to ancillary functions may also be more proactive, for instance when a list of ancillary functions is published. Private conduct should not give rise to doubts as to whether, when acting as a judge, he can transcend to institutional values.

I will look at two instruments that fall under the heading of rendering external accountability: the use of complaint procedures and the instrument of disqualification. Again, both instruments safeguard professional character as well.

*Complaint procedures* In many countries complaints can be made, which are not aimed at the decision but at other forms of conduct.[92] It is not always easy to

91 See Chapter 4 at section 3.1–3.3.

92 Take for instance the Office for Judicial Complaints (www.judicialcomplaints.gov.uk ), which will look into any complaint about the personal conduct of a judge, member of a tribunal or coroner in England and Wales, but which cannot deal with any complaints about a judge's decision or about how he has handled a case.

distinguish between a complaint about conduct and a complaint about a decision. For instance, is a complaint that a judge refuses to hear a witness a complaint about the conduct of the judge or about the resulting decision? Complaints about partiality are in some systems treated separately as they may lead to disqualification.

A complaint procedure has an external accountability function as it serves to provide an opportunity to disgruntled litigants or citizens to voice their complaint. It may also have a cathartic function.[93] A complaint procedure may thus meet the parameters to *defend* institutional values against the conduct of office holders and to demonstrate *actively* to the public that institutional values are upheld.

A complaint procedure may serve to safeguard professional character as well. After all, a complaint is free advice and courts do well to work it to their advantage, by for instance making an effort to avoid the same faults in the future. If internal sanctions follow from complaints, a complaint procedure might also serve to safeguard professional character in a negative sense.

In some countries complaints can be referred to an institution outside the judiciary, namely an ombudsman.[94] This is a 'diagonal'[95] form of complaint: the complaint is referred to an institution outside the judiciary, which then has powers to admonish, to advise or even demand prosecution.

*Disqualification* The instrument of disqualification is perhaps the best-known instrument to safeguard judicial integrity and more specifically, judicial impartiality.

93 See Bovens (2007:465). Also, an apology from the judge or the administrator of the court might satisfy the complainant (on the benefits of a complaint system see Laemers 2006:42f).

94 In Sweden, complaints about courts can be referred to the *justitieombudsman* (see the website: www.jo.se). This institution, that has roots dating back to 1766, focuses on control of the administration, which includes the courts. These complaints mainly concern matters such as delay in proceedings or lack of clarity in reasoning. In the annual report 2007/2008 359 cases were reported that have a bearing on courts of law: 136 cases were dismissed without investigation, 2 were referred to other agencies or state organs, in 190 cases there was no criticism after investigation, in 29 cases an admonition or other criticism followed, in 1 case guidelines were issued for good administration and in 1 case, preliminary criminal investigation was conducted but no prosecution followed (see *Justitieombudsman, Ämbetsberättelser* 2007–2008; available on www.jo.se). The example of the ombudsman has been followed throughout Europe. For example, in England an ombudsman assumed his responsibilities on 3 April 2006 to oversee specifically judicial appointments and conduct (see www.judicialombudsman.gov.uk). According to the 2007/2008 annual report, 314 complaints were received, of which 293 were related to conduct and 21 to appointments – 10 conduct cases and 1 appointment case were upheld (see Judicial Appointments & Conduct Ombudsman, *Annual Report* 2007–8; available at www.judicialombudsman.gov.uk).

95 Complaints now follow a 'two-step' process: vertical, from the forum to the ombudsman, and horizontal, from the ombudsman to the judge or the court, see Bovens (2007:460).

Judges can be disqualified or should disqualify themselves when the right to an impartial judiciary is at stake.

But when is this the case? Take, for example, the stance on impartiality by the European Court of Human Rights, which has developed substantial case law on the issue in relation to Art. 6 of the European Convention on Human Rights. Although the case law has no direct bearing on disqualification, it is of great value indirectly as the decisions on impartiality are relevant to the question when a judge should have disqualified himself or when disqualification by a party was justified.

Judicial impartiality has been described by the Court as the 'absence of prejudice or bias'. The Court makes a distinction between objective and subjective impartiality.[96] The subjective approach is used by the Court to focus on personal convictions of a specific judge, whereas the objective approach looks at whether guarantees offered by a judge are sufficient to exclude doubts about his impartiality.[97] The objective test[98] has been elaborated in the *Hauschildt* case:

---

96 See ECHR, 1 October 1982, *Piersack – Belgium* (Series A-53), § 30: 'Whilst impartiality normally denotes absence of prejudice or bias, its existence or otherwise can, notably under Article 6 § 1 (art. 6-1) of the Convention, be tested in various ways. A distinction can be drawn in this context between a subjective approach, that is endeavouring to ascertain the personal conviction of a given judge in a given case, and an objective approach, that is determining whether he offered guarantees sufficient to exclude any legitimate doubt in this respect'.

97 As these guarantees may also be provided on an organizational level, the distinction between objective impartiality and independence is rather blurred. This is especially true when a violation of impartiality concerns the 'tribunal'. In its famous *Procola* ruling (ECHR, 28 September 1995, *Procola – Luxembourg* (Series A-3236)) the Court held that in respect of the Luxembourg Conseil d'Etat the fact that 'four members carried out both advisory tasks and judicial functions in the same case … is capable of casting doubt on the institution's structural independence … That doubt in itself … is sufficient to vitiate the impartiality of the tribunal in question …' (§ 45). This sparked a strong debate in other European countries with similar institutions: were they impartial or should their structure be altered? For example, in its *Kleyn* judgment, the Court brought little clarity when it ruled on the Dutch Raad van State that the combination of judicial and advisory tasks can be problematic 'in certain circumstances' (ECHR, 6 May 2003, *Kleyn a.o. – Netherlands* (appl. nos. 39343/98 a.o.), §§ 190–202, esp. 196).

98 This objective test may concern both 'functional defects' and criticism of the judges 'personally'. For example, in *Kyprianou – Cyprus*, the Court held that a functional defect occurred when the same court 'in respect of which he [a lawyer defending a suspect in a murder trial – JS] allegedly committed contempt tried, convicted and sentenced him'. This raised objectively justified doubts as to the *functional* impartiality of the court. Since the criticism was directed at the judges personally – being the object of the applicant's criticisms – objectively justified doubts were raised as to their impartiality *as persons* when 'the same judges then took the decision to prosecute … determined his guilt and imposed the sanction' (ECHR, 24 January 2004, *Kyprianou – Cyprus* (appl. no. 73797/01), §§ 123–135). It was referred to the Grand Chamber which delivered judgment on 15 December 2005. In this case a violation of subjective impartiality was also attested by the Court.

> Under the objective test, it must be determined whether, quite apart from the judge's personal conduct, there are ascertainable facts which may raise doubts as to his impartiality. In this respect even appearances may be of a certain importance. What is at stake is the confidence which the courts in a democratic society must inspire in the public and above all, as far as criminal proceedings are concerned, in the accused. Accordingly, any judge in respect of whom there is a legitimate reason to fear a lack of impartiality must withdraw ... This implies that in deciding whether in a given case there is a legitimate reason to fear that a particular judge lacks impartiality, the standpoint of the accused is important but not decisive ... What is decisive is whether this fear can be held objectively justified.[99]

Thus with respect to integrity, disqualification is aimed not only at faults in professional character but also at the safeguarding of public trust in relation to the institutional value of impartiality.

The criterion that the Court uses for disqualification with respect to external accountability is 'legitimate fear'. With respect to this legitimacy, the Court points at the complex of facts that support such fear: 'what is decisive is whether this fear can be held objectively justified'. This shows the difficult relation between confidence on the one hand and the normative activity with respect to safeguarding it on the other. This difference is bound to sit uncomfortably at a theoretical level as it can only be resolved by careful deliberation in a specific legal culture.

The example of the European Court of Human Rights shows how institutional values take precedence over the professional character of office holders. The fear of partiality may find its justification not necessarily in the – lack of – professional character of the judge, but also with respect to external accountability as the value of impartiality should sometimes even be safeguarded against the office holder. The question about whether an appearance or fear of bias justifies disqualification or a retrial thus depends upon the relation between public confidence and institutional values.

### *3.3.3 Evaluation*

Integrity as virtue in conduct is safeguarded by the sharing of mores through professional organizations or through training facilities. These may provide a setting in which mores are passed and discipline is administered. Codes and principles may safeguard professional character in a positive sense as they may stipulate the values towards which the prudent person aspires. These instruments may also safeguard professional character in a negative sense as codes or guidelines stipulate the bandwidth of professional character.

Depending on the level of enforcement, codes and guidelines may safeguard external accountability as well. Likewise, a procedure for complaints about judicial conduct is to meet the norm of external accountability. Disqualification on

99 ECHR, 24 May 1989, *Hauschildt – Denmark* (Series A-154), § 48.

the count of partiality safeguards both against non-virtuous conduct and – in case of a legitimate fear – against the appearance of non-virtuous conduct.

With respect to the *first level* of safeguarding judicial integrity in conduct, there are other instruments available, such as impeachment procedures for bad conduct, declarations of assets of judges and their close relatives, or surveys among litigants as to 'customer satisfaction'.[100] Impartiality can also be actively safeguarded, for instance when a list of ancillary functions or interests is published.

The configuration of these mechanisms happens on the *second level* of safeguarding, in a meta-level discourse. Here the assessment of instruments takes place with institutional values in view, which focuses on the precise balancing of these instruments to safeguard professional character and external accountability. This may also concern a reification of symbols and rituals, so that they reflect institutional values rather than estrange people from them.

### *3.4 The Interplay of Safeguarding Instruments*

In section 3 so far I have been concerned mainly with the *first level* of safeguarding: considering which instruments are suitable to safeguard which parameters. I have looked at safeguarding the parameters of virtue and external accountability with respect to entry, judicial decision-making and the conduct of judges.

We now come to the question of the configuration against institutional values, designated as the *second level* of safeguarding. This configuration is a joint activity in which many may take part: for instance judges, the legislator, academics, the press, court administrators and others. It concerns an integral assessment of safeguarding instruments with institutional values in view, against the specific demands of a concrete legal culture, for instance its history and its peculiarities. Obviously, the configuration of a safeguarding mechanism may differ considerably between developing and established democracies. For example, the choice between codes or principles may depend on the level of corruption, the level of trust in the judiciary and the other mechanisms used. Such an integral assessment obviously lies beyond the scope of this book. As I said in section 1, this chapter should rather be read as an invitation to engage in such an assessment.

It has already been shown how the configuration of safeguarding instruments requires an understanding of the interplay between instruments. In the sphere of judicial decision-making there is a clear relation between the instruments of opinion writing, judging in judicial panels, lay participation and appeal. For example, in the United States one can generally not appeal on the facts as these are determined by juries. And opinion writing will take a different form when judicial

100 It must be said that this effort at 'customer-friendliness' is limited by the nature of the judicial process. Judges act upon authority; therefore the 'service' rendered by judges is often one 'by force' (cf. Ippel & Heeger-Hertter 2006:171). As a consequence, for some litigants the judicial process is a miserable experience, no matter how 'friendlily' the judge behaved.

panels are used from when a judge sits alone. In the same way, there is interplay between instruments that safeguard entry, decision-making and conduct. I will give some examples.

The safeguarding of professional character at entry is of importance for the configuration of parameters in decision-making and conduct. If effort is made to select the best candidates at entry, not only by means of a rigid procedure but also by offering excellent conditions, such as good career prospects, salary and social standing,[101] then in all spheres of safeguarding the attention may shift from securing minimum norms of behaviour to stimulating excellence.

The same is true with regard to safeguarding judicial decision-making. Let us look at two examples: lay participation and stating the grounds on which the decision is based.

First, with respect to lay participation, it is important to note that at entry only the non-virtuousness of magistrates or jury members is checked – for instance, the presence of a criminal record – while there is generally no rigid selection for virtue in a positive sense, as there is in most systems undertaken with professional judges. Equally, preliminary and continuing training is limited and in many countries merely voluntary.[102] Also, their conduct in private is generally not subjected to the same scrutiny as that of professional judges. On the other hand, questions about representation in the composition of lay judges can be more pertinent than with professional judges, as the decisive criterion is not merit but participation.[103]

Second, with respect to stating the grounds of the judicial decision, this also requires taking into account safeguarding at entry and safeguarding conduct. For example, with respect to entry, Lasser demonstrates how in France the trust in the judiciary is guaranteed by a rigid selection and career system.[104] There is therefore little doubt among the public about the technical legal competence of the judge and it is accepted that judges formulate in a crisp manner. In America, judges can be elected without having a technical legal background. Their juristic competence can thus be open to question, which must be resolved in the judgments proper.

Equally, in the sphere of conduct, safeguarding at entry and safeguarding in decision-making should be taken into account. If the entry levels are high, professional character may not have to be safeguarded rigidly – for instance by rules of strict compliance or by means of externally enforceable codes. Also, instruments that safeguard integrity in conduct can affect the integrity in decision-making. For example, the instrument of disqualification ensures in the eyes of the public that the judge is impartial – thus providing a check against biased deliberation.

---

101 On the importance of social status and the attractiveness of the judicial profession see Bell (2006:35, 39–40).

102 For example in Germany and France (see Bell 2006:155 and 90 respectively)

103 On religious or racial bias among juries see Gobert (1997:72–77).

104 Lasser (2004:307–311).

The understanding of the interplay between safeguarding instruments at all levels is thus necessary for an apt configuration against institutional values.

## 4. Conclusion

Judicial integrity is to be safeguarded by the interplay between two levels. On the *first level*, it is about meeting the following parameters. Professional character must be safeguarded in both a positive and a negative manner. Excellence of character is to be positively stimulated while the bandwidth of professional character is to be secured in a negative manner. External accountability must be safeguarded in a defensive and an active manner. In a defensive manner it is about securing the sacrosanctity of the office by dealing not only with non-virtuous conduct but also the appearance of it. In an active manner, trust in the judiciary may be actively stimulated.

The *second level* concerns the precise configuration of these parameters. This configuration is a prudent activity that happens in a meta-level discourse. It is performed by a plurality of actors and with other sectors of public life in view. Safeguarding on this second level can only be *actually* performed by those responsible for safeguarding integrity in concrete legal cultures. They can know, for instance, which institutional values are to be met by safeguarding and how these are interpreted, they may know which mechanisms are effective and how public confidence may be satisfied. In this chapter, I have only touched upon this level when discussing safeguarding integrity as a generic norm and when looking at the interplay between the levels of safeguarding at entry, decision-making and conduct.

Safeguarding at entry is of vital importance. Professional character is positively looked for, while the bandwidth of professional character serves to limit selection criteria. Selection criteria may also serve to exclude the *appearance* of non-virtuous behaviour. External accountability may be safeguarded actively when looking at, for instance, the composition of the judiciary. As a generic norm, safeguarding integrity at entry concerns the prudence of the selectors, of those who formulate the oath and those who organize continuing learning. It is up to them to look 'through' the instruments to institutional values and select virtuous judges in a representative corps.

As judicial decision-making is a professional activity, left to prudence, it is difficult to safeguard. With respect to professional character it is about safeguarding against non-virtuousness or bad deliberation and about stimulating excellence in deliberation. With respect to external accountability, it is about safeguarding against both bad deliberation and the appearance of it. It is also about active safeguarding, about finding new ways to enhance the acceptance of judgments. Again, as a generic norm, the safeguarding of integrity in conduct concerns the weighing of the demands of prudence and external accountability with institutional values in view.

When safeguarding integrity in conduct, one is to consider both the bandwidth of non-virtuous conduct and excellence in the enactment of institutional values. With respect to external accountability, not only bad conduct but also the fear of it should be dealt with. This is also true with regard to private conduct. As the profession resonates in the private conduct of judges, no doubts must arise about their ability to transcend to institutional values. To meet integrity as a generic norm, safeguarding judicial integrity entails balancing the prudence of judges and societal expectations with respect to institutional values.

In order to come to a meaningful configuration of safeguarding instruments, it is necessary to understand the interplay between safeguarding at the levels of selection, judicial decision-making and conduct. Understanding this interplay marks, however, only the outset of the second level of safeguarding. Judicial integrity must be safeguarded at various levels: the level of the courtroom, the level of the court organization, the level of civil society, the constitutional level and perhaps even European or international levels. In the end, safeguarding judicial integrity is a holistic activity that requires a configuration of instruments, which must be guided by institutional values, and which must be fine-tuned to the specific requirements of a concrete legal culture. This configuration is left to the prudence of those involved with safeguarding.

# Conclusion
# The Integrity of the Judge: A Philosophical Inquiry

This book is a philosophical inquiry into the professional integrity of judges who work within democracies under a rule of law. A comprehensive theory of judicial integrity has been developed and parameters have been proposed to safeguard judicial integrity.

To this end, this book has been structured around five questions: Is judicial integrity a norm (Chapter 1)? How can a theory of professional integrity of public officials be developed (Chapter 2)? How can this theory be applied to judges with respect to decision-making (Chapter 3) and conduct (Chapter 4)? Finally, by which parameters must judicial integrity be safeguarded (Chapter 5)?

Discussions about the integrity of the judge are part of the discourse on the *legitimacy* of public institutions. In order to answer the question whether integrity is a norm (Chapter 1), I have looked at the normative framework of this discourse, which is constituted by democracy and the rule of law. These two concepts provide the basic legitimacy for the judiciary. The legitimacy of the judiciary rests in the rule of law as the rule of law creates institutions and competences and stipulates general principles and rules. When it comes to its *realization*, the rule of law is, however, by itself an empty shell. The rule of law can only be upheld – and consequently exist – if the holders of its offices are of the right professional character. The democratic legitimacy of the judiciary lies ultimately in the *de facto* acceptance thereof by the public. To this public acceptance correlates the *norm* that institutions are trustworthy and show their trustworthiness. Integrity thus consists in both of these two norms: the norm that the office holder is of the right professional character and the norm that the institution accounts for its trustworthiness with respect to public acceptance. These two norms – and the tensions and relations between them – determine the specific dynamism of integrity in democracies under the rule of law.

In Chapter 2, a general theory of professional integrity of public officials has been developed. The norm to be of professional character can best be understood in virtue ethical terms. Professional character – or professional virtue – comes about by steadfastly acting prudently with institutional values in view. The second norm, that the institution is to demonstrate its trustworthiness, should be understood as the norm to render external accountability. With respect to external accountability, trust in the institution takes precedence over trust in the office holder. The rationale lies with institutional values as these provide a 'sacrosanctity' to the institution that must be upheld regardless of the professional character of the office holder.

Rendering external accountability is therefore a normative activity: public trust must be enhanced in such a manner that it is directed at the right institutional values. Integrity, however, is also to be understood as the norm that covers both the norm to be of professional character and the norm to render external accountability. As a *generic* norm, integrity is more than the sum of its parts. Speaking of integrity implies deliberating about the complex relation between professional character and external accountability, about its tensions, its reciprocities and its configuration. This deliberation is to be done by a 'second level' prudence in a 'meta-level' discourse. This prudence differs from the prudence on a virtue ethical level, but now concerns the configuration of virtue and external accountability. This discourse can be performed by many actors.

In Chapter 3, the theory of integrity has been applied to judicial decision-making. As virtue, integrity in the judicial decision-making comes about by prudence. I have elaborated upon three facets. Firstly, I have looked at the formation of character: as the judge prudently takes the right decisions over time, his professional character will develop. Secondly, as performed by prudence, judicial decision-making is purposive – or intentional – and guided by institutional values. Thirdly, the intricate relation between judicial decision-making and the character of the judge shows in the notion of judicial intuition. As external accountability, integrity in judicial decision-making is primarily concerned not with deliberation itself, but with making the decision accountable to public discourse. It is also concerned with protecting institutional values – sometimes even against the office holder. As a generic norm, integrity in judicial decision-making sees to the interplay between virtue and external accountability.

In Chapter 4, the theory of integrity has been applied to the conduct of judges other than judicial decision-making. As the institution is a symbol – meaning that it represents a number of values – the conduct of judges is by itself symbolic conduct: it should therefore bear witness to institutional values and enact them. In conduct, virtue and external accountability are intricately related, as conduct is to be performed prudently by the professional but is at the same time a direct point of reference for public trust. In *judicial* conduct, integrity needs to be shown in the enactment of symbols and rituals, for example in the treatment of litigants. There is no difference in principle between judicial conduct in the courtroom or outside the courtroom. Although in the latter context symbols and rituals are lacking, the conduct of the judge is still symbolic conduct. In *non-judicial* conduct, integrity needs to be shown (1) in the elimination of tragic convergence between personal and institutional interests, (2) in the choice between reticence and participation with respect to citizenship and (3) in avoiding behaviour at odds with institutional values. As a generic norm, a second level prudence is concerned with configuring the relation between virtue and accountability with institutional values in view. This is also done with regard to the configuration between decision-making and conduct, as integrity in conduct may influence integrity in decision-making and vice versa.

Safeguarding judicial integrity (Chapter 5) is done by taking into account the interplay between two levels. On the *first level*, parameters are developed and instruments are selected that can safeguard them. These parameters are the following. As *virtue*, integrity needs to be safeguarded both in a positive and a negative manner. In a positive manner it is about developing excellence in professional character. In a negative manner, the bandwidth of virtuous behaviour should be articulated and secured. As *external accountability*, integrity needs to be safeguarded in a defensive and an active manner. In a defensive manner, it is about safeguarding institutional values against non-virtuous behaviour and also against the *appearance* of it. In an active manner, it is about actively fashioning structural provisions so that public trust in institutional values is enhanced. At this level, I have looked at safeguarding the three spheres of entry, judicial decision-making and conduct. On the *second level*, safeguarding is about the configuration of these instruments against institutional values. Those involved with safeguarding ought to assess the *whole* of safeguarding activities against the specific demands of a concrete legal culture.

In this book the concept of integrity has thus been elucidated via a philosophical inquiry: it has been established that integrity is a norm, a theory of integrity has been developed that has been applied to judges with respect to judicial decision-making and conduct, and finally parameters have been developed for safeguarding judicial integrity.

This book aims to contribute to the understanding of both judicial integrity and safeguarding judicial integrity. With respect to the understanding of judicial integrity, this book shows that integrity is not simply a value or norm next to other values or norms. Instead, it is a norm that at the same time overarches and concretizes other norms. As virtue, it is a 'higher order' virtue. It sees to the virtuousness of office holders itself, which is necessary to enact and thereby concretize other values. It is also the norm that governs the relation between the institution and the public forum, as it stipulates that public confidence is directed at institutional values.

With respect to the understanding of safeguarding judicial integrity, this book shows that it is not realized by merely devising a code of conduct or by instating an appeal system, however important these instruments may be. Judicial integrity is certainly not realized by adopting a 'one size fits all' package of safeguarding mechanisms. Instead, safeguarding judicial integrity is a holistic activity that requires a configuration of safeguarding mechanisms against the specific demands of a concrete legal culture. As a consequence, safeguarding activities may differ considerably between legal cultures. This may be especially so with respect to differences between safeguarding judicial integrity in established or in developing democracies. Also, it is not just about 'negatively' avoiding violations, but also about positively stimulating the excellence in professional character and about actively rendering accountability so that public trust is furthered.

Further research can be recommended with respect to judicial integrity. First, empirical research is required. For instance, legal sociology is needed to investigate further the notions of public trust, the perception of public institutions, the knowledge of institutional values and the effectiveness of safeguarding instruments. Research is also needed to map processes of decision-making, either when a judge is sitting alone or when judges are sitting in judicial panels, and to assess the effect of the input by experts, lawyers, witnesses or victims.

Second, a discourse analysis of a second level prudence can be articulated further with respect to a specific legal culture. This 'second' level can itself be split into multiple levels: one can think of the discourse within the courtroom, a discourse on the level of the court organization, the discourse within civil society – in which academics and the media take part, the constitutional discourse and finally the international – or European – discourse. One may also think of deliberative discourses in a wider scope, focusing on safeguarding practices in the entire public sector. If integrity is to be safeguarded effectively in a concrete legal culture, the actors, the competences, the precise forms of accountability and the intra-level discourses need to be mapped and taken into account.

Third, I have been concerned with developing a theory of integrity in decision-making but not with respect to the application of law. Now that a theory of integrity has been developed, it may be seen how it connects to the application of law. A theory of integrity in decision-making may provide a framework for thinking about questions surrounding legal interpretation, the relation between law and morality, the status of legal norms and perhaps even a theory about integrity of law.

To conclude, in this book the concept of judicial integrity has been articulated, whilst both its normative structure and its difficulties have been examined. As for the normative structure, integrity is to be understood both as virtue and external accountability. The demand for external accountability is growing in present-day democratic societies, while the importance of prudence cannot be overestimated. Without continuous assessment with institutional values in view, we will not acquire excellent judges or excellent judicial organizations.

The concept of integrity is, however, also characterized by many difficulties: setting a norm against the fluid notion of public trust, the dependence on the intention of judges, the complexity of the purposiveness of decision-making, the symbolic enactment of institutional values, the difficulty of mapping discourses at a meta-level and the balancing of virtue and external accountability. These difficulties illustrate the great effort that must accompany the wish for judicial integrity.

# References


Adams, M. (2004), 'De verbeelding van de politieke democratie door het recht: inleidende beschouwingen', in M. Adams & P. Popelier (eds), *Recht en democratie. De democratische verbeelding van het recht.* Antwerp: Intersentia, 3–37.

Adams, M. & F. Tanghe (2009), 'Legitimacy and democracy *through* adjudication. Comparative reflections on the argumentative practice of the French and Belgian *Cour de Cassation*', in N. Huls, M. Adams & J. Bomhoff (eds), *The Legitimacy of Highest Courts' Rulings: Judicial Deliberations and Beyond.* The Hague: TMC Asser (forthcoming).

Allan, T.R.S. (1993), *Law, Liberty and Justice. The legal foundations of British constitutionalism.* Oxford: Clarendon.

Anagnostopoulos, G. (1994), *Aristotle on the Goals and Exactness of Ethics.* Berkeley: University of California Press.

Andrews, N. (2003), *English Civil Procedure.* Oxford: Oxford University Press.

Anscombe, G.E.M. & P.T. Geach (1961), *Three Philosophers.* Oxford: Blackwell.

Arendt, H. 'Franz Kafka. A (1994), Revaluation', in *Essays in Understanding 1930–1954. Formation, exile and totalitarianism.* New York: Schocken Books, 69–80.

Aristotle, (pseudo) (1952), *The Athenian Constitution.* London: Heinemann.

Armytage, L. (1996), *Educating Judges. Towards a new model of continuing judicial learning.* The Hague: Kluwer.

Ashford, E. (2000), 'Utilitarianism, Integrity, and Partiality'. *The Journal of Philosophy* 97(8):421–39.

Aubenque, P. (1963), *La Prudence chez Aristote.* Paris: Presses Universitaires de France.

Avinieri, Sh. (1972), *Hegel's Theory of the Modern State.* Cambridge: Cambridge University Press.

Baas, N.J. (2000), Rekrutering en (permanente) educatie van de rechtsprekende macht in vijf landen. Een internationale verkenning. The Hague: Ministry of Justice, Netherlands.

Baas, N.J. & E. Niemeijer (1999), *Kwaliteitssystemen voor de rechtsprekende macht. Een internationale verkenning.* The Hague: Ministry of Justice, Netherlands.

Bambrough, R. (1965), 'Aristotle on justice: A paradigm of philosophy', in R. Bambrough (ed.), *New Essays on Plato and Aristotle.* London: Routledge, 59–174.

Barak, A. (2005), *Purposive Interpretation in Law*. Princeton: Princeton University Press.

Bárd, K. (2004), 'Judicial independence in the accession countries of Central and Eastern European and the Baltics', in András Sajó (ed.), *Judicial Integrity*. Leiden: Brill, 265–313.

Bauman, Z. (1993), *Postmodern Ethics*. Oxford: Blackwell.

Bayles, M.D. (1990), *Procedural Justice. Allocating to individuals*. Dordrecht: Kluwer.

Beatson, J. (2005), 'Should judges conduct public inquiries?' *Law Quarterly Review* 121:221–252.

Becker, M. (1997), *Deugdethiek en pacifisme. Tolstojs pacifisme in gesprek met de deugdethiek van Aristoteles en Thomas van Aquino*. Amsterdam: Thesis.

Beebe, J. (1992), *Integrity in Depth*. Texas: Texas A&M University Press.

Bell, C. (1997), *Ritual. Perspectives and dimensions*. New York: Oxford University Press.

Bell, J.S. (1983), *Policy Arguments in Judicial Decisions*. Oxford: Clarendon.

Bell, J.S. (2006), *Judiciaries within Europe. A comparative review*. Cambridge: Cambridge University Press.

Berenbeim, R.E. (2004), 'Wittgenstein's bedrock: What business ethicists do', in G.C. Benkert (ed.), *Corporate Integrity and Accountability*. Thousand Oaks: Sage, 15–18.

Berge, J.B.J.M. ten (2006), 'Integriteit van en gedragsregels voor de rechterlijke macht?' in A.W. Heringa, A.M.L. Jansen, E.C.H.J. van der Linden & L.F.M. Verhey (eds), *Het bestuursrecht beschermd. Liber amicorum F.A.M. Stroink*. The Hague: Sdu, 45–55.

Berner, U. (2004), 'Symbol/Symbole/Symboltheorien. Religionswissenschaftlich', in H.D. Betz & D.S. Browning et al., *Religion in Geschichte und Gegenwart* 7. Tübingen: Mohr Siebeck, 1921–1922.

Berti, E. (1993), 'Phrónēsis et science politique', in P. Aubenque & A. Tordesillas, *Aristote politique. Etudes sur la Politique d'Aristote*. Paris: Presses Universitaires de France.

Bingham, T. (1995), 'Judicial ethics', in R. Cranston (ed.), *Legal Ethics and Professional Responsibility*. Oxford: Clarendon, 35–51.

Blackburn, S. (1994), 'Integrity', in *The Oxford Dictionary of Philosophy*. Oxford: Oxford University Press, 195.

Blair, V., J.E. Ma & A.P. Lenton (2001), 'Imagining stereotypes away: The moderation of implicit stereotypes through mental imagery'. *Journal of Personality and Social Philosophy* 81:828–841.

Bleicken, J. (1995), *Die athenische Demokratie* (4th ed.). Paderborn: Schöningh.

Böckenförde E.-W. (2002), *Geschichte der Rechts- und Staatsphilosophie. Antike und Mittelalter*. Tübingen: Mohr Siebeck.

Böcker, A. &. L.E. de Groot-van Leeuwen (2006), *Meer van minder in de rechterlijke macht. Etnische diversiteit onder rechters in zes landen*. Nijmegen: Wolf Legal.

Boegehold, A.L. (1995), *The Lawcourts at Athens. Sites, buildings, equipment, procedure, and testimonia* (The Athenian Agora XXVIII). Princeton: American School of Classical Studies at Athens.

Bogaert, V.V.R. van (2005), *De rechter beoordeeld. Over aansprakelijkheid en verantwoordelijkheid in civiel- en staatsrechtelijk perspectief.* Antwerp: Maklu.

Boone, M. & P. Langbroek (2007), *Financieren en verantwoorden. Het functioneren van de rechterlijke organisatie in beeld.* The Hague: Boom.

Bovend'Eert, P.P.T. (2008), *Rechterlijke organisatie, rechters en rechtspraak.* Alphen aan den Rijn: Kluwer.

Bovens, M.A.P. (1998), *The Quest for Responsibility. Accountability and citizenship in complex organisations.* Cambridge: Cambridge University Press.

Bovens, M.A.P. (2007), 'Analysing and assessing accountability: A conceptual framework'. *European Law Journal* 13(4):447–468.

Brants, C.H. (2006), *Criminal Cases Review Commission in Engeland en Wales.* Utrecht: Willem Pompe Instituut.

Brennan, W.J. (1999), 'In defense of dissents'. *Hastings Law Journal* 50:671–680.

Bukurura, S.H. (2006), 'A judiciary in transition: Reflections on the selection of judges in Namibia', in K. Malleson & P.H. Russell (eds), *Appointing Judges in an Age of Judicial Power. Critical perspectives from around the world.* Toronto: University of Toronto Press, 313–330.

Burckhardt, L. (2000), 'Eine Demokratie wohl, aber kein Rechtsstaat? Der Arginusenprozeß des Jahres 406 v. Chr.', in L. Burckhardt & J. von Ungern-Sternberg (eds), *Große Prozesse im antiken Athen.* München: Beck, 128–143.

Burckhardt, L. & J. von Ungern-Sternberg (eds) (2000), *Große Prozesse im antiken Athen.* München: Beck.

Burg, W. van der (1995), 'Morele beroepsinformatie. Enkele hypothesen over de professionele moraal van juristen', in L.E. de Groot-van Leeuwen & L.H.A.J.N. Quant (eds), *Ethiek en het juridisch beroep.* The Hague: VUGA, 13–34.

Caenegem, R.C. van (1987), *Judges, Legislators and Professors. Charters in European legal history.* Cambridge: Cambridge University Press.

Calhoun, C. (1995), 'Standing for something'. *The Journal of Philosophy* 92(5):235–260.

Cancik-Lindemaier, H. (2004), 'Symbol/Symbole/Symboltheorien. Griechisch-römische Antike', in H.D. Betz & D.S. Browning et al. (eds), *Religion in Geschichte und Gegenwart* 7. Tübingen: Mohr Siebeck, 1922–1923.

Cardozo, B.N. (1921), *The Nature of the Judicial Process.* New Haven: Yale University Press.

Carr, S. (1976), 'The integrity of a utilitarian'. *Ethics* 86(3): 241–246.

Carter, S.L. (1996), *Integrity.* New York: Basic Books.

Cartuyvels, Y. & L. Van Campenhoudt (2004), 'Comment étudier les attentes des citoyens à l'égard de la justice?' in S. Parmentier, G. Vervaeke, R. Doutrelepont & G. Kellens (eds), *Public Opinion and the Administration of Justice. Popular*

*perceptions and their implications for policy-making in Western countries.* Brussels: Politeia, 33–49.
Claes, E. (2002), 'Over rechtsvinding'. *Chroniques de Droit Public / Publiekrechtelijke Kronieken* 6(3):379–395.
Cohn, M. & D. Dow (2002), *Cameras in the Courtroom. Television and the pursuit of justice.* Lanham: Rowman & Littlefield.
Contini, F. & M. Fabri (2007), 'Case assignment in Italian courts', in Ph. M. Langbroek & M. Fabri (eds), *The Right Judge for Each Case. A study of case assignment and impartiality in six European judiciaries*. Antwerp: Intersentia, 233–270.
Coulthard, M. (1977), *An Introduction to Discourse Analysis.* Harlow: Longman.
Cox, D., M. la Caze & M.P. Levine. (2003), *Integrity and the Fragile Self.* Aldershot: Ashgate.
Crombag, H., P.J. van Koppen & W.A. Wagenaar (1992), *Dubieuze zaken. De psychologie van strafrechtelijk bewijs.* Amsterdam: Contact.
Cronin, J.F. (1936), *The Athenian Juror and his Oath.* Chicago: University of Chicago Libraries.
Cross, R. & J.W. Harris (1992), *Precedent in English Law* (4th ed.). Oxford: Oxford University Press.
Davis, M. (2002), *Profession, Code and Ethics*. Aldershot: Ashgate.
Delden, A.H. van (2006), *Wat is de rechter waard? Rechtspraaklezing* 2006. The Hague: Raad voor de Rechtspraak.
Della Porta, D. (2001), 'A judges' revolution? Political corruption and the judiciary in Italy'. *European Journal of Political Research* 39:1–21.
Devlin, P. (1981), *The Judge.* Oxford: Oxford University Press.
Dewey, J. (1924), 'Logical method and the law'. *Cornell Law Quarterly* (10): 17–27.
Dienhart, J.W. (2004), 'Global business ethics and sustainability: A multi-institutional approach', in G.C. Benkert (ed.), *Corporate Integrity and Accountability.* Thousand Oaks: Sage, 186–202.
Di Federico, G. (2004), 'Independence and accountability of the judiciary in Italy: The experience of a former transitional country in a comparative perspective', in A. Sajó (ed.), *Judicial Integrity*. Leiden: Brill, 181–205.
Dobel, J. (1999), *Public Integrity.* Baltimore: John Hopkins University Press.
Du Bois, F. (2006), 'Judicial selection in post-apartheid South Africa', in K. Malleson & P.H. Russell (eds), *Appointing Judges in an Age of Judicial Power. Critical perspectives from around the world.* Toronto: University of Toronto Press, 280–312.
Duff, R.A. (2006), 'The Virtues and Vices of Virtue Jurisprudence', in T. Chappell (ed.), *Values and Virtues. Aristotelianism in contemporary ethics.* Oxford: Oxford University Press, 90–104.
Dumont, L. (1986), *Essays on Individualism. Modern ideology in anthropological perspective*. Chicago: University of Chicago Press.
Dworkin, R. (1982), 'Law as Interpretation'. *Texas Law Review* 60:529–550.

Dworkin, R. (1986), *Law's Empire*. Cambridge: Harvard University Press.

Dyzenhaus, D. (1998), *Judging the Judges, Judging Ourselves. Truth, reconciliation and the apartheid legal order*. Oxford: Hart.

Ebert, Th. (1995), 'Phronêsis. Anmerkungen zu einem Begriff der Aristotelischen Ethik (VI 5,8–13)', in O. Höffe (ed.), *Aristoteles. Die Nikomachische Ethik*. Berlin: Akademie Verlag,165–85.

Elster, J., C. Offe & U.K. Preuss (1998), *Institutional Design in Post-Communist Societies. Rebuilding the ship at sea*. Cambridge: Cambridge University Press.

Ferrara, A. (1998), *Reflective authenticity. Rethinking the project of modernity*. London: Routledge.

Flood, J., A. Whyte, R. Banakar & J. Webb (2007), 'Case assignment in English courts', in Ph. M. Langbroek & M. Fabri (eds), *The Right Judge for Each Case. A study of case assignment and impartiality in six European judiciaries*. Antwerp: Intersentia, 133–187.

Forschner, M. (1993), 'Glück als erfülltes Tätigsein. Zum Aristotelischen Konzept der Eudaimonia', in *Über das Glück des Menschen. Aristoteles, Epikur, Stoa, Thomas von Aquin, Kant*. Darmstadt: Wissenschaftliche Buchgesellschaft, 1–21.

Fortenbaugh, W.W. (1975), *Aristotle on Emotion. A contribution to philosophical psychology, rhetoric, poetics, politics and ethics*. London: Duckworth.

Franken, H. (1997). *Onafhankelijk en verantwoordelijk. Een paradox in de positie van de rechter?* Deventer: Gouda Quint.

Frankfurt, H.G. (1971), 'Freedom of the will and the concept of a person'. *The Journal of Philosophy* 68(1):5–20.

Frankfurt, H.G. (1987), 'Identification and wholeheartedness', in F. Schoeman (ed.), *Responsibility, Character and Emotions. New essays in moral psychology*. New York: Cambridge University Press, 27–45.

Freidson, E. (2001), *Professionalism. The third logic*. Cambridge: Polity.

Friedman, B. (2004), 'History, politics and judicial independence', in András Sajó (ed.), *Judicial Integrity*. Leiden: Brill, 99–123.

Fritz, K. von (1964), *Die* e.vpagwghv *bei Aristoteles*. München: Verlag der Bayerischen Akademie der Wissenschaften.

Fritz, K. von (1984), *Beiträge zu Aristoteles*. Berlin: Walter de Gruyter.

Frost, M. (1994), 'Ethos, pathos & legal audience'. *Dickinson Law Review* 99:85–116.

Fuller, L.L. (1969), *The Morality of Law* (Revised ed.). New Haven: Yale University Press.

Gadamer, H.-G. (1986), *Wahrheit und Methode. Gründzüge einer philosophischen Hermeneutik* (GW 1). Tübingen: Mohr Siebeck.

Gaffney, P. (1996), *Ronald Dworkin on Law as Integrity. Rights as principles of adjudication*. Lewiston: Mellen University Press.

Garapon, A. (1997), *Bien juger. Essay sur le ritual judiciaire*. Paris: Odile Jacob.

Garapon, A., J. Allard & F. Gros (2008), *Les vertus du juge*. Paris: Dalloz.

Gargarella, R. (2004), 'In search of democratic justice – what courts should not do: Argentina, 1983–2002', in S. Gloppen, R. Gargarella & E. Skaar (eds), *Democratization and the Judiciary. The accountability function of courts in developing democracies*. London: Frank Cass, 181–197.

Gény F. (1922), *Science et technique en droit privé positif. Nouvelle contribution à la critique de la méthode juridique*. Paris: Recueil Sirey.

Glei, R. & S. Natzel (1992), 'Ritus. Antieke und Mittelalter', in J. Ritter & K. Gründer (eds), *Historisches Wörterbuch der Philosophie* 8. Darmstadt: Wissenschaftliche Buchgesellschaft, 1052–1053.

Gloppen, S. (2004), 'The accountability function of the courts in Tanzania and Zambia', in S. Gloppen, R. Gargarella & E. Skaar (eds), *Democratization and the Judiciary. The accountability function of courts in developing democracies*. London: Frank Cass, 112–136.

Gloppen, S., R. Gargarella & E. Skaar (eds) (2004), *Democratization and the Judiciary. The accountability function of courts in developing democracies*. London: Frank Cass.

Gobert, J. (1997), *Justice, Democracy and the Jury*. Aldershot: Ashgate.

Graham, L.M. (1996), 'Aristotle's ethics and the virtuous lawyer: Part one of a study on legal ethics and clinical legal education'. *Journal of the Legal Profession* 20:5–49.

Griffith, J.A.G. (1997), *The Politics of the Judiciary* (5th ed.). London: Fontana.

Groot-van Leeuwen, L.E. de (1997), 'De feminisering van juridische beroepen; een overzicht van de onderzoeksresultaten'. *Justitiële Verkenningen* 23(8):103–116.

Groot-van Leeuwen, L.E. de (2003), 'Rechters onder controle', in P.P.T. Bovend'Eert, L.E. de Groot-van Leeuwen & Th.J.M. Mertens (eds), *De rechter bewaakt: over toezicht en rechters*. Deventer: Kluwer, 269–283.

Guarnieri, C. & P. Pederzoli (2002), *The Power of Judges. A comparative study of courts and democracy*. Oxford: Oxford University Press.

Guthrie, C., J.J. Rachlinski & A.J. Wistrich (2007), 'Blinking on the bench: How judges decide cases'. *Cornell Law Review* 93:1–44.

Gutmann, J. (1945), 'Integrity as the standard of valuation'. *Journal of Philosophy* 42(8):210–216.

Haarscher, G. (2004), 'Integrity and neutrality of legal institutions', in A. Sajó (ed.), *Judicial Integrity*. Leiden: Martinus Nijhoff, 43–67.

Habermas, J. (1994), *Faktizität und Geltung. Beiträge zur Diskurstheorie des Rechts und des demokratischen Rechtsstaats*. Frankfurt am Main: Suhrkamp.

Halfon, M. (1989), *Integrity. A Philosphical Inquiry*. Philadelphia: Temple University Press.

Hall, E. (1997), 'The sociology of Athenian tragedy', in P. Easterling (ed.), *The Cambridge Companion to Greek Tragedy*. Cambridge: Cambridge University Press, 93–126.

Harcourt, E. (1998), 'Integrity, practical deliberation and utilitarianism'. *Philosophical Quarterly* 48(191):189–198.

Hardimon, M.O. (1994), *Hegel's Social Philosophy. The project of reconciliation.* Cambridge: Cambridge University Press.

Harris, J. (1974), 'Williams on negative responsibility and integrity'. *Philosophical Quarterly* 24(96):265–273.

Hartendorp, R.C. (2008), *Praktisch gesproken. Alledaagse civiele rechtspleging als praktische oordeelsvorming*. Rotterdam: Erasmus Press.

Hawes, C. (2006), 'Improving the quality of the judiciary in China: Recent reforms to the procedures for appointing, promoting, and discharging judges', in K. Malleson & P.H. Russell (eds), *Appointing Judges in an Age of Judicial Power. Critical perspectives from around the world.* Toronto: University of Toronto Press, 395–419.

Hazard, G.C. & A. Dondi (2004), *Legal Ethics. A comparative study.* Stanford: Stanford University Press.

Hensler, D.R. & J. Resnik (2000), 'Contested identities: Task forces on gender, race, and ethnic bias and the obligations of the legal profession', in D.L. Rhode (ed.), *Ethics in Practice. Lawyers' roles, responsibilities, and regulation.* Oxford: Oxford University Press, 240–263.

Hepburn, R. (1995), 'Integrity', in T. Honderich (ed.), *Oxford Companion to Philosophy*. Oxford: Oxford University Press, 410–411.

Herodotus (1997), *Historiae*. Vol. II. Edited by H.B. Rosén. Stuttgart: Teubner.

Hert, P. de (2004), 'Leve de republiek, leve de jury. Historische, bewijstechnische, democratische en politieke argumenten', in M. Adams & P. Popelier (eds), *Recht en democratie. De democratische verbeelding van het recht.* Antwerp: Intersentia, 459–491.

Hettinger, V.A., S.A. Lindquist & W.L. Martinek (2006), *Judging on a Collegial Court. Influences on federal appellate decision making.* Charlottesville: University of Virginia Press.

Heyde (1987), *De verwerkelijking van de vrijheid. Een inleiding in Hegels rechtsfilosofie*. Leuven: Universitaire Press Leuven.

Höffe O. (ed.) (1995), *Aristoteles, Die Nikomachische Ethik*. Berlin: Akademie Verlag.

Hol, A.M. (2006), 'Rituelen en symbolen in de rechtspraak. Hun functie en hun betekenis'. *Ars Aequi*: 805–817.

Hol, A.M. &. M.A. Loth (2004), *Reshaping Justice. Judicial reform and adjudication in the Netherlands*. Maastricht: Shaker.

Honeyball, S. &. J. Walter (1998), *Integrity, Community and Interpretation.* Dartmouth: Ashgate.

Honneth, A. (1992), *Kampf um Anerkennung. Zur moralischen Grammatik sozialer Konflikte*. Frankfurt am Main: Suhrkamp.

Hooft Graafland, J.A.Z. (2005), 'Beroepsethiek van rechters'. *Trema* 7: 286–292.

Horst, M. van der (2006), 'Scheidend voorzitter De Savornin Lohman over de Commissie Aantrekken Leden Rechterlijke Macht'. *Trema* 5:191–198.

Huberts, L.W.J.C. (2003), *Mag het ietsje meer zijn? Integriteitsonderzoek in het mijnenveld van de moraal*. Amsterdam: VU Press.

Huizinga, J. (1938), *Homo ludens. Proeve ener bepaling van het spelelement der cultuur*. Groningen: Wolters-Noordhoff.
Hutcheson jr., J.C. (1929), 'The judgment intuitive: The function of the "hunch" in judicial decision'. *Cornell Law Quarterly* 14:274–288.
Ippel, P. & S. Heeger-Hertter (2006), *Sprekend de rechtbank. Alledaagse communicatie in de Utrechtse zittingszaal*. Nijmegen: Wolf Legal.
Janssen, J.F.M. (2008), 'De persoonlijke aansprakelijkheid van de rechter'. *Nederlands Juristenblad* 20:1212–1218.
Joppke C. & S. Lukes (1999), 'Introduction. Multicultural questions', in C. Joppke & S. Lukes (eds), *Multicultural Questions*. Oxford: Oxford University Press, 1–24.
Kahn, H. (1979), 'Sensation and consciousness in Aristotle's psychology', in J. Barnes, M. Schofield & R. Sorabji (eds), *Articles on Aristotle 4. Psychology and aesthetics*. London: Duckworth, 1–31.
Kant, I. (1902), *Grundlegung zur Metaphysik der Sitten* [1786]. *Kants gesammelte Schriften* IV. Akademie Ausgabe. Berlin: De Gruyter.
Kant, I. (1912), *Zum Ewigen Frieden. Ein philosophischer Entwurf* [1795]. *Kants gesammelte Schriften* VIII. Akademie Ausgabe. Berlin: De Gruyter.
Kant, I. (1917), *Anthropologie in pragmatischer Hinsicht* [1798]. *Kants gesammelte Schriften* VII. Akademie Ausgabe. Berlin: De Gruyter.
Kant, I. (1922), *Metaphysik der Sitten* [1797]. Hamburg: Felix Meiner.
Kawakami, K., J.F. Dovidio, J. Moll, S. Hermsen & A. Russin (2000), 'Just say no (to stereotyping): Effects of training in the negation of stereotypic activation'. *Journal of Personality and Social Philosophy* 78:871–888.
Keijser, J.W. de, P.J. van Koppen & H. Elffers (2006), *Op de stoel van de rechter. Oordeelt het publiek net zo als de strafrechter?* The Hague: Raad voor de Rechtspraak.
Kekes, J. (1983), 'Constancy and purity'. *Mind* XCII:499–518.
Kelly, P.J. (2004), 'Impartiality. A philosophical perspective', in A. Sajó (ed.), *Judicial Integrity*. Leiden: Martinus Nijhoff, 17–42.
Kenny, A.J.P. (1979), *Aristotle's Theory of the Will*. London: Duckworth.
Kierkegaard, S. (1987), *Either/Or* I. Edited and translated by H. Hong and E. Hong. Princeton: Princeton University Press.
Klein, D.E. & R.J. Hume (2003), 'Fear of reversal as an explanation for lower court compliance'. *Law and Society Review* 37:579–606.
Klift, A.H.E. van de (2003), 'Wie bewaakt de rechter binnen het gerecht?' in P.P.T. Bovend'Eert, L.E. de Groot-van Leeuwen & Th.J.M. Mertens (eds), *De rechter bewaakt: over toezicht en rechters*. Deventer: Kluwer, 89–107.
Köhne-Hoegen, E. (2006), 'Over de socialisatie en (her)opvoeding van de raio'. *Trema* 5:186–190.
Kronman, A. (1987), 'Living in the Law'. *University of Chicago Law Review* 54:835–876.
Kronman, A. (1993), *The Lost Lawyer. Failing ideals of the legal profession*. Cambridge: Belknap Press.

Kronman, A.T. (2000), 'The law as a profession', in D.L. Rhode (ed.), *Ethics in Practice. Lawyers' roles, responsibilities, and regulation*. Oxford: Oxford University Press, 29–41.

Kuhn, H. (1960), 'Der Begriff der Prohairesis in der Nikomachischen Ethik', in *Die Gegenwart der Griechen im neueren Denken. Festschrift für Hans-Georg Gadamer zum* 60. *Geburtstag*. Tübingen: Mohr Siebeck, 123–140.

Kuijer, M. (2004), *The Blindfold of Lady Justice*. Nijmegen: Wolf Legal.

Kymlicka, W. (1995), 'Introduction', in W. Kymlicka (ed.), *The Rights of Minority Cultures*. Oxford: Oxford University Press, 1–27.

Laemers, M.T.A.B. (2006), 'Open opstelling van rechters en aandacht voor kwaliteit. Een bijdrage over klachten van burgers als reactie op rechterlijke ongehoorzaamheid en effecten van klachten op kwaliteit', in L.E. de Groot-van Leeuwen, A.M. van den Bossche & Y. Buruma (eds), *De ongehoorzame rechter. Rechter versus andere rechters, de wetgever, de bevolking en het Europees recht*. Deventer: Kluwer, 33–54.

Langbroek, Ph.M. (2007), 'Case assignment in Dutch courts', in Ph. M. Langbroek & M. Fabri (eds), *The Right Judge for Each Case. A study of case assignment and impartiality in six European judiciaries*. Antwerp: Intersentia, 105–131.

Langseth, P. & O. Stolpe (2003), 'The United Nations' approach to helping countries help themselves by strengthening judicial integrity: A case study from Nigeria', in C. Fijnaut & L. Huberts (eds), *Corruption, Integrity and Law Enforcement*. The Hague: Kluwer, 309–334.

Lasser, M. de S.,-O.,–l'E. (2004), Judicial deliberations. A comparative analysis of judicial transparency and legitimacy. Oxford: Oxford University Press.

Lee, S. (1988), *Judging Judges*. London: Faber and Faber.

Leest, J.E. (2007), *Een redelijk ritueel. Bemiddelen tussen strafrecht en leefwereld*. The Hague: Boom.

Lent, L. van (2008), *Externe openbaarheid in het strafproces*. The Hague: Boom.

Luijk, H. van (2002), 'Integriteit in het publieke domein. Contouren van een representatieve ethiek', in R. Jeurissen & A.W. Musschenga (eds), *Integriteit in bedrijf, organisatie en openbaar bestuur*. Assen: Van Gorcum, 58–77.

Machiavelli, N. (2006), *The Prince* [1513]. Translated by G. Bull. London: Penguin.

MacIntyre, A. (1981), *After Virtue. A study in moral theory*. London: Duckworth.

Mackor, A.-R. (2001), 'Rechtvaardigheid, barmhartigheid en empathie'. *Algemeen Nederlands Tijdschrift voor Wijsbegeerte* 93(1):29–45.

Malleson, K. (1999), *The New Judiciary. The Effects of Expansionism and Activism*. Aldershot: Ashgate.

Malleson K. & P.H. Russell (eds) (2006), *Appointing Judges in an Age of Judicial Power. Critical perspectives from around the world*. Toronto: University of Toronto Press.

Malsch, M. (2007), 'Samenwerking tussen rechters en leken'. *Rechtstreeks* 1: 64–77.

Mandeville, B. (1924), *The Fable of the Bees: or, Private Vices, Public Benefits*. With a Commentary by F.B. Kaye. Oxford: Clarendon Press.

Marmor, A. (2004), 'The rule of law and its limits'. *Law and Philosophy* 23:1–43.

Matyszak, D (2006), 'Creating a compliant judiciary in Zimbabwe, 2000–2003', in K. Malleson & P.H. Russell (eds), *Appointing Judges in an Age of Judicial Power. Critical perspectives from around the world.* Toronto: University of Toronto Press, 331–354.

Mautner, T. (1996), 'Integrity', in T. Mautner (ed.), *A Dictionary of Philosophy*. Oxford: Blackwell Publishers, 210.

McDowell, J. (1979), 'Virtue and reason'. *The Monist* 62(3):331–350.

McFall, L. (1987), 'Integrity'. *Ethics* 98:5–20.

Meier-Oeser, S. (1998), 'Symbol. Antike, Mittelalter, Neuzeit', in J. Ritter & K. Gründer (eds), *Historisches Wörterbuch der Philosophie* 10. Darmstadt: Wissenschaftliche Buchgesellschaft, 710–723.

Mincke, G.W. (1998), 'Haftung für richterliches Handeln in Deutschland', in A.W. Jongbloed (ed.), *Aansprakelijkheid voor optreden van de rechterlijke macht.* The Hague: Boom, 65–76.

Mirhady, D.C. (2007), 'The Dikasts' oath and the question of fact', in A.H. Sommerstein, & J. Fletcher (2007), *Horkos. The oath in Greek society*. Bristol: Phoenix, 48–58.

Moats, B. (2004), 'The next generation of codes of conduct', in G.C. Benkert (ed.), *Corporate Integrity and Accountability*. Thousand Oaks: Sage, 177–185.

Moliterno, J.E. & G.C. Harris (2007), *Global Issues in legal ethics*. St. Paul: Thomson West.

Montesquieu, C. de (1868), *De l'esprit des lois*. Paris: Garnier.

Müri, W. (1976), *Griechische Studien. Ausgewählte wort- und sachgeschichtliche Forschungen zur Antike*. Basel: Friedrich Reinhardt.

Murphy, W.F. (1966), 'Courts as small groups'. *Harvard Law Review* 79:1565–1572.

Musschenga, A.W. (2002), 'Integrity – personal, moral and professional', in A.W. Musschenga, W. van Haaften, B. Spiecker & M. Slors (eds), *Personal and Moral Identity*. Dordrecht: Kluwer, 169–201.

Musschenga, A.W. (2004), Integriteit. Over de eenheid en heelheid van de persoon. Utrecht: Lemma.

Ng, G.Y. (2007), *Quality of Judicial Organisation and Checks and Balances*. Antwerp: Intersentia.

Nussbaum, M.C. (1994), *Therapy of Desire. Theory and Practice in Hellenistic Ethics*. Princeton: Princeton University Press.

Nussbaum, M.C. (2004), *Hiding from Humanity. Disgust, shame and the law*. Princeton: Princeton University Press.

O'Brien, B.M. (2006), 'The politics of judicial selection and appointments in Japan and ten South and Southeast Asian Countries', in K. Malleson & P.H. Russell

(eds), *Appointing Judges in an Age of Judicial Power. Critical perspectives from around the world.* Toronto: University of Toronto Press, 355–374.
Oksenberg Rorty, A. (ed.) (1980), *Essays on Aristotle's Ethics*. Berkeley: University of California Press.
Ommeren F.J. van & E. Zijlstra (eds) (2003), *De rechtsstaat als toetsingskader.* The Hague: Boom.
Oostrum, H.A.J. van (2002), *Toevallige weetbaarheden. Een onderzoek naar integriteitsbewaking in advocatenkantoren*. The Hague: Boom.
O'Neill, O. (1989), *Constructions of Reason. Explorations of Kant's Practical Philosophy*. Cambridge: Cambridge University Press.
O'Neill, O. (2002), *A Question of Trust. The BBC Reith Lectures* 2002. Cambridge: Cambridge University Press.
Osborne, D.T &. T. Gaebler (1992), *Reinventing Government. How the entrepreneurial spirit is transforming the public sector*. New York: Addison-Wesley.
Paterson, A. (1982), *The Law Lords*. London: Macmillan.
Peperzak, A.Th. (1997), 'Hegels Pflichten- und Tugendlehre. Eine Analyse und Interpretation der *Grundlinien der Philosophie des Rechts* §§ 142–156', in L. Siep (ed.), *G.W.F. Hegel. Grundlinien der Philosophie des Rechts.* Berlin: Akademie Verlag, 167–191.
Peperzak, A.Th. (2001), Modern Freedom. Hegel's legal, moral and political philosophy. Dordrecht: Kluwer.
Pettit, P. (1997), *Republicanism. A theory of freedom and government*. Oxford: Clarendon.
Pizzaro D.A. & P. Bloom (2003), 'The intelligence of the moral intuitions'. *Psychological Review* (1):193.
Plescia, J. (1970), *The Oath and Perjury in Ancient Greece*. Tallahassee: Florida State University Press.
Posner, R.A. (2008), *How Judges Think*. Cambridge: Harvard University Press.
Price, A.W. (1989), *Love and Friendship in Plato and Aristotle*. Oxford: Oxford University Press.
Pritchard, M. (1972), 'Human dignity and justice'. *Ethics* 82:299–313.
Prodi, P. (1992), *Der Eid in der europäischen Verfassungsgeschichte*. München: Stiftung Historisches Kolleg.
Provine, D.M. & A. Garapon (2006), 'The selection of judges in France: Searching for a new legitimacy', in K. Malleson & P.H. Russell (eds), *Appointing Judges in an Age of Judicial Power. Critical perspectives from around the world.* Toronto: University of Toronto Press, 176–195.
Quante, M. (1997), 'Personal autonomy and the structure of the will', in: J. Kotkavirta (ed.), *Right, Morality, Ethical Life. Studies in G.W.F. Hegel's philosophy of right.* Jyväskylä: SoPhi, 45–74.
Radin, M. (1925), 'The theory of judicial decision: Or how judges think'. *American Bar Association Journal* (11):357–362.
Ramsay, H. (1997), *Beyond Virtue: Integrity and morality*. London: Macmillan.

Rassin, E. (2005), *Tussen sofa en toga. Inleiding in de rechtspsychologie*. The Hague: Boom.

Rawls, J. (1971), *A Theory of Justice*. Cambridge: Harvard University Press.

Raz, J. (2004), 'Speaking with one voice: On Dworkinian integrity and coherence', in J. Burley (ed.), *Dworkin and His Critics*. Oxford: Blackwell, 285–290.

Recki, B. (2004), 'Symbol/Symbole/Symboltheorien. Philosophisch', in H.D. Betz & D.S. Browning et al. (eds), *Religion in Geschichte und Gegenwart* 7. Tübingen: Mohr Siebeck, 1923–1924.

Resnik, J. (1982), 'Managerial judges'. *Harvard Law Review* 96:374–448.

Ricoeur, P. (1995), *Le Juste*. Paris: Éditions Esprit.

Riedel M. (1976), 'Der Begriff der "Bürgerlichen Gesellschaft" und das Problem seines geschichtlichen Ursprungs', in E.-W. Böckenförde (ed.), *Staat und Gesellschaft*. Darmstadt: Wissenschaftliche Buchgesellschaft, 77–108.

Robbers, G. (2002), *Einführung in das deutsche Recht*. 3. Auflage. Baden-Baden: Nomos.

Robertshaw, P. (1995), *Jury and Judge. The Crown Court in action*. Dartmouth: Ashgate.

Rottier, H. (2003), 'Integriteit binnen de rechterlijke macht', in Capra, *Bestuurlijke en ambtelijke integriteit*. The Hague: Elsevier, 23–42.

Rousseau J.J. (1963), *Du Contrat Social ou Principes du Droit Politique* [1762]. Paris: Garnier.

Roussel, V. (2002), *Affaires de juges. Les magistrates dans les scandales politiques en France*. Paris: Éditions la Découverte.

Salzberger, E.M. (2006), 'Judicial appointments and promotions in Israel: Constitution, law and politics', in K. Malleson & P.H. Russell (eds), *Appointing Judges in an Age of Judicial Power. Critical perspectives from around the world*. Toronto: University of Toronto Press, 241–259.

Santiso, C. (2004), 'Economic reform and judicial governance in Brazil: Balancing independence with accountability', in S. Gloppen, R. Gargarella & E. Skaar (eds), *Democratization and the Judiciary. The accountability function of courts in developing democracies*. London: Frank Cass, 161–180.

Schauer, F. (1995), 'Opinions as rules'. *University of Chicago Law Review* 62:1455–1475.

Scheltema, M. (1995), 'Constitutional developments in the Netherlands. Towards a weaker parliament and stronger courts?', in J.J. Hesse & N. Johnson (eds), *Constitutional Policy and Change in Europe*. Oxford: Oxford University Press, 200–213.

Scheltema, M. (2005), *Het recht van de toekomst. De gevolgen van de internationalisering voor het recht*. Deventer: Kluwer.

Schilder, A. &. W.H.J.M. Nuijts (2005), 'De accountant. Onafhankelijkheid in een meervoudig spanningsveld', *Justitiële verkenningen* 3:77–98.

Schipper, F. (2007), 'Transparency and integrity: Contrary concepts?' in K. Homann, P. Koslowski & C. Luetge (eds), *Globalisation and Business Ethics*. Aldershot: Ashgate, 101–117.

Scholten, P. (1949), *Verzamelde Geschriften* 1. Zwolle: W.E.J. Tjeenk Willink.
Scholten, P. (1974), Mr. C. Asser's handleiding tot de beoefening van het Nederlands burgerlijk recht. Algemeen deel.* Zwolle: W.E.J. Tjeenk Willink.
Scholz, O.R. (1998), 'Symbol. 19. und 20. Jh.', in J. Ritter & K. Gründer, *Historisches Wörterbuch der Philosophie* 10. Darmstadt: Wissenschaftliche Buchgesellschaft, 723–737.
Scholz, P. (2000), 'Der Prozeß gegen Sokrates. Ein ‚Sündenfall' der athenischen Demokratie?' in L. Burckhardt & J. von Ungern-Sternberg (eds), *Große Prozesse im antiken Athen*. München: Beck, 157–173.
Sharp Paine, L. (1994), 'Managing for organizational integrity'. *Harvard Business Review* (March–April), 106–117.
Sherman, N. (1989), *The Fabric of Character. Aristotle's theory of virtue*. Oxford: Clarendon.
Sherman, N. (1997), *Making a Necessity of Virtue*. Cambridge: Cambridge University Press.
Sherman, N. (1999), 'The habituation of character', in *Aristotle's Ethics. Critical essays*. Lanham: Rowman & Littlefield, 231–260.
Shetreet, Sh. (1976), *Judges on Trial. A study of the appointment and accountability of the English judiciary*. Amsterdam: North Holland.
Sieder, R. (2004), 'Renegotiating "law and order": Judicial reform and citizen responses in post-war Guatemala', in S. Gloppen, R. Gargarella & E. Skaar (eds), *Democratization and the Judiciary. The accountability function of courts in developing democracies*. London: Frank Cass, 137–160.
Siep, L. (1979), *Anerkennung als Prinzip der praktischen Philosophie. Untersuchungen zu Hegels Jenaer Philosophie des Geistes*. Freiburg: Karl Alber.
Siep, L. (1997), 'Vernunftrecht und Rechtsgeschichte', in L. Siep (ed.), *G.W.F. Hegel, Grundlinien der Philosophie Des Rechts*. Berlin: Akademie Verlag, 5–30.
Siep L. (2003), 'Hegel und der Holismus in der politischen Philosophie', in R. Geiger et al. (eds), *Modelle politischer Philosophie*. Paderborn: Mentis, 63–77.
Sigrist, Ch. (1992), 'Ritus. Religionswissenschaft des 19. und 20. Jh.', in J. Ritter & K. Gründer, *Historisches Wörterbuch der Philosophie* 8. Darmstadt: Wissenschaftliche Buchgesellschaft, 1053–1058.
Smart, J.J.C. &. B. Williams (1973), *Utilitarianism. For and against*. Cambridge: Cambridge University Press.
Soeharno, J.E. (2005), 'Over rechterlijke intuïtie. Over rechterlijke intuïtie. Paul Scholtens intuïtieleer en een alternatief model van Aristoteles'. *Tijdschrift voor Rechtsfilosofie & Rechtstheorie* 3:235–261.
Soeharno, J.E. (2006), 'From guardian of the *Rechtsstaat* to ruler in the rule of law: An inquiry into the increased role of the judiciary', in A. van Hoek, T. Hol, O, Jansen, P. Rijpkema and R. Widdershoven (eds), *Multilevel Governance in Enforcement and Adjudication*. Antwerp: Intersentia, 157–178.

Soeharno, J.E. (2007), 'Freedom as a second nature. Exploring the value of Hegel's concept of autonomous personality for global institutional theory'. *Archiv für Rechts- und Sozialphilosophie*. Beiheft 107:61–72.

Soetjipto, A. (2002), 'The battle against corruption in the context of a developing country: The case of Indonesia', in C. Fijnaut & L. Huberts (eds), *Corruption, Integrity and Law Enforcement.* The Hague: Kluwer, 57–72.

Solomon, P.H. (2004), 'Courts in Russia: Independence, power and accountability', in András Sajó (ed.), *Judicial Integrity*. Leiden: Brill, 225–252.

Solomon, R.C. (1993), *Ethics and Excellence. Cooperation and integrity in business.* Oxford: Oxford University Press.

Solum, L.B. (1988), 'The virtues and vices of a judge. An Aristotelian guide to judicial selection'. *Southern California Law Review* 61:1735.

Solum, L.B. (2003), 'Virtue jurisprudence. A virtue-centered theory of judging'. *Metaphilosophy* 34(1/2):178–213.

Solum, L.B. (2005a), 'Judicial selection. Ideology versus character'. *Cardozo Law Review* 26:659.

Solum, L.B. (2005b), 'A Tournament of Virtue'. *Florida State University Law Review* 32:1365.

Sorabji, R. (1980), 'Aristotle on the role of intellect in virtue', in A. Oksenberg Rorty (ed.), *Essays on Aristotle's Ethics*. Berkeley: University of California Press, 201–219.

Spitzer, M. & E. Talley (2000), 'Judicial auditing'. *Journal of Legal Studies* 29:649–683.

Sterk, C.H.W.M. & C.R.L.R.M. Ficq (2008), 'Promis: inzicht in de gedachtegang van de rechter'. *Nederlands Juristenblad* 3:153–157.

Stevens, R. (2005), *The English Judges. Their role in the changing constitution.* Oxford: Hart.

Stone Sweet, A. (2000), *Governing with Judges. Constitutional politics in Europe.* Oxford: Oxford University Press.

Storr, A. (1960), *The Integrity of the Personality.* London: Heinemann.

Sunstein, C.R., D. Schkade, L.M. Ellman & A. Sawicki (2006), *Are Judges Political? An empirical analysis of the federal judiciary.* Washington: Brookings Institution Press.

Tacitus, P.C. (1965), *Annales* 1–6. Edited by J.W. Fuchs. The Hague: Van Goor Zonen.

Taekema, S. (2004), 'What ideals are: Ontological and epistemological issues', in W. van der Burg & S. Taekema (eds), *The Importance of Ideals. Debating their relevance in law, morality and politics.* Brussels: Peter Lang, 39–58.

Tamanaha, B.Z. (2004), *On the Rule of Law. History, politics, theory.* Cambridge: Cambridge University Press.

Tate, C.N. & T. Vallinder (1995), *The Global Expansion of Judicial Power.* New York: New York University Press.

Taylor, G. (1985), *Pride, Shame and Guilt. Emotions of self-assessment.* Oxford: Clarendon.

Terry, L.D. (1998), 'Administrative leadership, neo-managerialism, and the public management movement'. *Public Administration Review* 58(3).

Teuben, K. (2004), *Rechtersregelingen in het burgerlijk (proces)recht*. Deventer: Kluwer.

Thomas, E.W. (2005), *The Judicial Process. Realism, pragmatism, practical reasoning and principles*. Cambridge: Cambridge University Press.

Todd, S.C. (1993), *The Shape of Athenian Law*. Oxford: Clarendon.

Tolley, M.C. (2006), 'Legal controversies over federal judicial selection in the United States: Breaking the cycle of obstruction and retribution over judicial appointments', in K. Malleson & P.H. Russell (eds), *Appointing Judges in an Age of Judicial Power. Critical perspectives from around the world.* Toronto: University of Toronto Press, 80–102.

Tonkens-Gerkema, W. & P. van Kesteren (2005), 'Kritiek op kwaliteit, kritiek op de organisatie?' *Trema* 4:137–38.

Transparency International (2007), *Global Corruption Report* 2007. *Corruption in Judicial Systems*. Cambridge: Cambridge University Press.

Trochev, A. (2006), 'Judicial selection in Russia: Towards accountability and centralization', in K. Malleson & P.H. Russell (eds), *Appointing Judges in an Age of Judicial Power. Critical perspectives from around the world.* Toronto: University of Toronto Press, 375–394.

Urmson, J.O. (1990), *The Greek Philosophical Vocabulary*. London: Duckworth.

Velasquez, M. (2004), 'Is corruption always corrupt?' in G.C. Benkert (ed.), *Corporate Integrity and Accountability*. Thousand Oaks: Sage, 148–165.

Verbrugge, A. (1996), 'Aristoteles' begrip van de fro,nhsij''. *Algemeen Nederlands Tijdschrift voor Wijsbegeerte* 87(1):89–124.

Verhaeghe, J. (1980), *Het mensbeeld in de Aristotelische Ethiek.* Brussel: Paleis der Academiën.

Voermans, W. (2007), 'Judicial transparency furthering public accountability for new judiciaries'. *Utrecht Law Review* 3(1):148–159.

Voermans, W. & P. Albers (2003), *Councils for the Judiciary in EU Countries.* Strasbourg: European Commission for the Efficiency of Justice (CEPEJ), Council of Europe.

Vogenauer, S. (2001), *Die Auslegung von Gesetzen in England und auf dem Kontinent. Eine vergleichende Untersuchung der Rechtsprechung und ihrer historischen Grundlagen*. Bd II. Tübingen: Mohr Siebeck.

Vrieze, G. (2005a), 'Zijn rechters zonder gedragscode nog wel te vertrouwen? (I)'. *Trema* 4:139–50.

Vrieze, G. (2005b), 'Zijn rechters zonder gedragscode nog wel te vertrouwen? (II)'. *Trema* 5:194–08.

Wade, H. &. C. Forsyth (2004), *Administrative Law* (9th ed.). Oxford: Oxford University Press.

Wedin, M.V. (1993), 'Tracking Aristotle's *Noûs*', in M. Durrant (ed.), *Aristotle's De Anima in Focus*. London: Routledge, 128–161.

Willemsen, H. (1992), 'Integriteit', in H. Willemsen (ed.), *Woordenboek der Filosofie*. Assen: Van Gorcum, 218.
Williams, B. (1981), 'Persons, character and morality', in *Moral Luck. Philosophical papers 1973–1980*. Cambridge: Cambridge University Press, 1–19.
Williams, B. (1985), *Ethics and the Limits of Philosophy*. London: Fontana Press.
Wolfe, C. (1986), *The Rise of Modern Judicial Review. From constitutional interpretation to judge-made law*. New York: Basic Books.
Wróblewski, J. (1992), *The Judicial Application of Law*. Edited by Z. Bankowski & N. MacCormick. Dordrecht: Kluwer Academic.
Zippelius, R. (2003), *Rechtsphilosophie*. München: Beck.

# Index